IMAGES
of America

WAYNE COUNTY

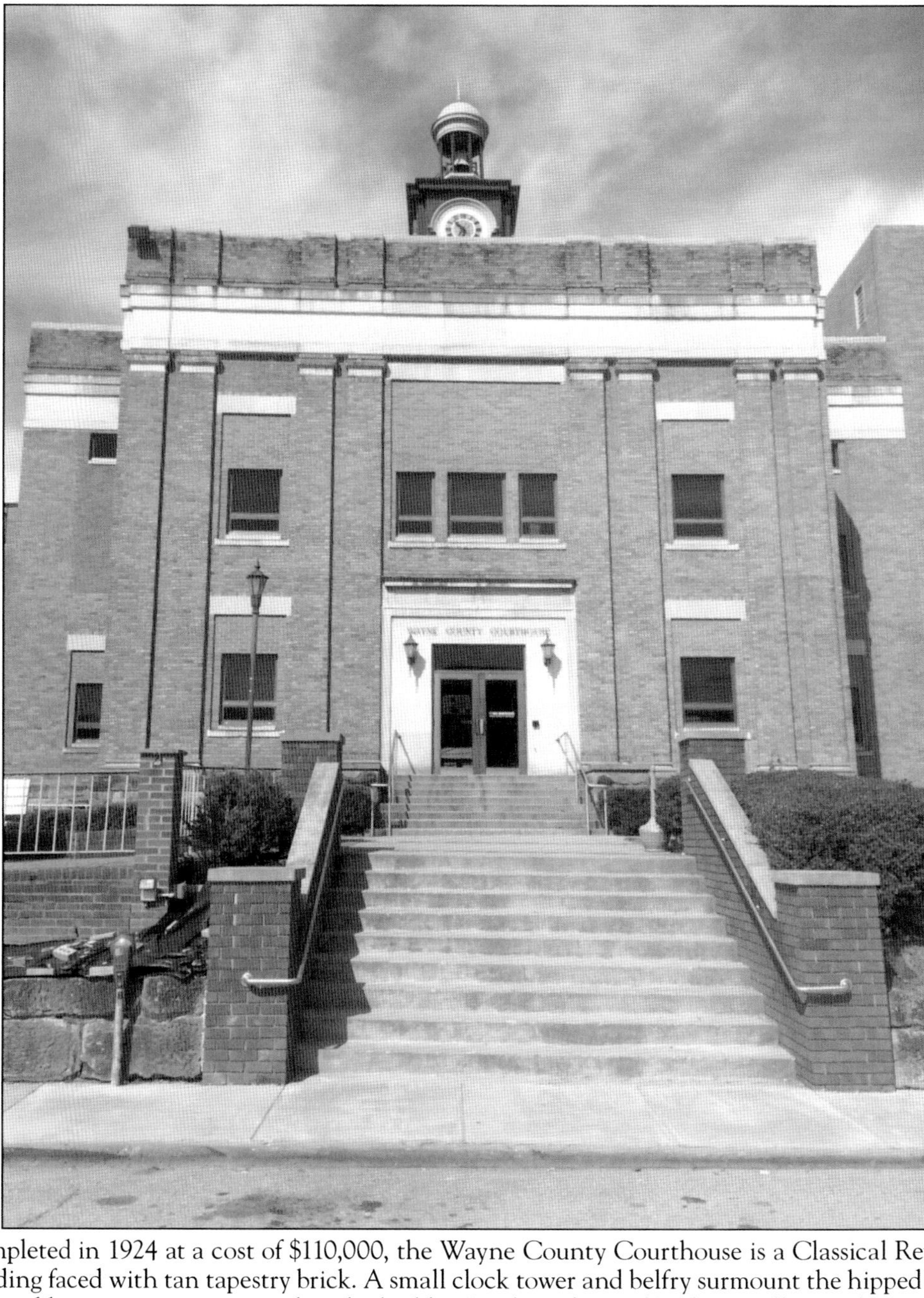

Completed in 1924 at a cost of $110,000, the Wayne County Courthouse is a Classical Revival building faced with tan tapestry brick. A small clock tower and belfry surmount the hipped roof. Later additions were constructed to the building's side and rear. (Author's collection.)

ON THE COVER: The Norfolk & Western (now Norfolk Southern) Railroad Bridge at Kenova is a true Wayne County landmark and an engineering marvel that has stood for more than 100 years. Workers such as these began constructing the span in 1890, a task that was not completed until 1913, when the first train rumbled across the steel-truss span. As the bridge took shape, the town of Kenova grew up around it. (Author's collection.)

IMAGES
of America

WAYNE COUNTY

James E. Casto

ARCADIA
PUBLISHING

ISBN 978-1-4671-3423-1

Published by Arcadia Publishing
Charleston, South Carolina

Printed in the United States of America

Library of Congress Control Number: 2015940580

For all general information, please contact Arcadia Publishing:
Telephone 843-853-2070
Fax 843-853-0044
E-mail sales@arcadiapublishing.com
For customer service and orders:
Toll-Free 1-888-313-2665

Visit us on the Internet at www.arcadiapublishing.com

Contents

ACKNOWLEDGMENTS

Let me say right up front that this slim book is by no means a comprehensive history of Wayne County. Such an effort would require a far larger book than this—and hands more capable than mine.

Instead, this book's vintage postcards, old photographs, and contemporary images are offered as a scrapbook of sorts that proffers a sample of Wayne County's fascinating story. It is my hope that as you leaf through the book, you will stop at some point and exclaim, "I remember that!" If so, I will have accomplished my mission.

Gathering the images included here was a demanding task. Fortunately, I had willing helpers. As in the past with my previous books, my former colleagues at the *Herald-Dispatch* were enormously helpful. Once again, editor and publisher Ed Dawson gave me a green light to rummage in the newspaper's archives for the photographs and information that I would require. "I'm sure Andrea can help you find what you need," he said, and online editor Andrea Copley did exactly that, smilingly responding to my many, many requests. Thank you, Andrea.

Jack Houvouras, whose *Huntington Quarterly* magazine has long chronicled our community's story, again granted me permission to use some of the magazine's striking photographs. Thank you, Jack.

Special collections at the Marshall University Library is a treasure chest of vintage photographs and other items, and Nat Debruin and Jack Dickinson were quick to respond when I turned to them for help. Thank you, Nat and Jack.

The photographs herein that are from the *Herald-Dispatch* are identified by the initials *H-D* at the end of their captions. Those from *Huntington Quarterly* are identified by the initials *HQ*. And those from Marshall are identified by the initials MU. Images from the author's personal collection are so indicated. Photographs provided from other sources are individually credited.

Finally, let me say that if this book has any interest or merit, it is because so many people were willing to help me with it. If there are mistakes in it, the fault is not theirs but solely mine.

INTRODUCTION

Wayne County is the westernmost of the 55 counties that make up West Virginia. Its total area of 440 square miles (281.6 acres) is bounded on the northwest by the Ohio River, the northeast by Cabell County, the east by Lincoln County, and the west by the Big Sandy River. The Ohio and the Big Sandy Rivers would play important roles in the county's history.

Dividing the county in two nearly equal parts is Twelve Pole Creek. The county's lowest elevation is that of Virginia Point in Kenova, which is 516 feet above sea level. Its highest point is at the county courthouse in Wayne, which is 600 feet above sea level. The county's estimated population in 2014 was 41,122.

Thousands of years before the first Europeans came to North America, ancient people sometimes referred to as Paleo Indians lived in what is now Wayne County. Later, the Adena, or mound builders, inhabited the region.

It is generally believed that the first white men to set foot in what is now Wayne County were members of what historians have labeled the Big Sandy Expedition of 1758. In the year before, the Shawnee Indians had attacked and destroyed a number of settlements. To avenge the attacks, Virginia governor Robert Dinwiddie ordered a force of militia to journey into the Indian country north of the Ohio River and subdue the Indians there. To avoid discovery, the militia traveled north along the Big Sandy River rather than the more frequented route along the Kanawha River.

When they were within 10 miles of the Ohio River and in the present limits of Wayne County, Francis Fauquier, who had newly arrived from England and replaced Dinwiddie as governor, ordered the men to turn around and return home. Discouraged and disheartened, they nevertheless obeyed the order, but with their provisions exhausted and winter's cold at its worst, many failed to survive the arduous return journey.

On December 15, 1772, Virginia governor Lord Dunmore, acting at the direction of King George III, granted 28,627 acres along the Ohio, Big Sandy, and Guyandotte Rivers to John Savage and 59 other former soldiers who had fought for England in the French and Indian War. The tract stretched from Greenbottom at the eastern end of today's Cabell County; west along the Ohio River to Catlettsburg, Kentucky; and south on the Big Sandy to the forks of the river at present-day Fort Gay. The Wayne County towns of Ceredo and Kenova are now located on land that was included in the Savage Grant.

Apparently, none of the old soldiers ever lived on their newly acquired land, but in 1775, some of the grantees met on the land for a partial division, and all of the properties were eventually claimed by descendents or assignees of the 60 men.

Wayne County was established on January 18, 1842, from part of Cabell County and was named for Gen. "Mad Anthony" Wayne, a Revolutionary War hero who retired from the Army in 1783 but later was recalled by President Washington in the hopes he could put a halt to continued Indians attacks on the Virginia frontier.

Nicknamed "Mad Anthony" for his impetuous nature, the general proved singularly cautious in his new assignment. He spent two years gathering and training his troops before leading them to victory over the Indians in the Battle of Fallen Timbers on the Maumee River near the present-day site of Toledo, Ohio. In the ensuing Treaty of Greenville, the defeated Indians ceded any claim to lands in southern Ohio and parts of Indiana.

General Wayne died in 1796 at the age of 51. There are 16 counties and 12 cities in the country that are named for him.

Established by the same 1842 legislation that created the county, the town of Wayne is the county seat. Wayne originally was named Trout's Hill, after miller Abraham Trout, who donated the land where the county's first courthouse was built. The town was later incorporated as Fairview but was still commonly known as Wayne Courthouse. In 1890, the Norfolk & Western Railway placed the name Wayne on its schedule, and the name caught on. The town's name was officially changed to Wayne in 1911.

Wayne has always been the county seat, but it more than once had to defend that status against challenges from other towns. In 1905, Ceredo made a campaign to see the county seat moved there from Wayne, even offering to pay for tearing down the courthouse in Wayne and building a new one in Ceredo. In February 1906, the county's voters firmly rejected Ceredo's bid. In 1921, Kenova campaigned to have the county seat moved there. Again, the voters said no.

Although the southern half of the county was the first to be settled, it remained sparsely populated and was slow to develop. The northern part, bordering Cabell County, expanded rapidly after the Civil War. The city of Huntington, Cabell's county seat, was founded as the western terminus of the Chesapeake & Ohio Railway in 1871 and grew rapidly. In 1921, Huntington expanded its corporate limits westward into Wayne County. The Wayne County portion of Huntington is known as Westmoreland.

In the 19th century, timbering and farming were the county's economic mainstays. Later, coal mining would provide good-paying jobs for many men. Today, many of the county's residents drive to jobs in Huntington or across the Big Sandy River in Ashland, Kentucky.

In addition to its portion of Huntington and the town of Wayne, the county has three other incorporated communities—Ceredo, Kenova, and Fort Gay.

A New England abolitionist and member of the US House of Representatives, Eli Thayer founded the town of Ceredo in 1857, the same year he was elected to Congress. In founding Ceredo, Thayer wanted to show Southerners that a community could function successfully without slave labor. He named his new settlement after Ceres, the Roman goddess of grain and harvest, equivalent to the Greek goddess Demeter. Thayer's new town attracted 500 or so residents.

Kenova's founders chose its site because it was where the Norfolk & Western Railway planned to build the first bridge across the Ohio River between Wheeling, West Virginia, and Cincinnati, Ohio. Work on the bridge began in 1890, and Kenova was incorporated in 1894. The completion of the N&W to the Ohio River and the new town of Kenova touched off a growth spurt in the county's southern end.

The town of Fort Gay traces its history back to 1789, when a dozen people established a settlement at the junction of the Tug and Big Sandy Rivers, across from what is now Louisa, Kentucky. In 1875, it was chartered as Cassville—though it was simultaneously known as Fort Gay. In 1932, the town's name was officially changed to Fort Gay. While there is no evidence as to why the name was changed, there are several theories. One theory notes that there is another West Virginia town named Cassville, and either the N&W or the post office did not want two Cassvilles on the same route or in the same state. The other theory holds that a Civil War nurse named Gay became synonymous with the town.

Well-known unincorporated communities in the county include Kiasville, Crum, Dunlow, Genoa, East Lynn, Wilsondale, Prichard, Shoals, and Lavalette.

Recreation plays an important role in Wayne County life. The county is home to Beech Fork State Park and Lake, East Lynn Lake, Cabwaylingo State Forest, Heritage Farm Museum and Village, Dreamland Pool, and Camden Park, West Virginia's only surviving amusement park.

Today, Wayne County is experiencing a modest resurgence of manufacturing, with new and expanded plants at the A. Michael Perry Industrial Park in Prichard and other locales. And the county is anticipating a major economic impact from the $30 million intermodal freight facility being developed by the West Virginia Public Port Authority at a 100-acre site adjacent to the Perry Industrial Park in Prichard.

One

Beginnings

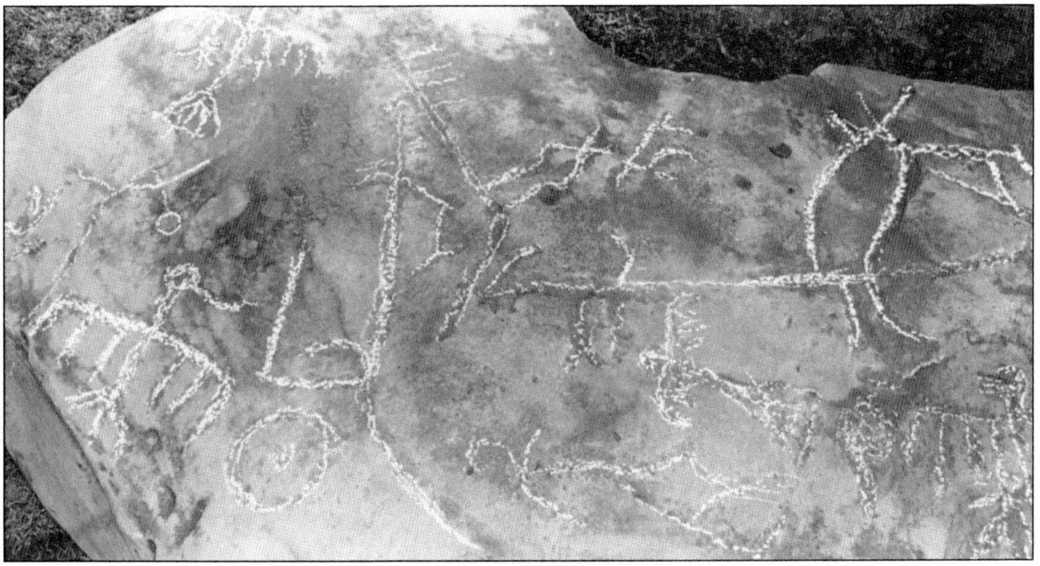

Thousands of years before the first Europeans came to North America, ancient people sometimes referred to as Paleo Indians lived in what is now Wayne County. Later, the mound-building Adena inhabited the region. The early Indians used crude tools to make rock carvings depicting their daily lives. Frontier settlers thoughtlessly destroyed many, but some—such as this example found near Fort Gay on the Big Sandy River—have survived and been preserved. Chalk has been applied to make the carvings stand out. They appear to represent a goose and a beaver. (Courtesy of *H-D*.)

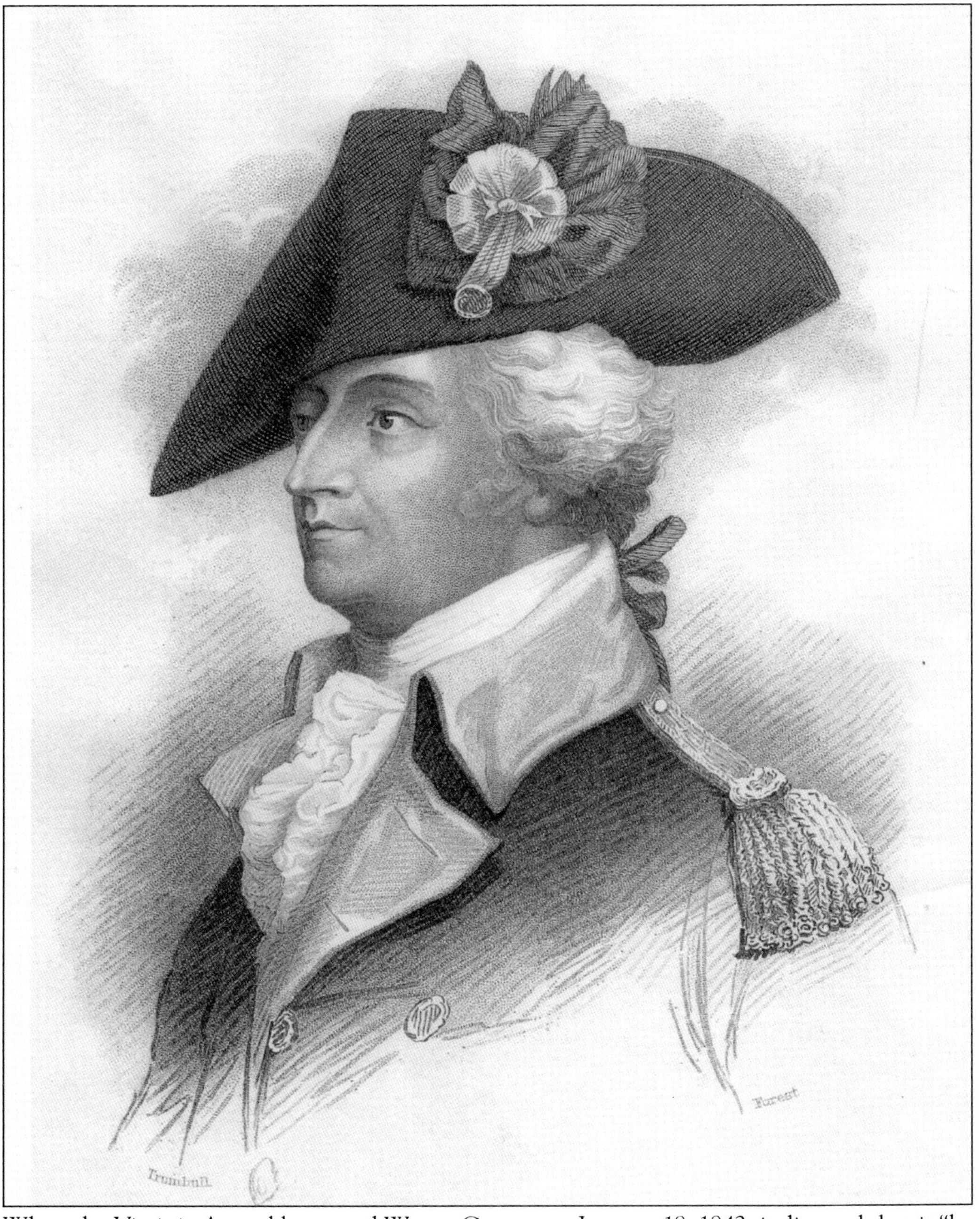

When the Virginia Assembly created Wayne County on January 18, 1842, it directed that it "be called and known by the name of Wayne County, in memory of and in honor of General Anthony Wayne." Wayne served with distinction in the American Revolution. Among his victories was a successful surprise attack on the British in July 1779 at New York's Stoney Point on the Hudson River. Wayne retired from the Army in 1783 but was called back to duty to deal with the Indian raids on settlers in the Ohio Valley. He crushed the Indians at the Battle of Fallen Timbers in August 1794. He is generally known as Mad Anthony Wayne, not because he was a lunatic, but because of his legendary quick temper. Again retiring, he divided his time between business and politics. He died in 1796 at the age of 51. (Courtesy of the Library of Congress.)

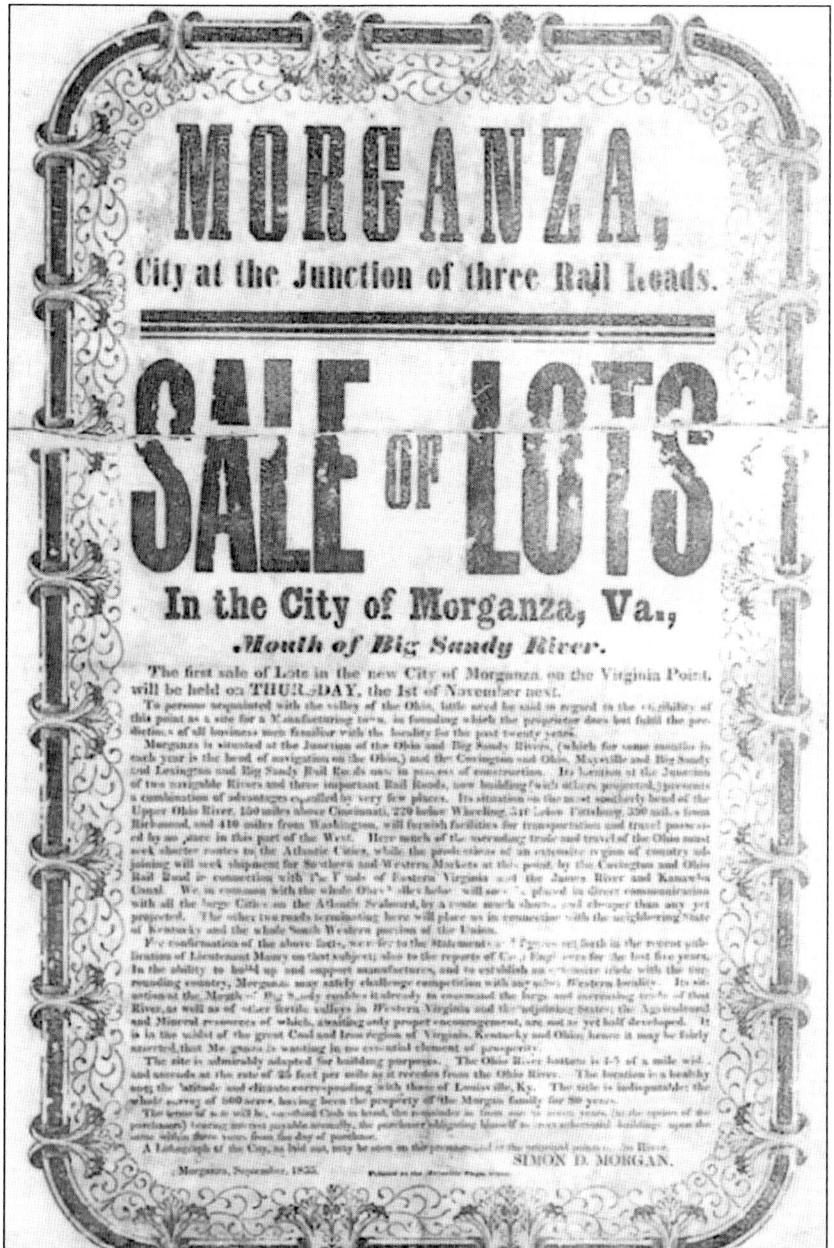

Morganza, Virginia, is a Wayne County town that never was. On November 9, 1858, Jeremiah Wellman presented to the Wayne County Court a plan for a town to be built at Virginia Point (where the Big Sandy and Ohio Rivers meet). The plan identified the new town as Morganza, presumably in honor of the Morgan brothers, who at that time owned 800 acres of land on the Ohio and Big Sandy Rivers. Flyers were printed and posted announcing the first public sale of lots on November 1, 1885. The results of that sale are not known, but the town never developed. The flyer boasted that Morganza would be situated on two rivers and three railroads. In 1890, the town of Kenova would be built at the same location, watered by two rivers and served by three railroads. (Author's collection.)

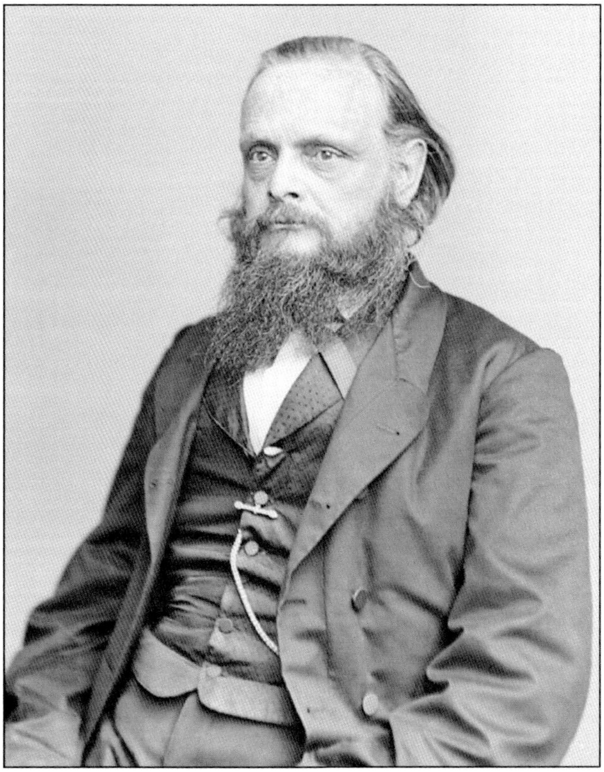

Abolitionist politician John C. Underwood founded the American Emigrant Aid and Homestead Company to plant abolitionist colonies in slave-holding states. The idea appealed to New England abolitionist Eli Thayer, who initially partnered with Underwood but ultimately took control of the project. (Courtesy of the Library of Congress.)

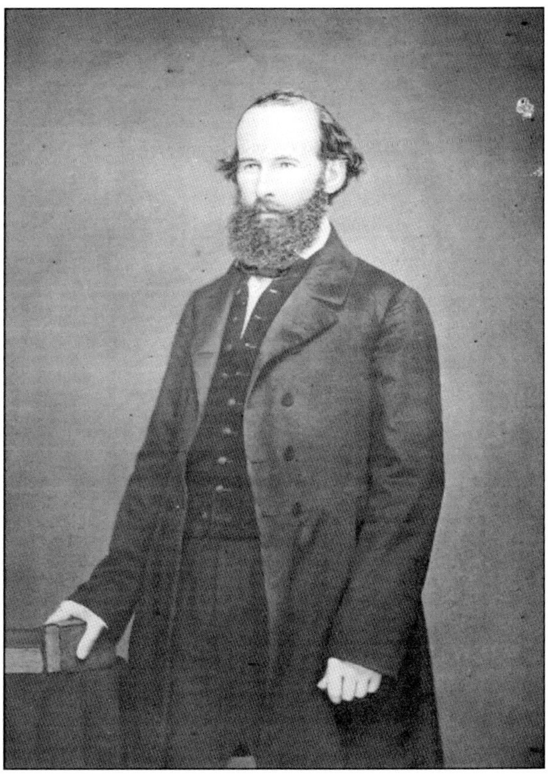

A New England abolitionist and member of the US House of Representatives, Eli Thayer founded the Wayne County town of Ceredo in 1857, the same year he was elected to Congress. In founding Ceredo, Thayer wanted to show Southerners that a community could function without slave labor. He named his new settlement after Ceres, the Roman goddess of grain and harvest, equivalent to the Greek goddess Demeter. Thayer's new town attracted 500 or so residents. He is represented here in a photograph by famed Civil War photographer Mathew Brady. (Courtesy of the Library of Congress.)

The Civil War brought hard times to Ceredo, and most of the New England settlers fled. One who did not was Zopher D. Ramsdell, the owner of a boot and shoe factory, and he became the city's postmaster. The Ramsdell family home, built in 1858 at Ceredo's B and Fourth Streets, is thought to have been a stop on the Underground Railroad, which smuggled runaway slaves north to freedom. Today, the house is a museum. (Courtesy of *HQ*.)

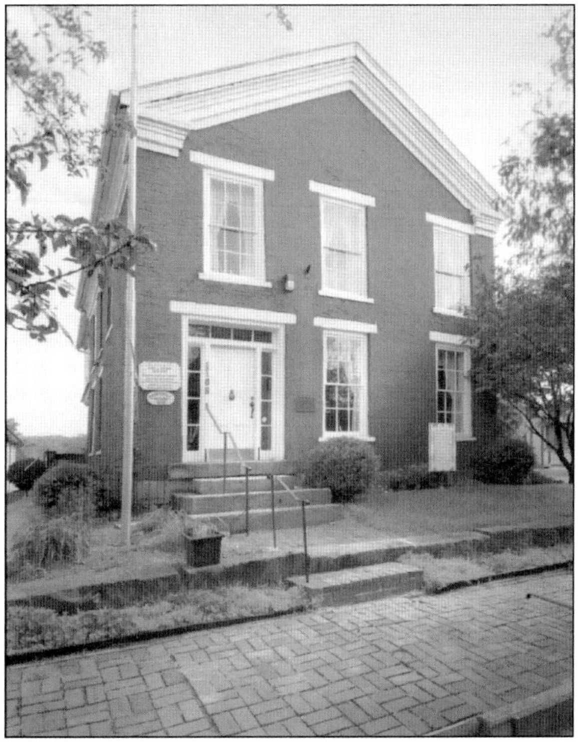

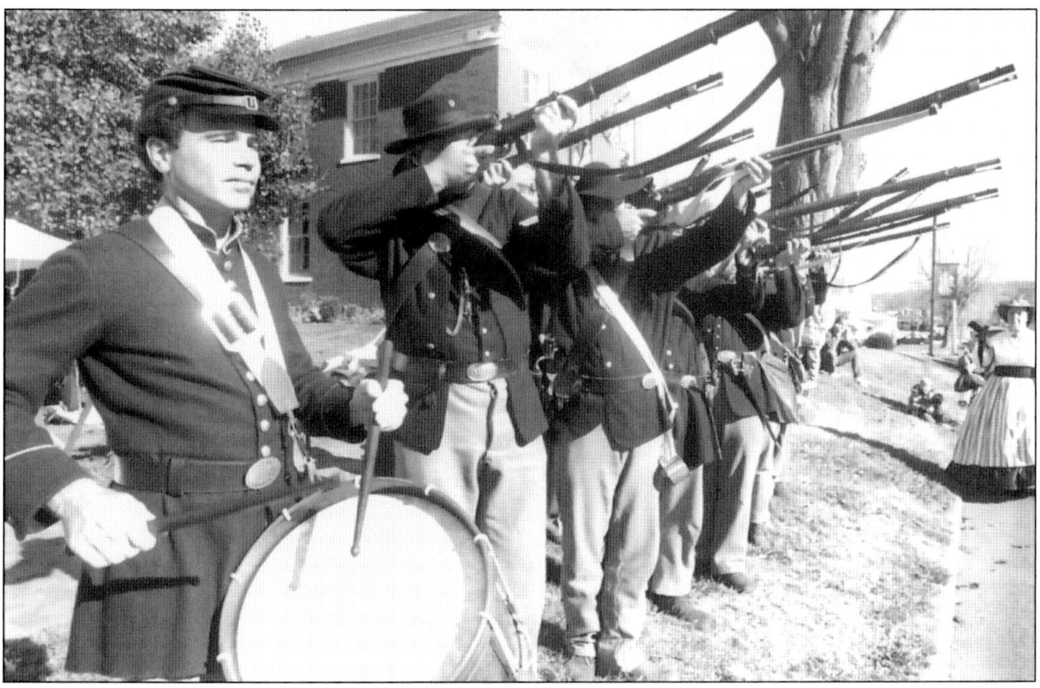

A drummer raps his drum to signal the troops to fire their guns during a 1990 Civil War reenactment at Ceredo's Ramsdell House. Most of the participants were members of the Confederate 36th Virginia Infantry, but they occasionally portray Union soldiers, as they did this day. (Courtesy of *H-D*.)

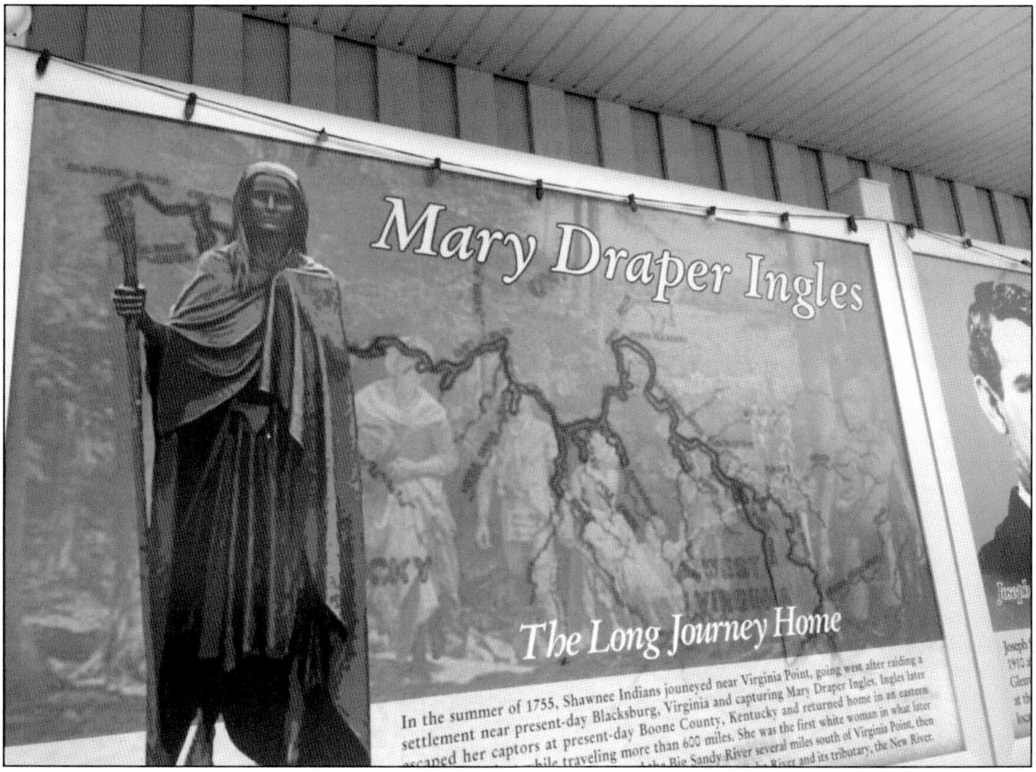

A row of posters along Kenova's Chestnut Street celebrates Wayne County's history. This one portrays Mary Draper Ingles. In 1755, Indians captured Ingles at her Virginia home and took her to Ohio. She managed to escape and make her way on foot through more than 600 miles of wilderness to return home, an incredible trek that made her the first white woman to set foot in Wayne County. (Author's collection.)

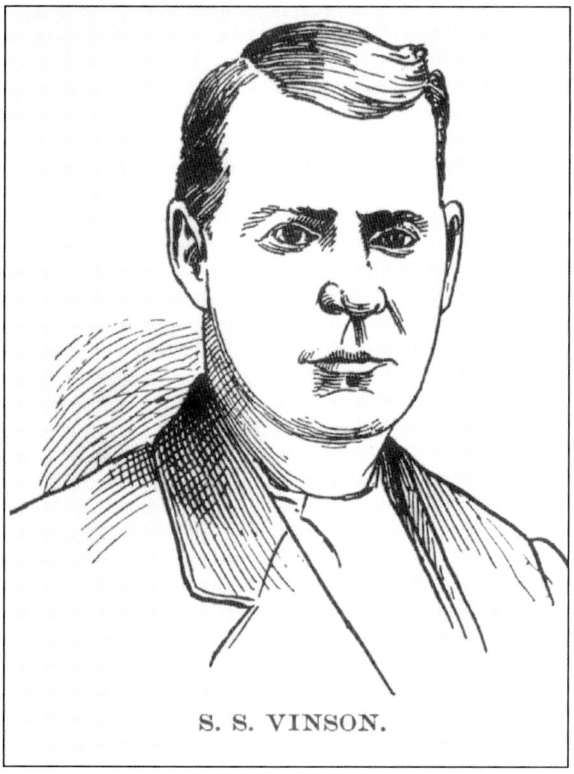

S. S. VINSON.

Samuel Sperry Vinson, known as "Uncle Sam," was born on the Tug Fork of the Big Sandy River in Kentucky in 1833 but lived most of his life in Wayne County, where he was prominent in business and political circles. When the Civil War began, he rallied to the Confederate cause. He was wounded twice before being captured, then paroled. He died in 1904. (Courtesy of Jack Dickinson.)

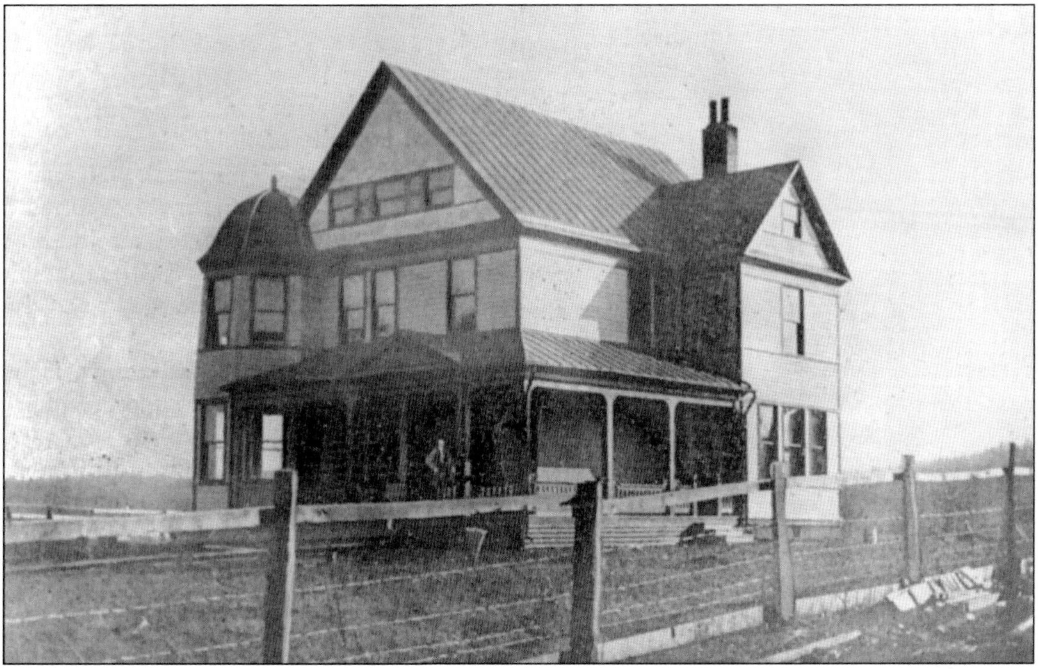

Wayne County's James Ferguson could not read or write but had a head for figures, which enabled him to have a big farm, worked by slaves. When the Civil War began, he sent his seven sons to join the Confederacy. One son, called "Big Wayne," was only 14 when he joined up. He survived the war and is shown here on the porch of his home in Wayne around 1890. (Courtesy of *H-D*.)

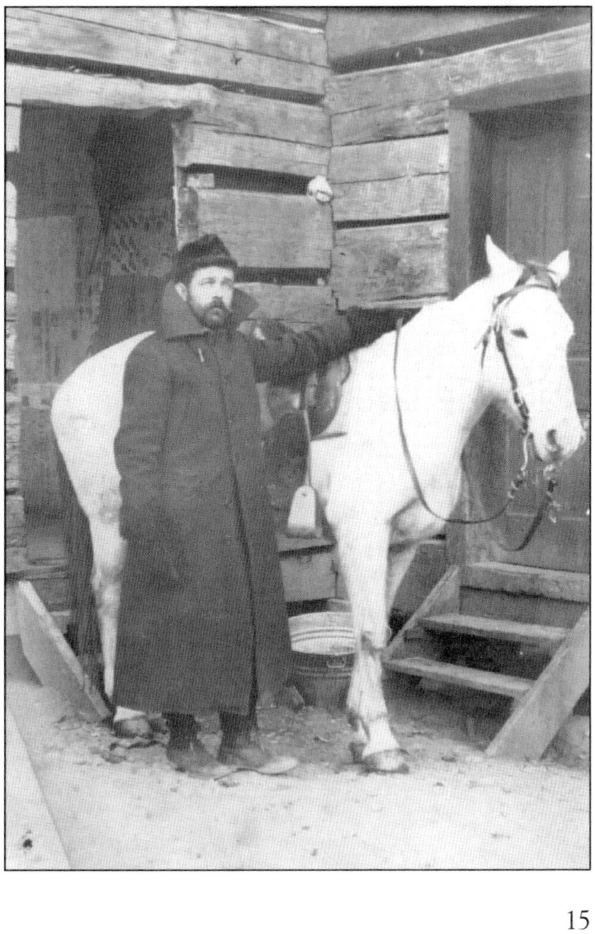

In the early 1900s, Dr. Oscar T. Hines learned that the small Wayne County town of East Lynn needed a coal company doctor. Local legend says he turned down a fancy job at Tulane University in New Orleans, Louisiana, to accept the East Lynn job, where he would minister not just to the health needs of the miners and their families, but also nearby families. (Courtesy of MU.)

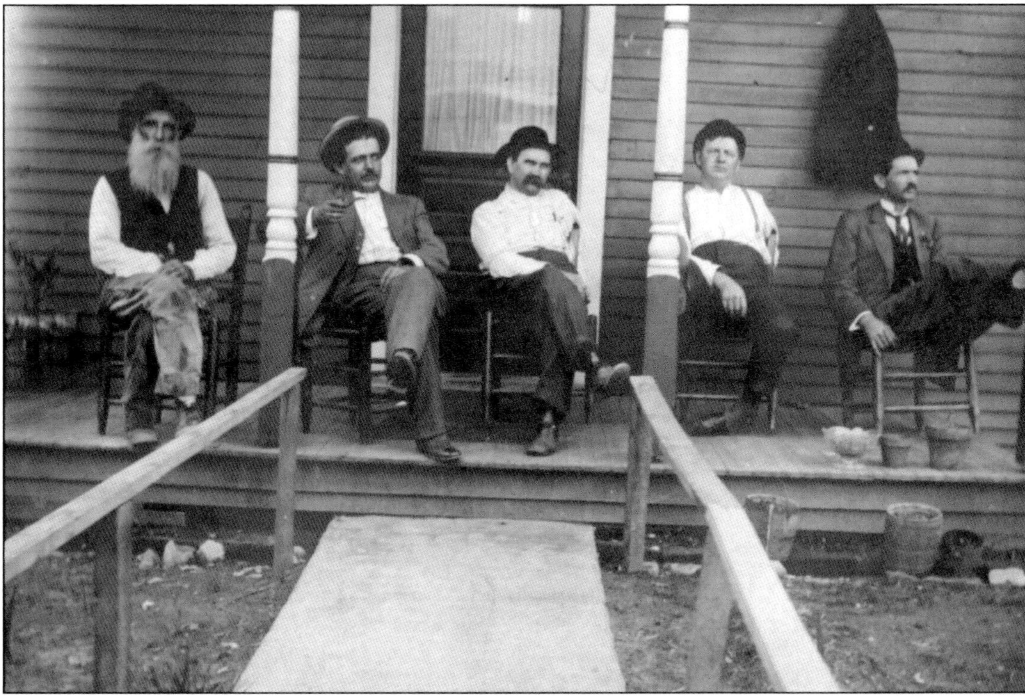

Postmarked in 1910, this postcard shows a group of local men gathered on the front porch of a building known variously as the East Lynn Hotel and the Golden Rule Lodge Hall. From left to right are John Ward Lloyd, Dr. Hines, Walker Osburn, an unidentified man, and a man identified only as "Mr. Clay." (Courtesy of MU.)

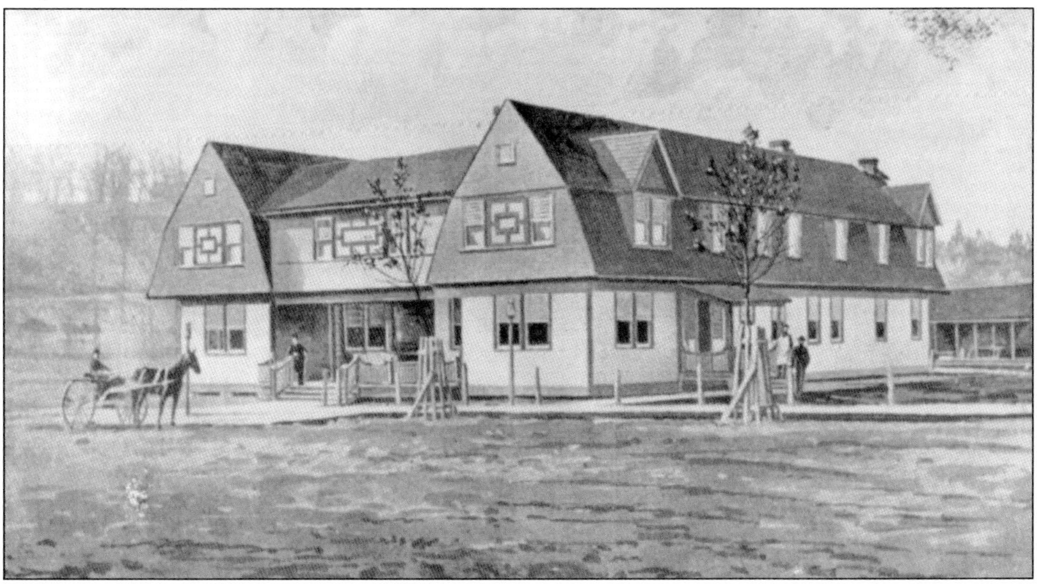

When L.T. Peck and Floyd Hoard of Ceredo announced their plans for the Glenwood Hotel in Kenova, they proposed a five-story brick building costing $100,000. But the Panic of 1893 delayed things. What was finally completed in 1902 was a much more modest two-story hotel. Despite its smaller size, the building was a showplace until 1917, when declining business forced its closure. (Courtesy of *H-D.*)

Two

WAYNE

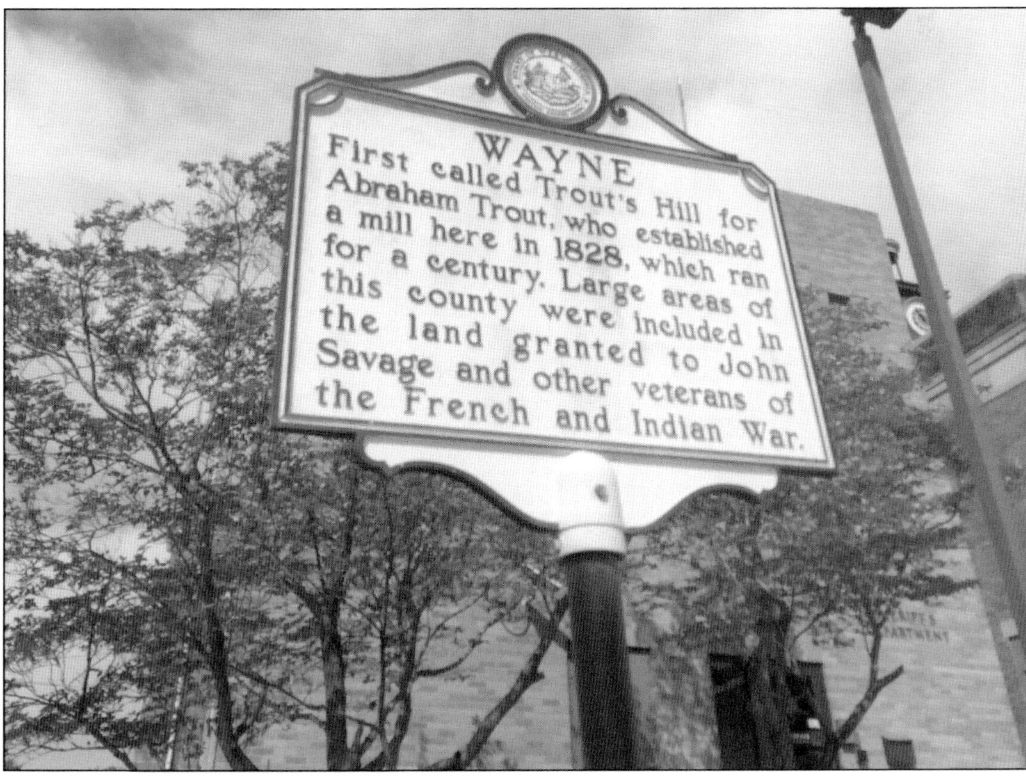

As this historical marker on the courthouse grounds proclaims, the town of Wayne initially was named Trout's Hill, after miller Abraham Trout. Trout donated the land where the county's first courthouse was built. The town of Wayne was established in 1842 by the same act of the Virginia General Assembly that created Wayne County. (Author's collection.)

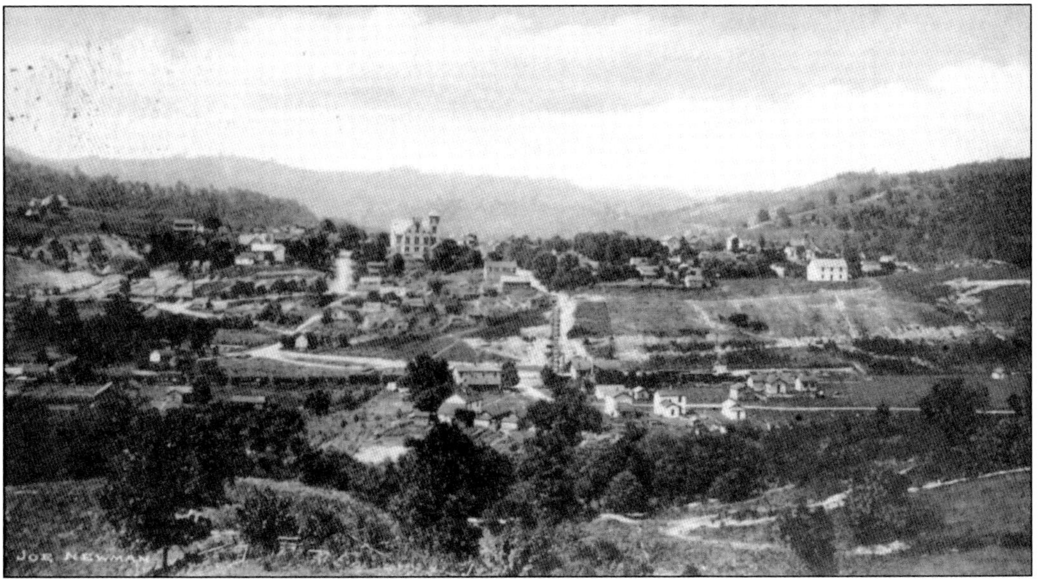

The Wayne Courthouse Post Office was also established in 1842, and for many years the town was known simultaneously as Trout's Hill and Wayne Courthouse. The town was incorporated in 1860 and again in 1882 as Fairview but was still commonly known as Wayne Courthouse. In 1890, the Norfolk & Western Railway placed the name Wayne on its schedule, and the name caught on. The town's name was officially changed to Wayne in 1911. (Author's collection.)

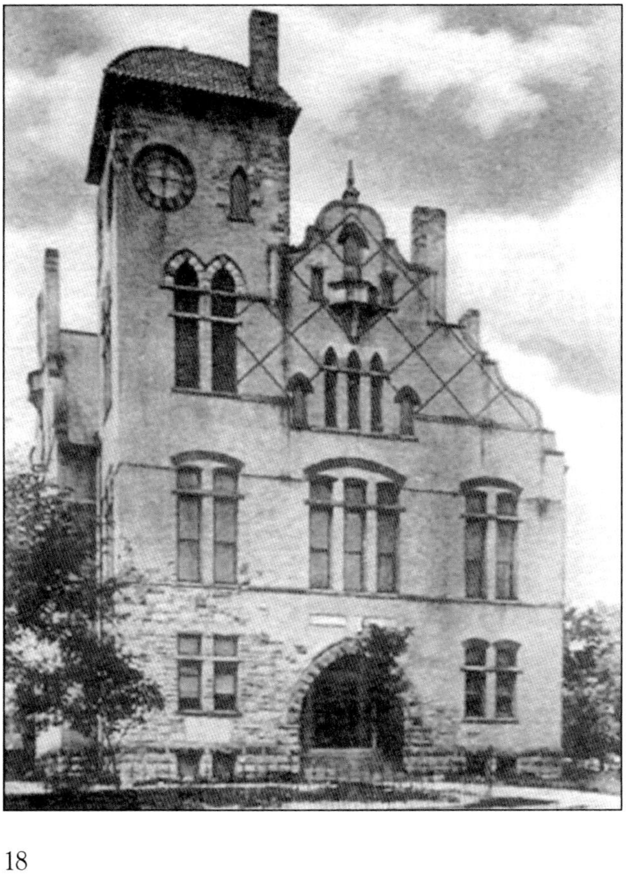

Wayne County's first courthouse was built of logs. A brick building followed in 1852 and a new larger structure in 1891. When it burned down a few years later, Frank P. Milburn designed this replacement structure. When it burned in 1921, Milburn's successor firm designed the present structure. (Author's collection.)

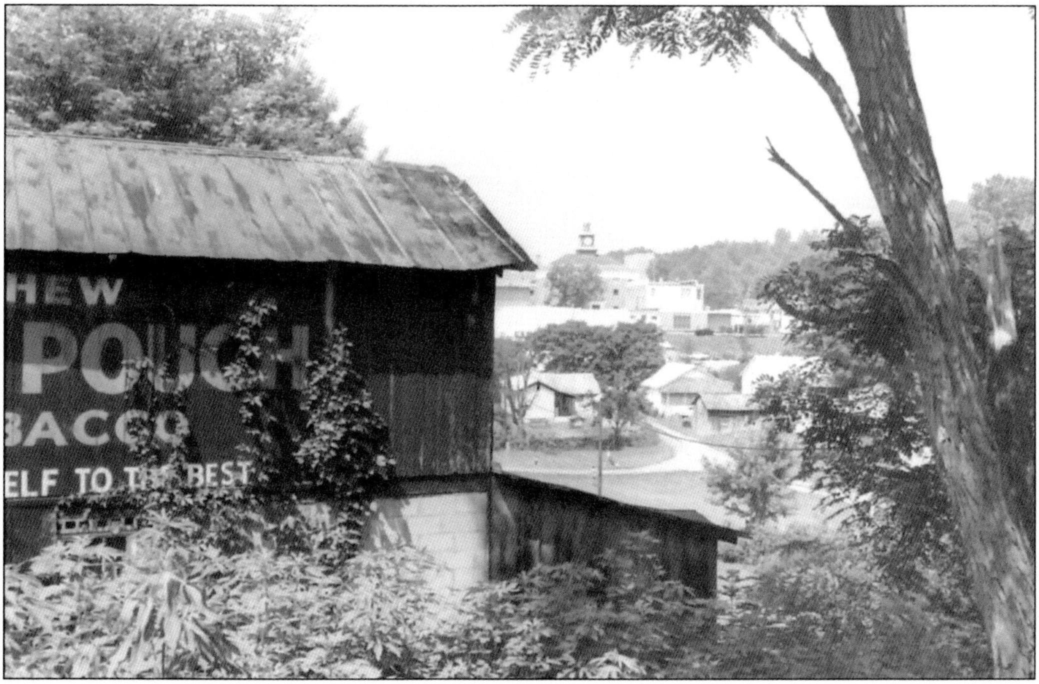

Barns painted with giant signs advertising Mail Pouch chewing tobacco once dotted the rural landscape in West Virginia and nearly two dozen other states. The Bloch Brothers Tobacco Company in Wheeling paid farmers a few dollars for the advertisements. But more importantly, a farmer received a fresh coat of paint on his barn. The signs were seldom seen as close to town as this one photographed on the outskirts of Wayne in 1981. Note the clock tower atop the courthouse, visible in the distance. (Courtesy of *H-D*.)

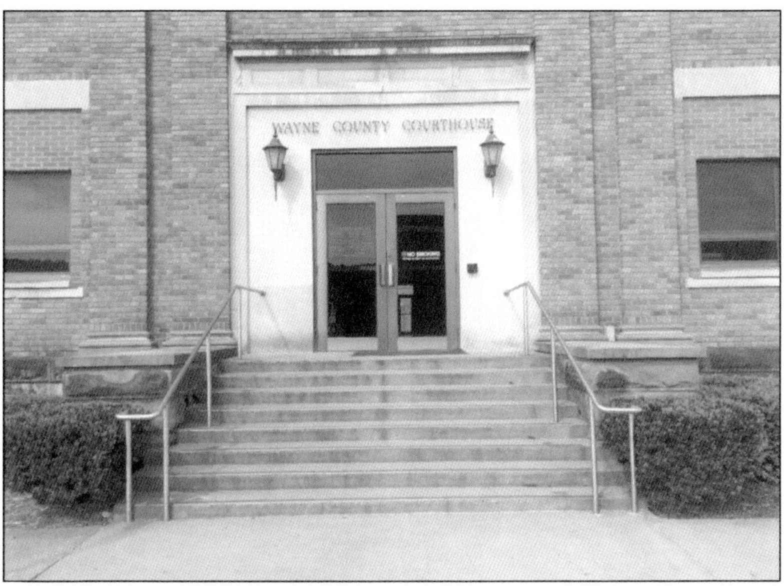

The central double entrance doors at the Wayne Courthouse have a simple stone surround. While the original window openings have been infilled with smaller window units, the original stone lintels and sills remain. (Author's collection.)

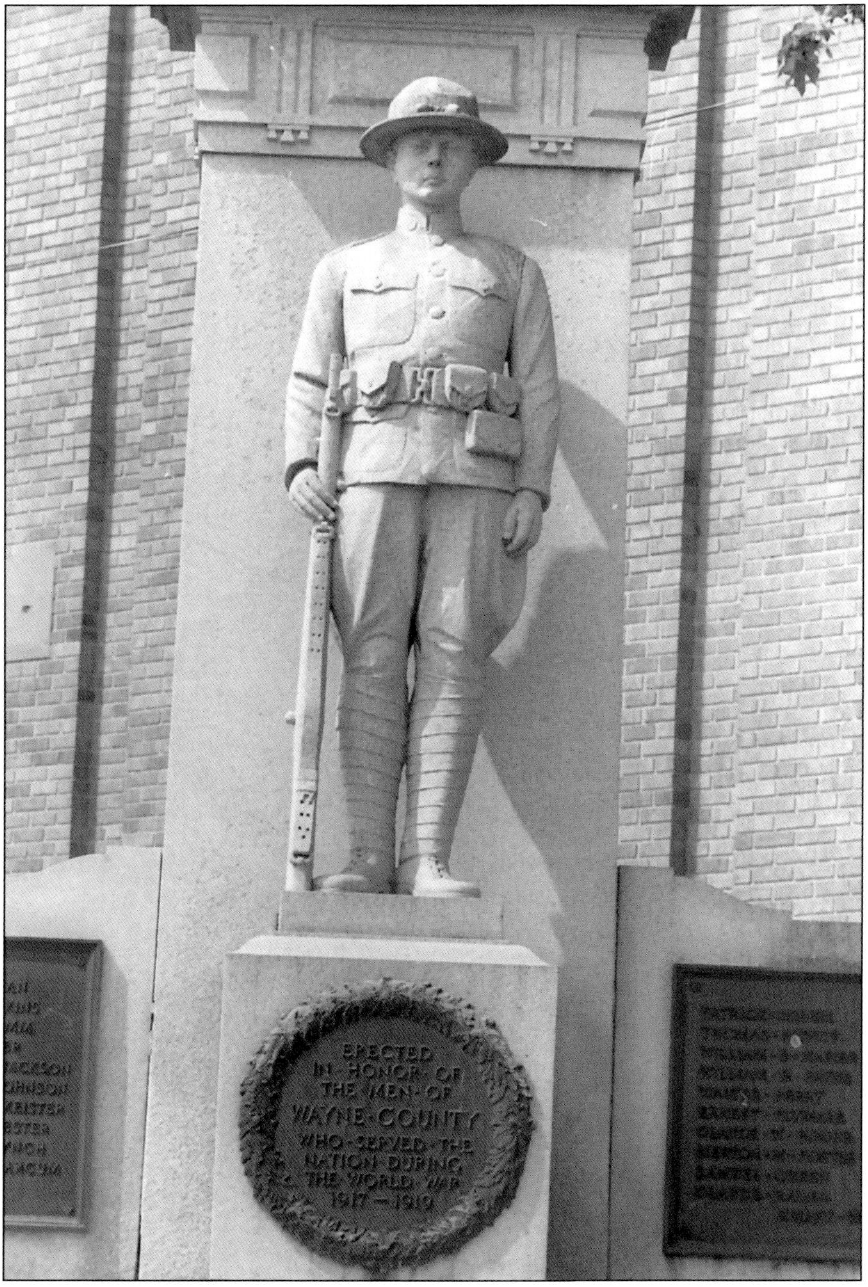

There were 42 men from Wayne County killed in World War I, a terrible toll for a county so small. In the 1920s, a memorial to the fallen men was erected on the courthouse lawn. The county spent $12,000 on a statue of a World War I doughboy carved from New England granite by Sears Monument Company of Charleston, West Virginia. The names of the 42 men from the county who died during the war were placed on a bronze plaque at the base of the statue. At the dedication ceremony for the monument on May 30, 1923, the names of the fallen were read, "Taps" was sounded, and the American flag draped over the monument was pulled off, revealing the statue. Inside the courthouse, both walls in the main entryway display photographs of veterans, some dating back to the Spanish-American War. (Courtesy of *H-D*.)

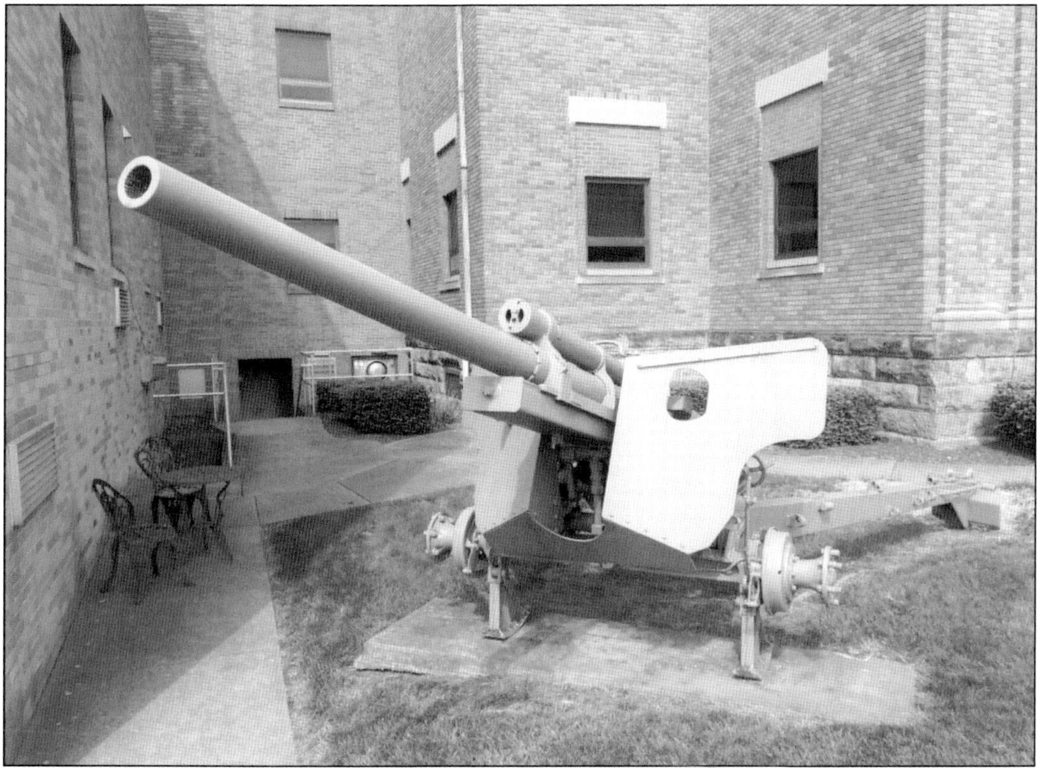

After World War I, Wayne County, like many others across the nation, was given old cannons to put on display. When World War II began, the old cannons were donated for scrap metal to aid the war effort. After the war, Wayne received World War II cannons to replace them. They are on display at the courthouse and the Veterans Park. (Author's collection.)

Large additions have been added to the side and rear of the Wayne Courthouse. While the additions provided badly needed space, they are out of scale with the rest of the structure and make the original clock tower and belfry appear too small for the building. (Courtesy of *H-D*.)

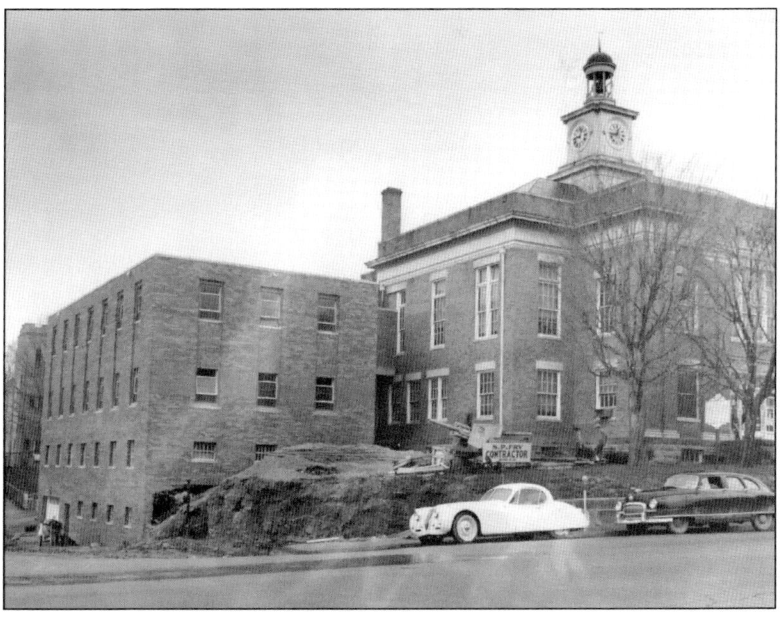

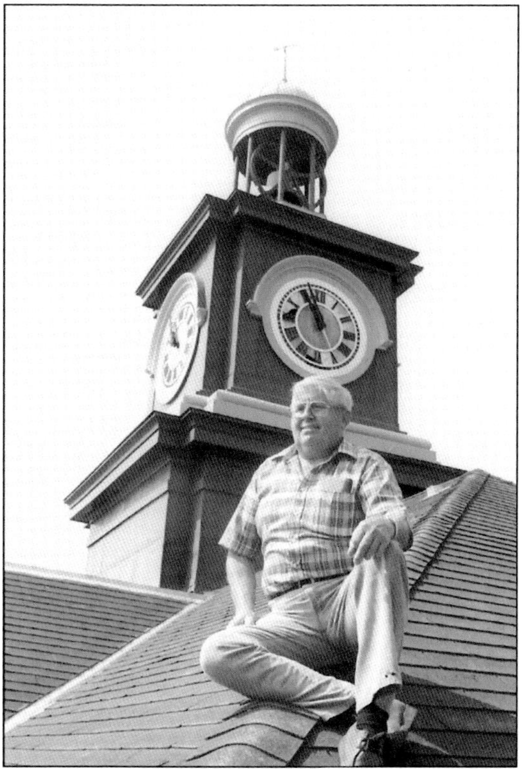

As part of a 1981 photographic essay titled "Wayne, USA," the *Herald-Dispatch* photographed Wayne mayor Otis Skeans perched on the roof of the county courthouse. In the brief text with the photograph, the newspaper did not divulge how or why it lured the mayor to pose in such an odd setting. (Courtesy of *H-D*.)

In 2014, Wayne County opened a courthouse annex across the street from the courthouse to house operations of family court, the assessor's office, and the probation office. In West Virginia, family court judges hear cases involving divorce and other family issues, including final hearings in domestic violence civil proceedings. (Author's collection.)

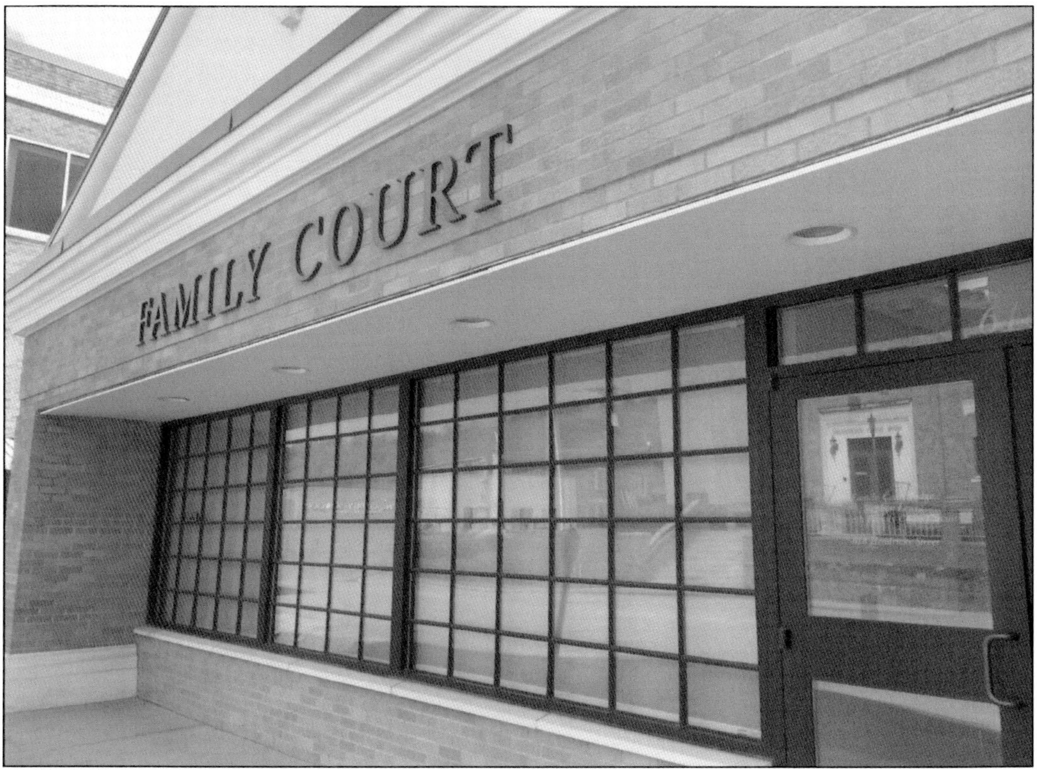

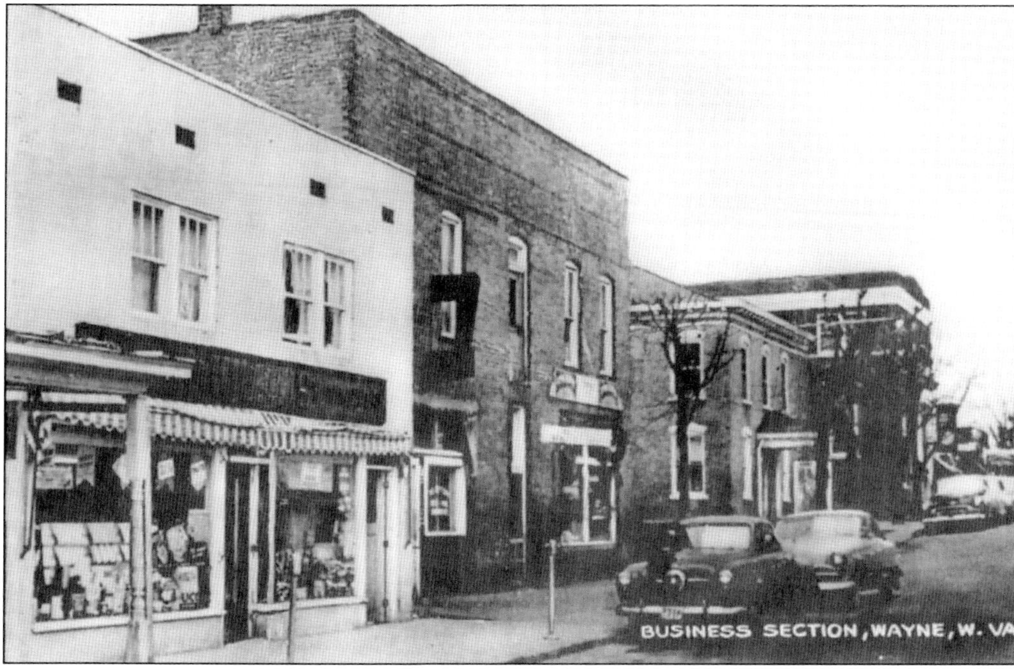

This old postcard provides a great view of a major Wayne thoroughfare, Hendricks Street, during the 1950s. The street was one of the first laid out when Wayne was established in 1842 and is thought to have been named Main Street at the time. In the election of 1884, the people of Wayne supported Pres. Grover Cleveland and Vice Pres. Thomas Hendricks and named two streets for them. (Author's collection.)

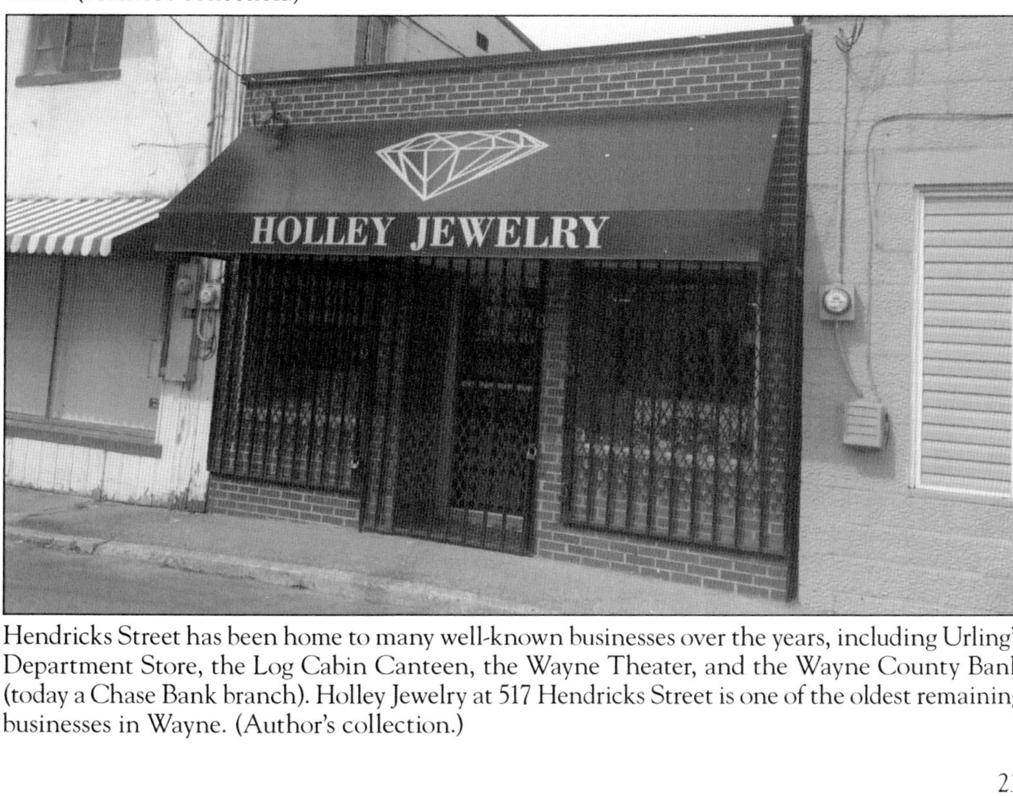

Hendricks Street has been home to many well-known businesses over the years, including Urling's Department Store, the Log Cabin Canteen, the Wayne Theater, and the Wayne County Bank (today a Chase Bank branch). Holley Jewelry at 517 Hendricks Street is one of the oldest remaining businesses in Wayne. (Author's collection.)

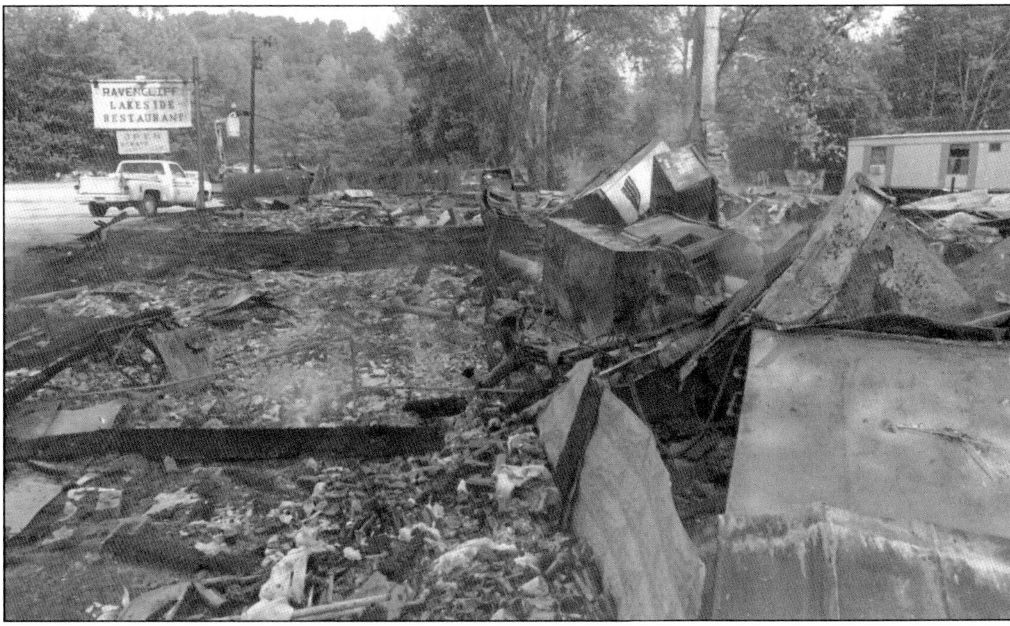

Its formal name was the Ravencliff Restaurant, but most folks just called it Zip's. The roadside tavern-restaurant about three miles north of Wayne on US 52 was a popular hangout for Marshall University students and other young people. Hatfield "Zip" Brubeck, a former member of the West Virginia State Senate, owned and operated the Ravencliff for about 35 years until his death in 1973. An early-morning fire on June 7, 1976, reduced it to ashes. (Courtesy of *H-D*.)

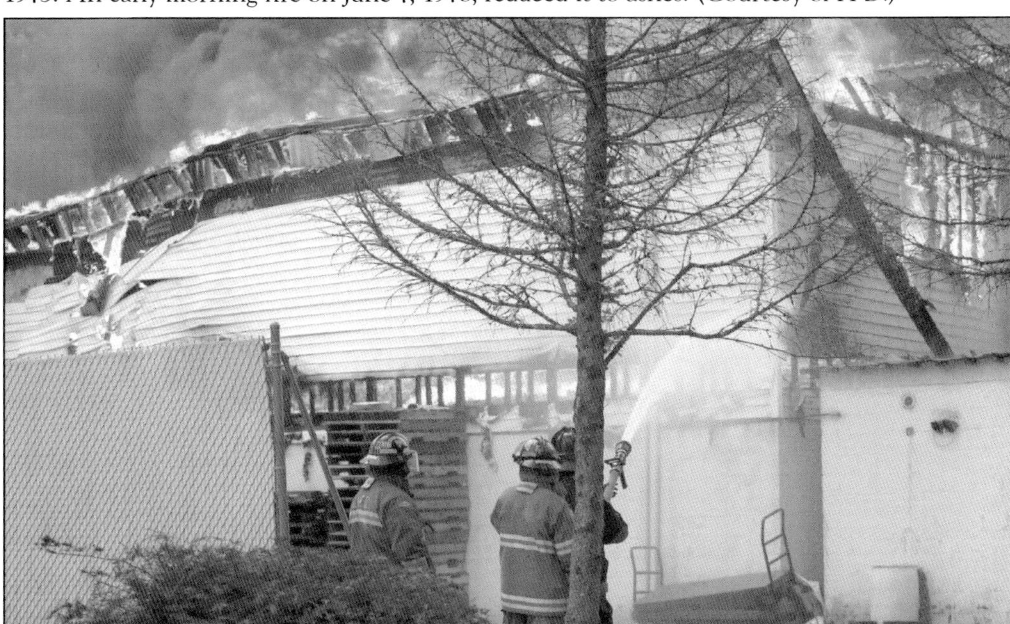

Only a few concrete walls remained following a massive August 4, 2014, fire that destroyed the Ballards Farm Sausage plant on the Right Fork of Wilson Creek in Wayne County. Operated by the Ballard family for three generations, the sausage company was one of the best-known businesses in the county. (Courtesy of *H-D*.)

Three

Ceredo and Kenova

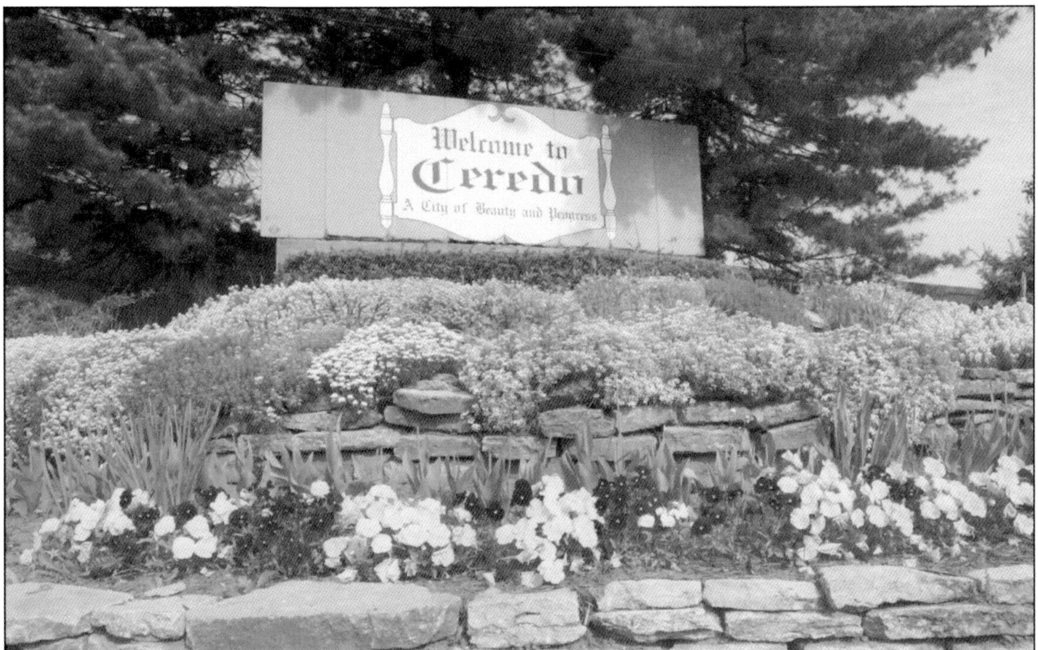

This beautifully landscaped sign welcoming visitors to Ceredo is an example of the work done by members of the town's beautification committee. Over the years, the committee has planted hundreds of trees, installed and maintained flowers in planters, and perhaps most importantly, encouraged homeowners and businesses to spruce up their own properties. As one committee member puts it, "The better job we do, the more ambition people have to work on their own property." (Courtesy of *HQ*.)

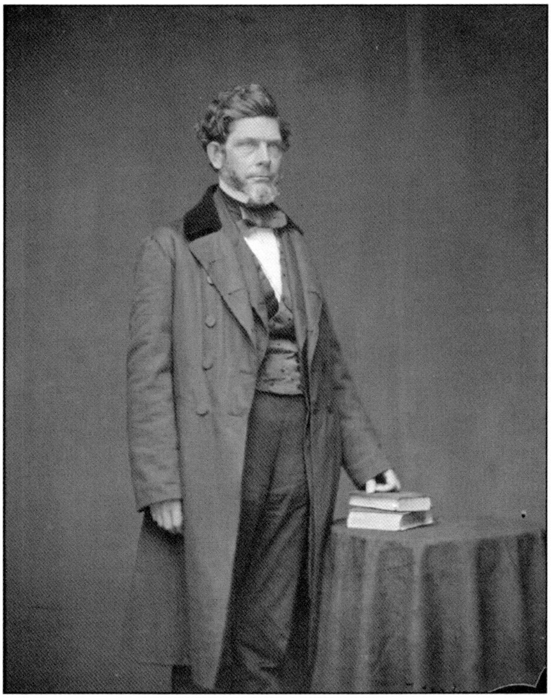

Manufacturer Charles B. Hoard loaned Eli Thayer some of the funds he needed to establish his new Wayne County town. During the Civil War, Hoard lost money as the result of a dispute with the War Department over a contract he had entered into for the manufacture of rifles. In 1870, looking for a new start, he relocated to Ceredo. (Courtesy of the Library of Congress.)

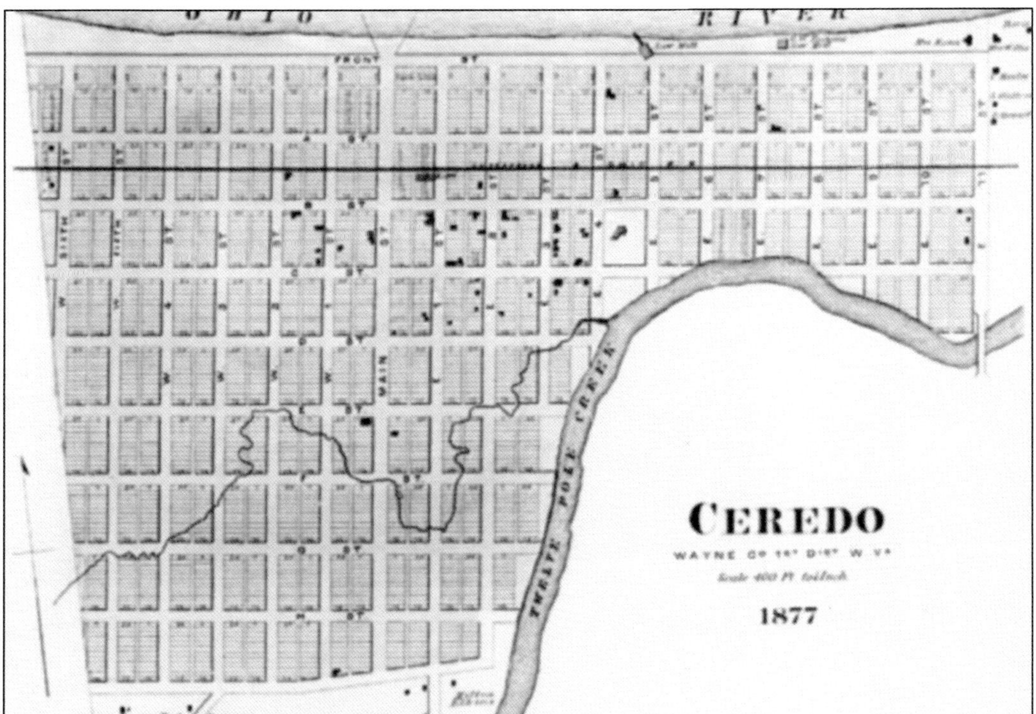

In 1868, Thayer sold his interest in Ceredo to Hoard. From 1870, when he moved to Ceredo, until his death in 1886, Hoard devoted most of his energy to developing the town. His efforts to improve Ceredo and repair his fortunes proved successful. This 1877 map reflects a number of changes Hoard made to Thayer's original town plan. (Author's collection.)

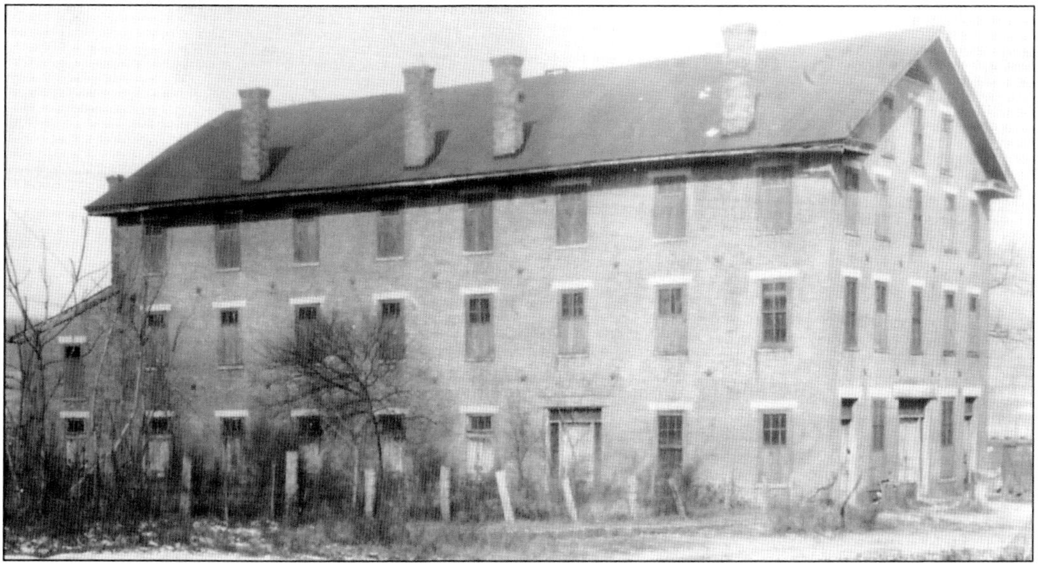

In Ceredo's earliest years, a newspaper, the *Ceredo Crescent*, was published in this building, variously known as the Ceredo House or the Thayer Hotel. Charles B. Webb was the paper's editor. The building served as an armory and a hospital during the Civil War. (Author's collection.)

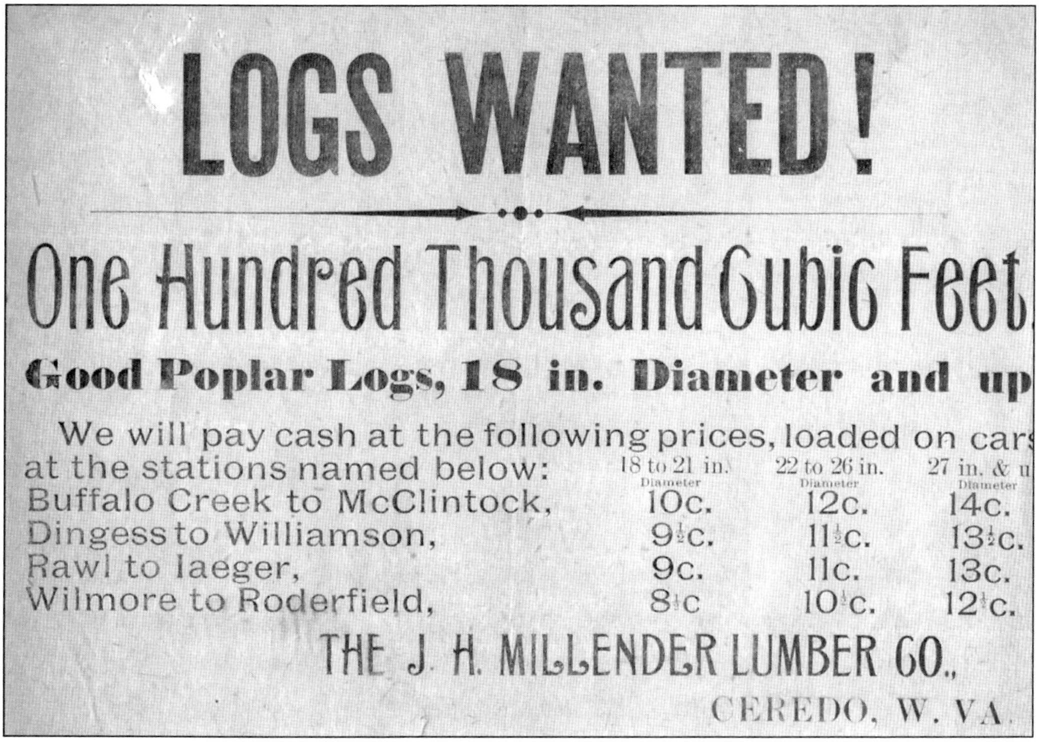

Another family that came to Ceredo in its early years was the Millender family, which formed the J.H. Millender Lumber Co. "LOGS WANTED!" proclaimed this early flyer. The mill operated until about 1904, when it burned down and was not rebuilt. The Millenders also built a commercial building on B Street between First and Second Streets. It, too, burned down in the 1920s and was not rebuilt. (Author's collection.)

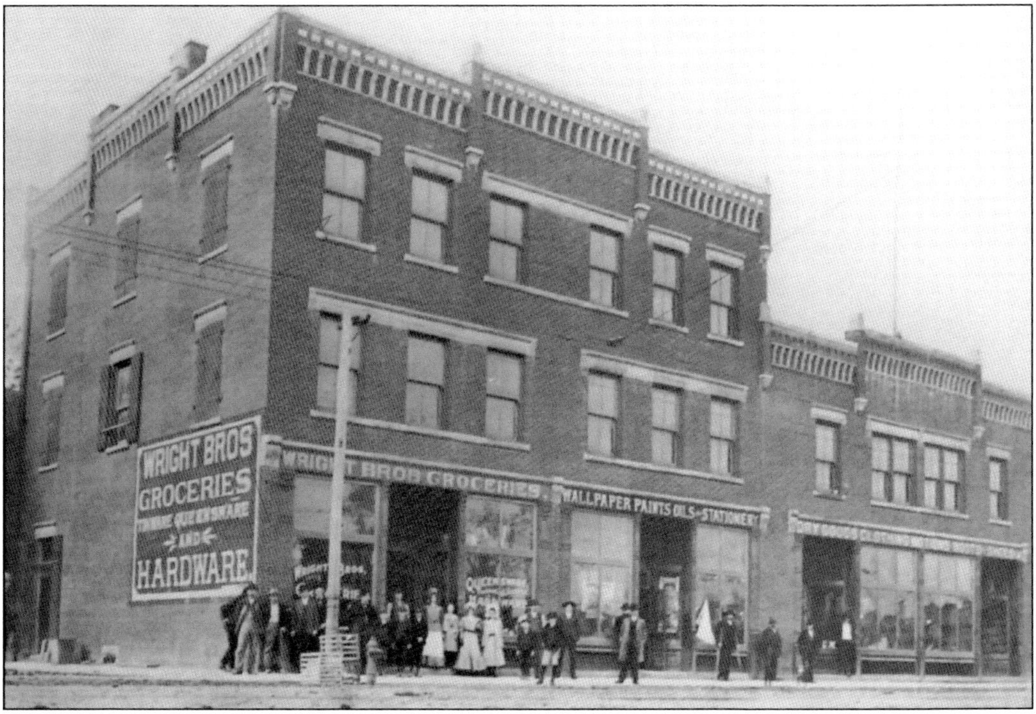

One of the first families to come to Ceredo was the Wright family. They were also one of the largest families in Wayne County—10 boys and 2 girls. A close-knit hardworking family, they established one of the most successful stores between Cincinnati and Pittsburgh, building a large three-story structure on B Street across from the present city hall. As this photograph from the 1890s shows, they sold groceries, paint, wallpaper, and more. (Courtesy of *H-D*.)

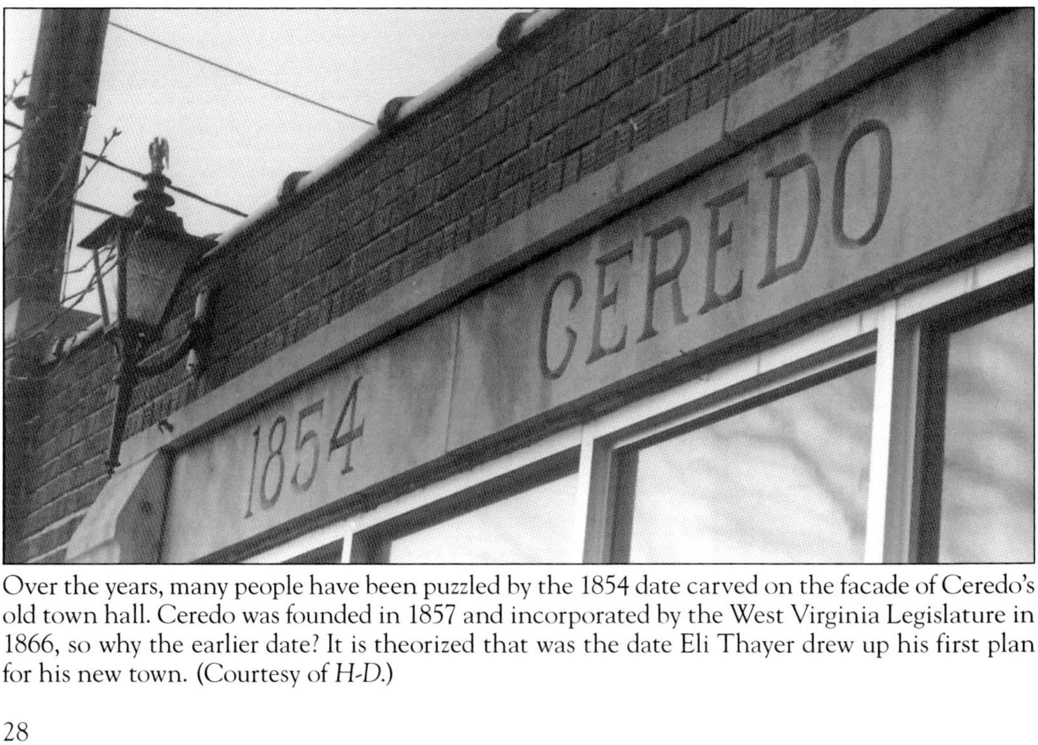

Over the years, many people have been puzzled by the 1854 date carved on the facade of Ceredo's old town hall. Ceredo was founded in 1857 and incorporated by the West Virginia Legislature in 1866, so why the earlier date? It is theorized that was the date Eli Thayer drew up his first plan for his new town. (Courtesy of *H-D*.)

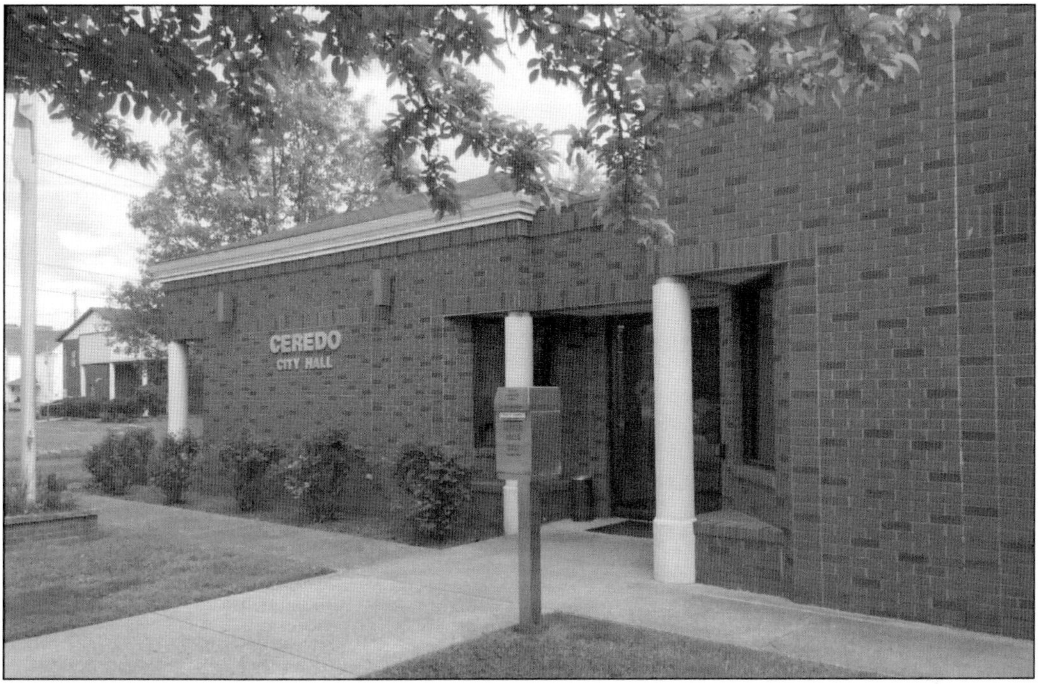

Ceredo's current city hall is a modern structure that was built adjacent to the old town hall, which now houses the police department. The Ceredo Volunteer Fire Department is next door to the police station. (Author's collection.)

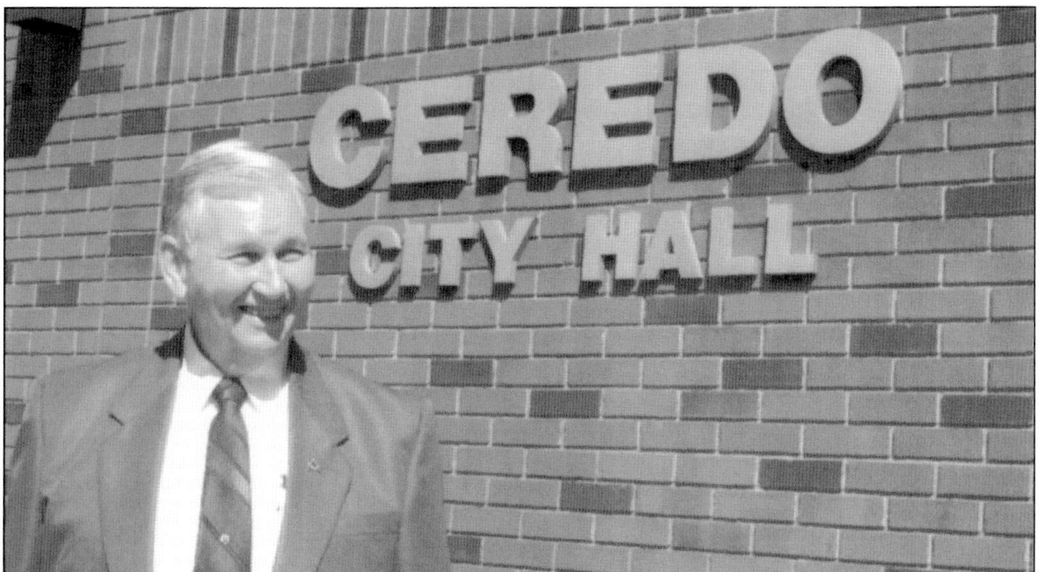

Mose A. Napier (1931–2011) was elected mayor of Ceredo in 1969, and he held that post for an amazing 40 years. During Napier's time as mayor, many in Ceredo were born, went to school, grew to adulthood, and started their own families, never knowing another mayor. A graduate of Marshall University, he was a longtime teacher and administrator in Wayne County schools. After retiring as the county's superintendent of schools, he went back to Ceredo-Kenova to teach, as teaching was his first love. (Courtesy of *H-D*.)

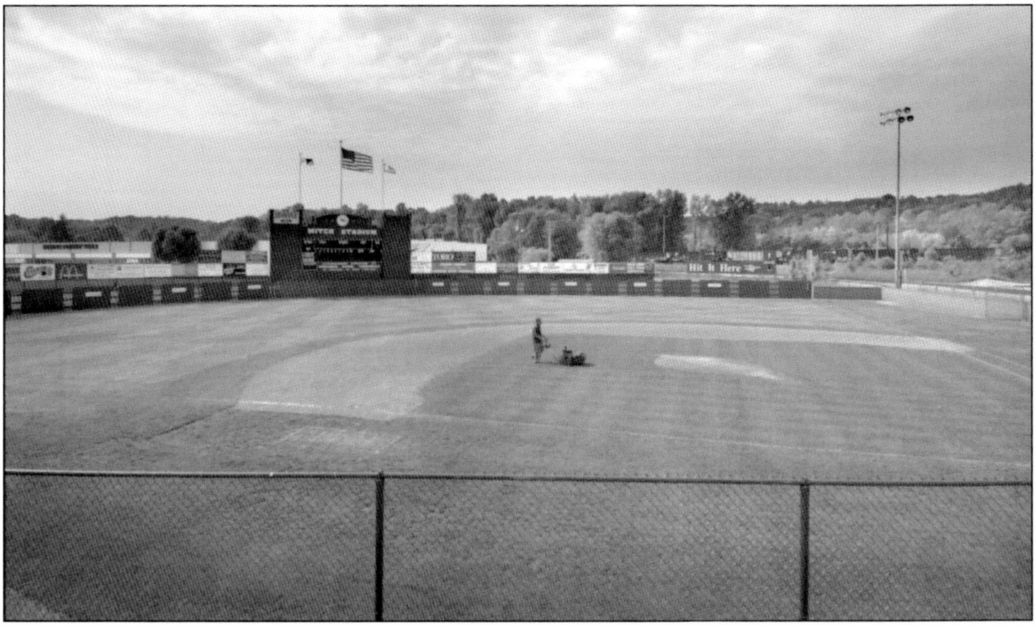

Located on the boundary line between the towns of Ceredo and Kenova, Mitch Stadium is home to the Ceredo-Kenova Little League and regularly plays host to state and regional Little League play. Created in 1955, the stadium is named in honor of Elmer "Big Mitch" Mitchell, who served as the field's groundskeeper for 27 years, until his death in 1981. (Courtesy of *HQ*.)

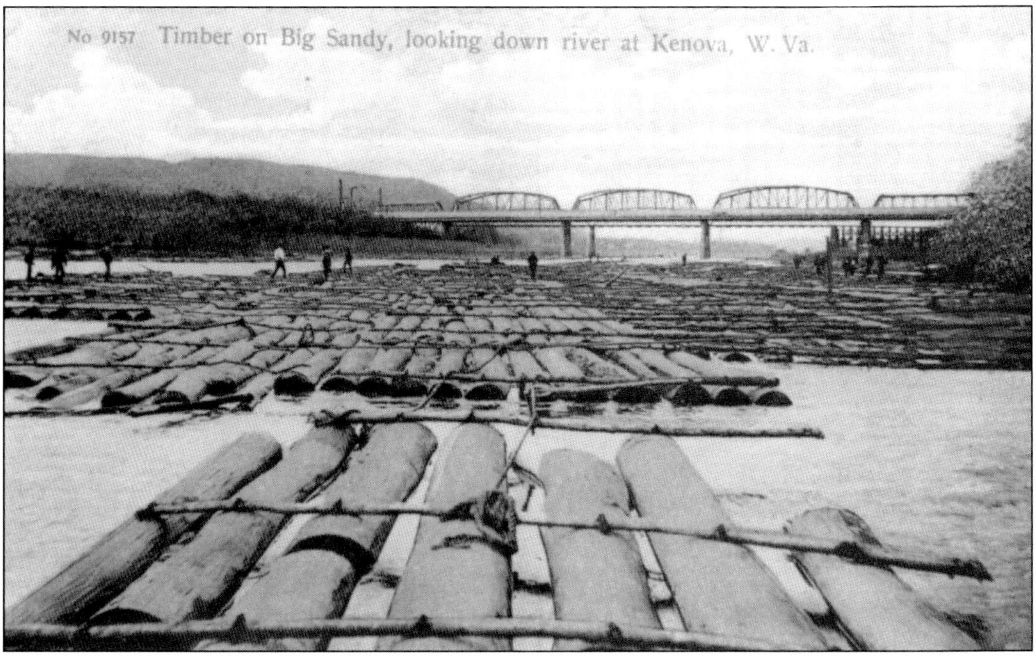

Kenova is the largest city in Wayne County. Its history was shaped by its location on the Ohio and Big Sandy Rivers where Kentucky, Ohio, and West Virginia meet—hence the town's name. It sounds like an Indian name, but in fact it was devised by taking a few letters from each of the three states' names. Timber was big business in Kenova's early days, with logs felled in the southern end of the county and then floated down the Big Sandy to Kenova. (Author's collection.)

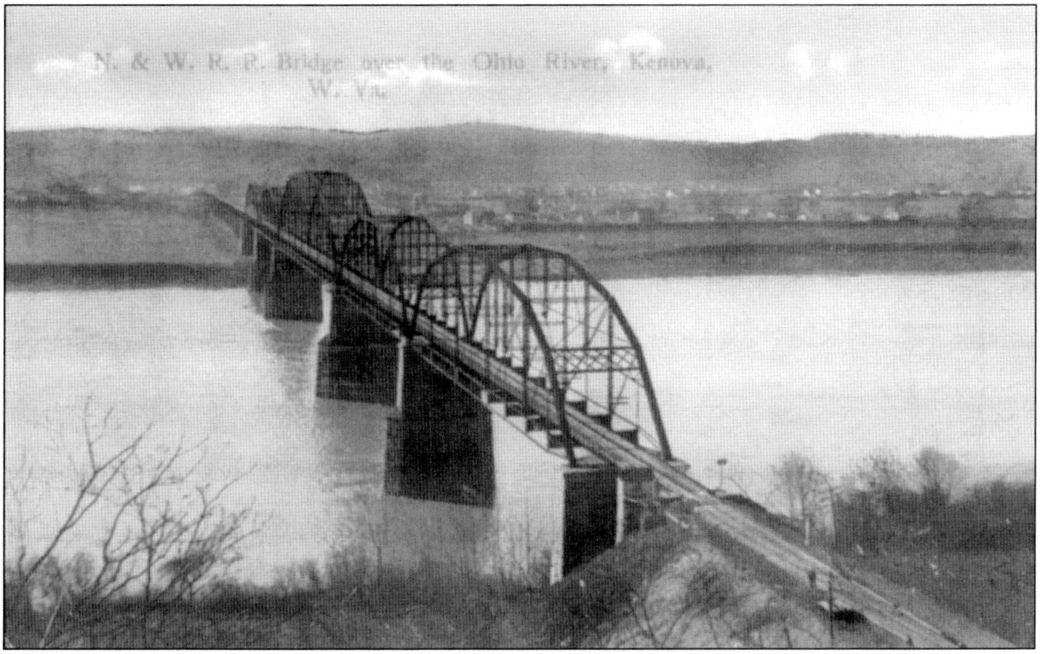

Kenova's founder chose its site because it was where the Norfolk & Western planned to build the first bridge across the Ohio River between Wheeling and Cincinnati. Work on the bridge began in 1890, and Kenova was incorporated in 1894. (Author's collection.)

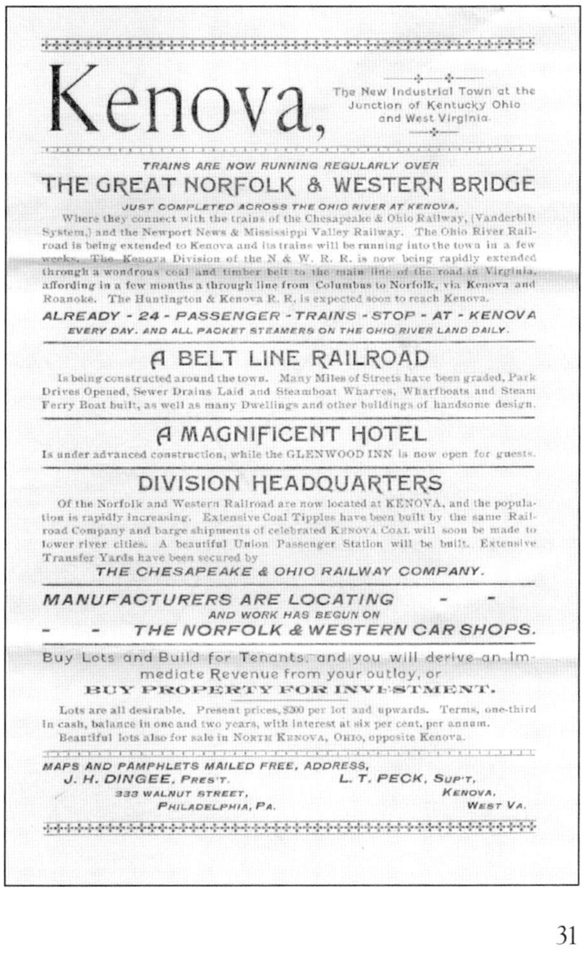

Kenova,

The New Industrial Town at the Junction of Kentucky Ohio and West Virginia.

TRAINS ARE NOW RUNNING REGULARLY OVER

THE GREAT NORFOLK & WESTERN BRIDGE

JUST COMPLETED ACROSS THE OHIO RIVER AT KENOVA.

Where they connect with the trains of the Chesapeake & Ohio Railway, (Vanderbilt System,) and the Newport News & Mississippi Valley Railway. The Ohio River Railroad is being extended to Kenova and its trains will be running into the town in a few weeks. The Kenova Division of the N & W. R. R. is now being rapidly extended through a wondrous coal and timber belt to the main line of the road in Virginia, affording in a few months a through line from Columbus to Norfolk, via Kenova and Roanoke. The Huntington & Kenova R. R. is expected soon to reach Kenova.

ALREADY - 24 - PASSENGER - TRAINS - STOP - AT - KENOVA EVERY DAY. AND ALL PACKET STEAMERS ON THE OHIO RIVER LAND DAILY.

A BELT LINE RAILROAD

Is being constructed around the town. Many Miles of Streets have been graded, Park Drives Opened, Sewer Drains Laid and Steamboat Wharves, Wharfboats and Steam Ferry Boat built, as well as many Dwellings and other buildings of handsome design.

A MAGNIFICENT HOTEL

Is under advanced construction, while the GLENWOOD INN is now open for guests.

DIVISION HEADQUARTERS

Of the Norfolk and Western Railroad are now located at KENOVA, and the population is rapidly increasing. Extensive Coal Tipples have been built by the same Railroad Company and barge shipments of celebrated KENOVA COAL will soon be made to lower river cities. A beautiful Union Passenger Station will be built. Extensive Transfer Yards have been secured by

THE CHESAPEAKE & OHIO RAILWAY COMPANY.

MANUFACTURERS ARE LOCATING - - AND WORK HAS BEGUN ON - - THE NORFOLK & WESTERN CAR SHOPS.

Buy Lots and Build for Tenants, and you will derive an Immediate Revenue from your outlay, or

BUY PROPERTY FOR INVESTMENT.

Lots are all desirable. Present prices, $200 per lot and upwards. Terms, one-third in cash, balance in one and two years, with interest at six per cent. per annum.

Beautiful lots also for sale in NORTH KENOVA, OHIO, opposite Kenova.

MAPS AND PAMPHLETS MAILED FREE, ADDRESS,

J. H. DINGEE, PRES'T.
333 WALNUT STREET,
PHILADELPHIA, PA.

L. T. PECK, SUP'T,
KENOVA,
WEST VA.

This undated flyer from Kenova's early years boasted about the fledgling town's many attractions, including the Great Norfolk & Western Bridge, a "magnificent hotel," the N&W shops, and more. The appeal was well received, and the town grew rapidly. (Author's collection.)

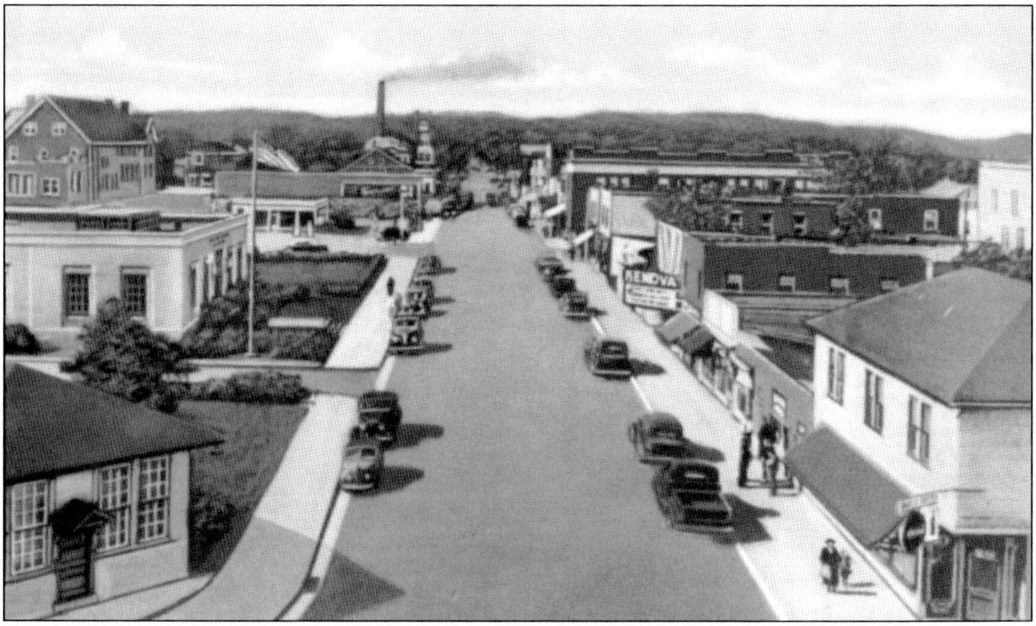

Given the importance of the timber industry in early Kenova, it is hardly coincidental that many of the town's streets were named for trees. This 1940s postcard offers a view along Chestnut Street. Other Kenova street names include Oak, Beech, Walnut, and Poplar. (Author's collection.)

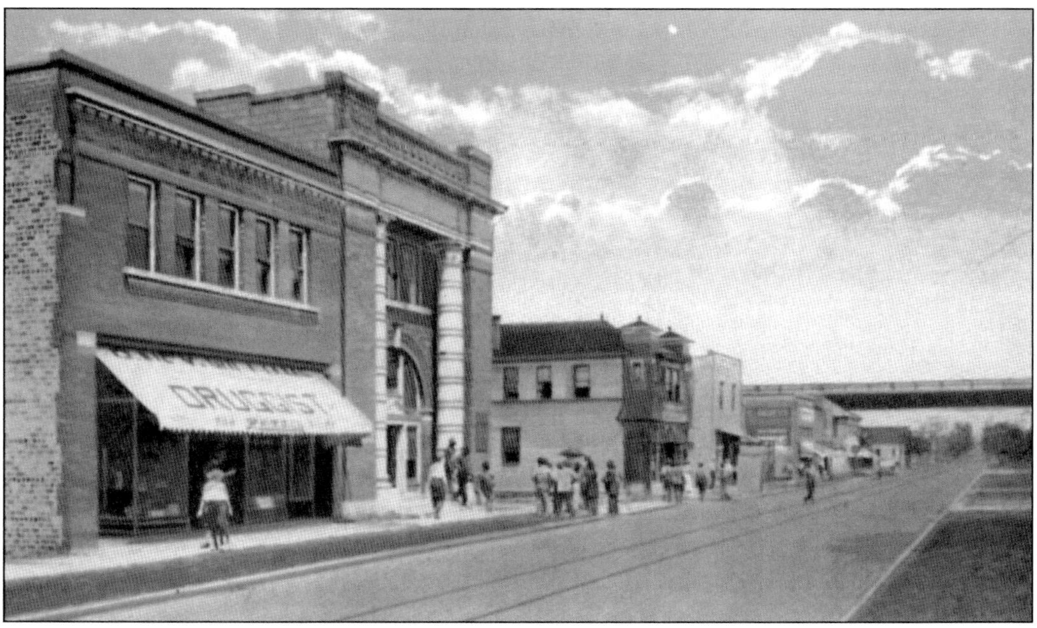

Here is a vintage view of the north side of Chestnut Street. The store with the awning is the Griffith & Feil drugstore. Over the years, the store has had various locations and ownerships, but it has been part of Kenova since 1892. The building next to it, with the tall white columns, is the former First National Bank of Kenova, which opened in 1910 and closed in 1992. (Author's collection.)

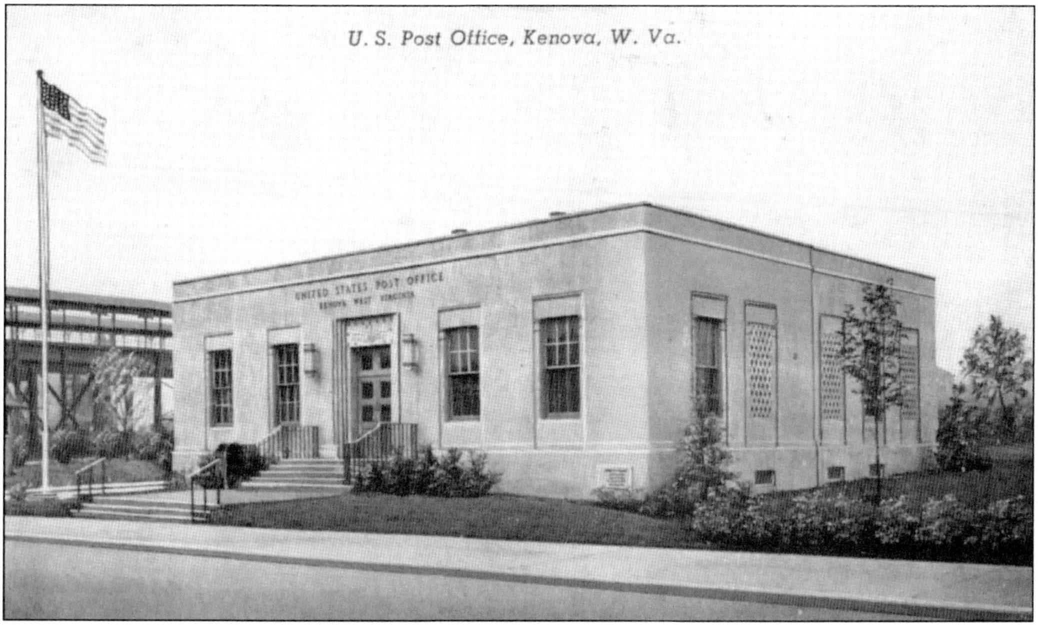

Kenova's post office, at 1300 Chestnut Street, is an Art Deco–style structure built in 1939 as a New Deal public works project. To the left of the building can be seen a glimpse of the long trestle leading to the Norfolk Southern (NS) Ohio River bridge. (Author's collection.)

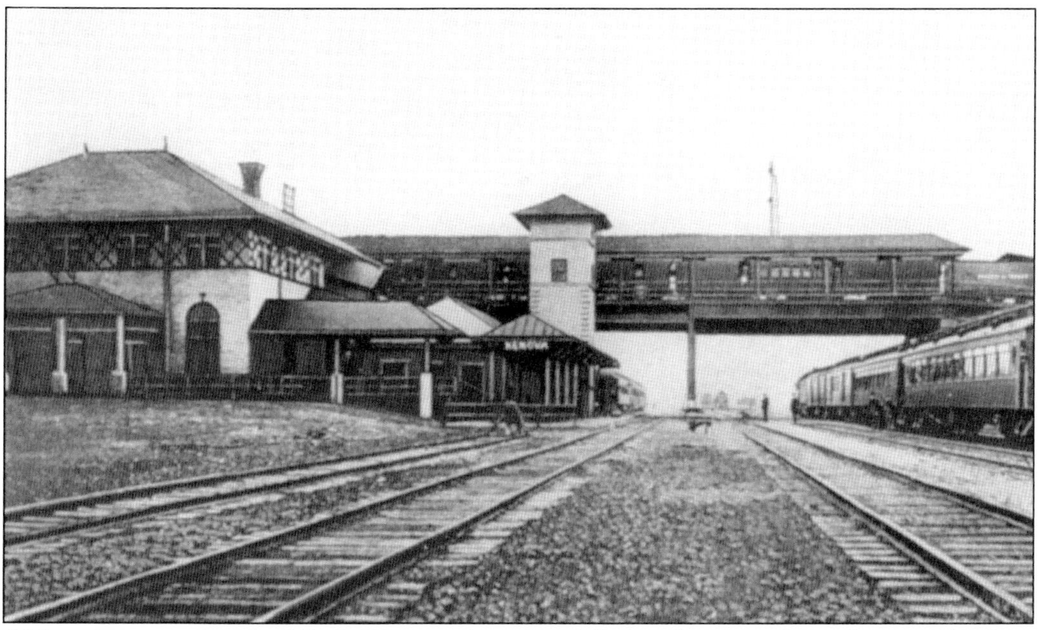

Although it was the Norfolk & Western (now Norfolk Southern) Railway that gave birth to Kenova, the Chesapeake & Ohio Railway and the Baltimore & Ohio Railroad (the two now combined as CSX) also found their way to Kenova, making it a busy rail hub. It is said that more coal passed through Kenova than any other place in the world. And back in the day when the passenger train was still the way people traveled any long distance, all three railroads stopped at Kenova's Union Station. Today, the station is long gone, as is the former N&W roundhouse. (Author's collection.)

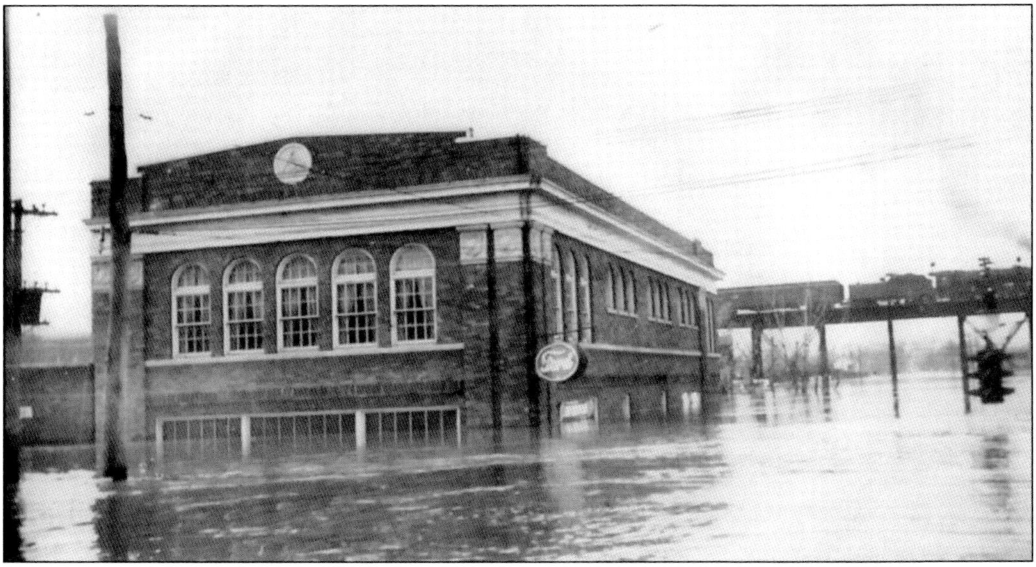

In 1937, raging floodwaters brought devastation to Ohio River communities large and small, driving a million people from their homes and recording $500 million in damages. Kenova was hard hit. Here is a view of the town's flooded Ford dealership. In the background, an N&W passenger train can be seen making its way along the trestle leading to the railroad's Ohio River bridge. (Courtesy of the US Army Corps of Engineers.)

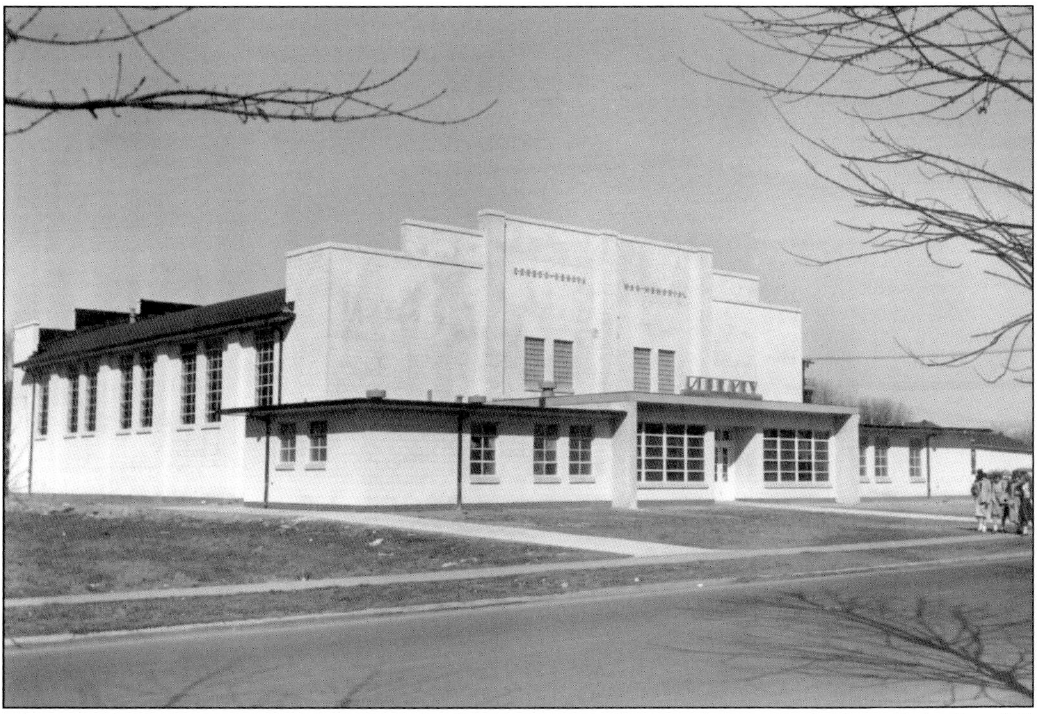

The Ceredo-Kenova War Memorial was built in 1950 in tribute to those who had "paid the last full measure" in the nation's defense and designed for use as both a sports facility and for community events. Known today as the C-K Community Center, the nonprofit organization works to serve both youth and adult fitness needs and host events of community interest. (Courtesy of *H-D*.)

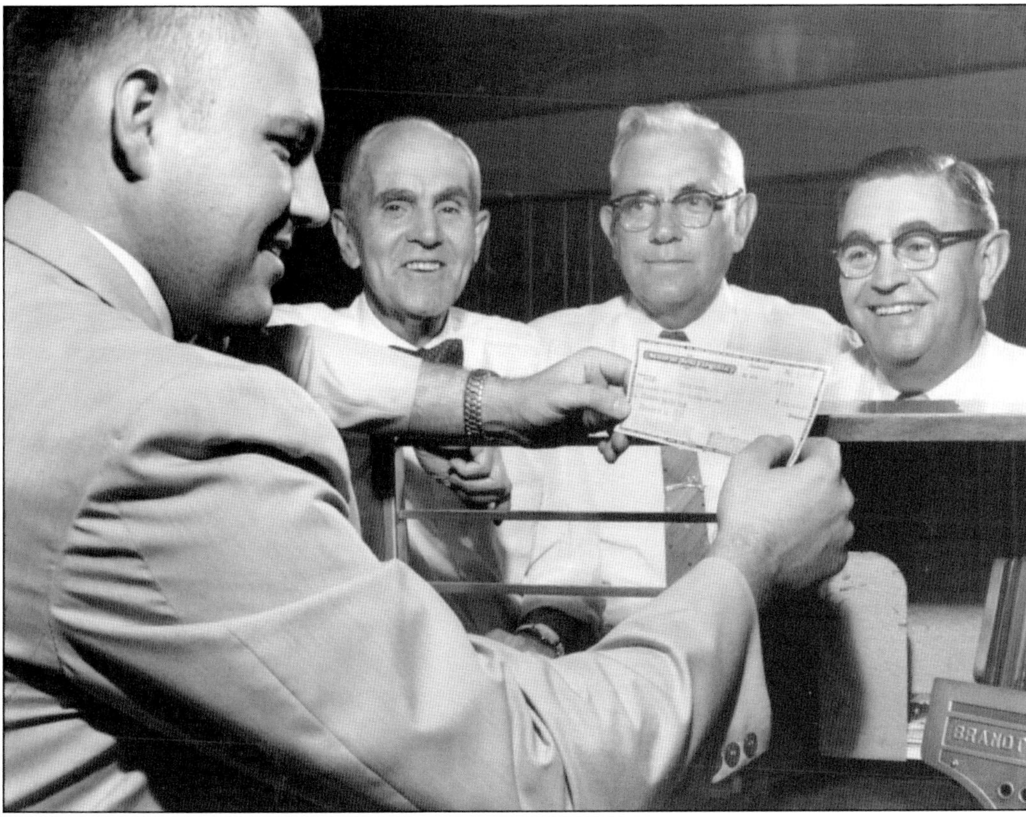

On July 10, 1958, Kenova mayor Paul Shingleton deposited a $425,000 check in the First National Bank there. The check represented the proceeds from a bond issue approved by the voters to finance a broad street-improvement program. From left to right are Mayor Shingleton, W.R. Turner (vice president of the bank), Lawson D. Willis (member of the town council and chairman of its finance committee), and Raymond Turner (teller). (Courtesy of *H-D*.)

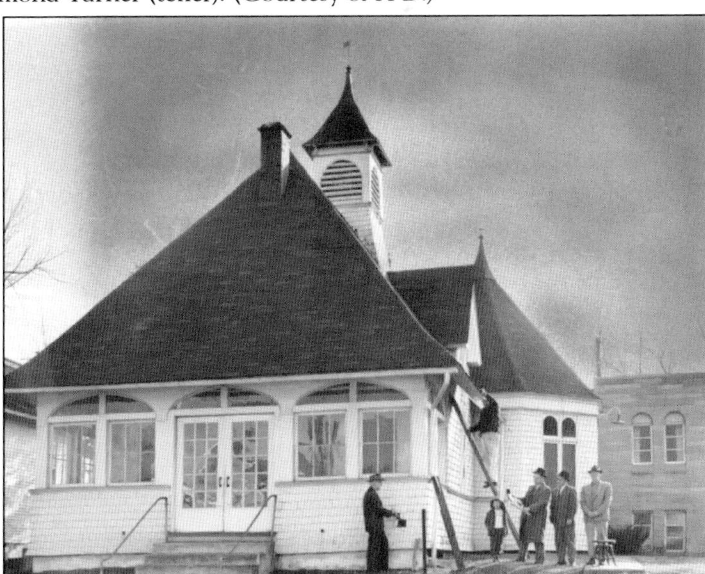

In 1960, the Kenova Presbyterian Church razed a landmark structure to make way for construction of a new chapel. Erected in 1890, the building was designed as an assembly hall for the town. Shortly after the structure was built, the Norfolk & Western took it over as a YMCA for its employees. (Courtesy of *H-D*.)

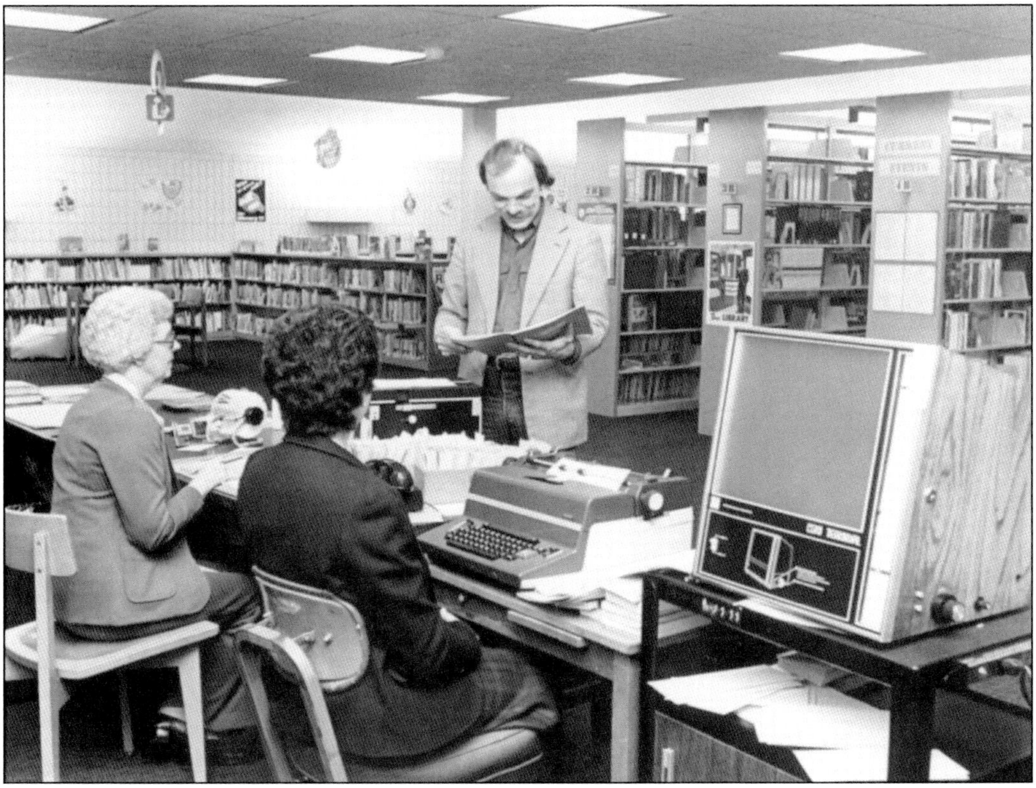

The Woman's Club of Kenova established Ceredo-Kenova's first library in 1950 in a building on Pine Street in Kenova. In 1952, the library moved to the C-K War Memorial building, remaining there until 1984 when a new library building was constructed at 1200 Oak Street. This photograph was taken in January 1985, shortly after the new library opened. Arn Winter, library director, can be seen talking with assistant librarians Kathryn Hatfield (left) and Brenda Francis (right). (Courtesy of *H-D.*)

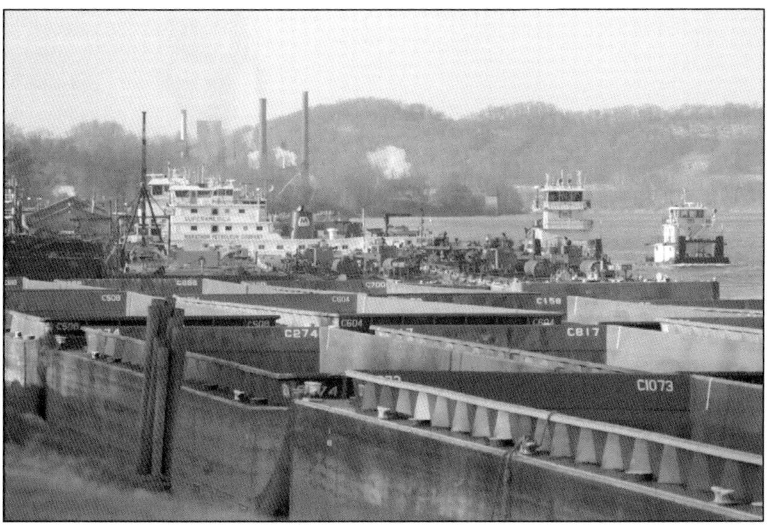

Marathon Petroleum's giant refinery at Catlettsburg, Kentucky, just across the Big Sandy River from Kenova, is a major employer in the area. Marathon facilities can also be found on the West Virginia side of the river, where it operates a tank farm and a marine transportation dock. Courtesy of Jim Ross.)

Erected in 1911, the old Kenova City Hall at Pine and Fifteenth Streets served the town for 67 years before it was destroyed in a spectacular fire. Judging from the automobile parked in front of the structure, this vintage postcard dates from the 1950s. (Author's collection.)

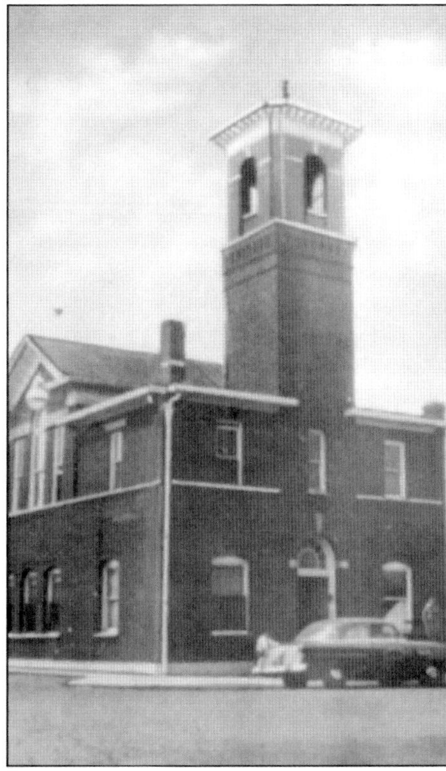

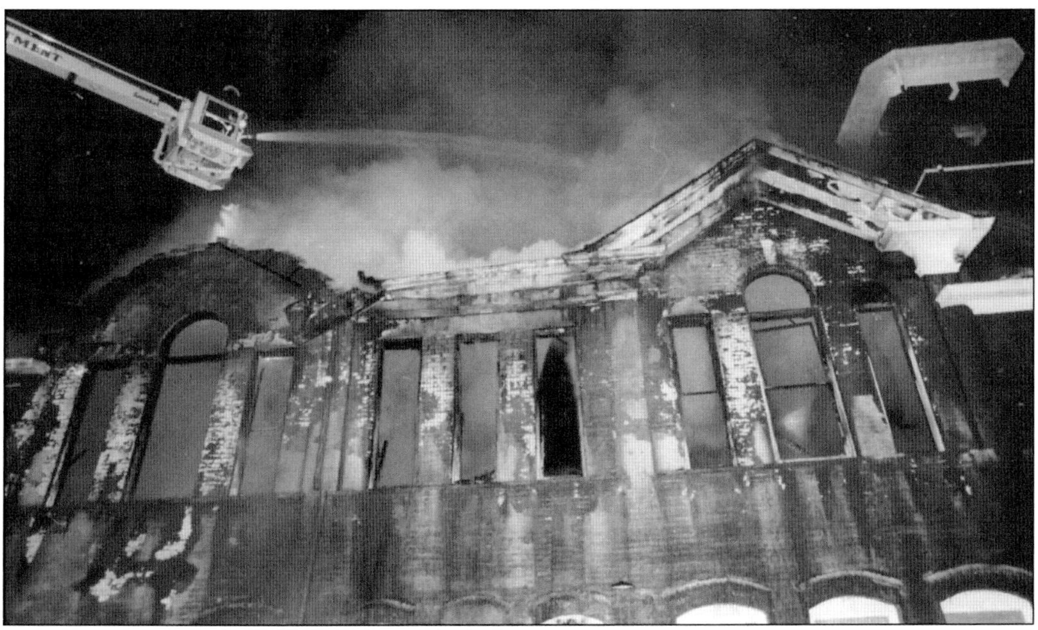

Efforts to replace the old Kenova City Hall were well under way when an early-morning fire on January 16, 1978, left the building a smoking ruin. The Huntington and Ceredo Fire Departments aided in battling the blaze. The building was largely vacant. City offices had moved to temporary quarters a few weeks before when a $598,000 grant for a new building was approved. (Courtesy of *H-D*.)

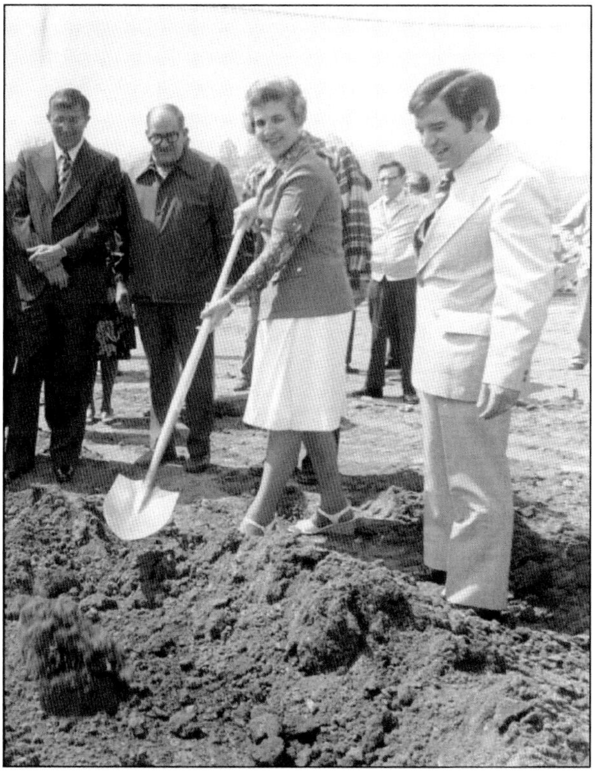

Lucy Rollins stood in for her husband at an April 27, 1978, ground-breaking for a new Kenova City Hall. Rollins is flanked by, from left to right, Kenova council members Tom Wilson and John Spangler and US representative Nick J. Rahall. Mayor Harold Rollins was ill and could not attend the ceremony. (Courtesy of *H-D*.)

The new city hall that Kenova erected is starkly modern on the outside. But inside, the town proudly displays its history. The walls of the council chamber are lined with vintage photographs of the members of the Kenova Hall of Fame. And the stairwells display an array of green-and-white banners representing the many athletic championships won by the teams of long-closed Ceredo-Kenova High School. (Author's collection.)

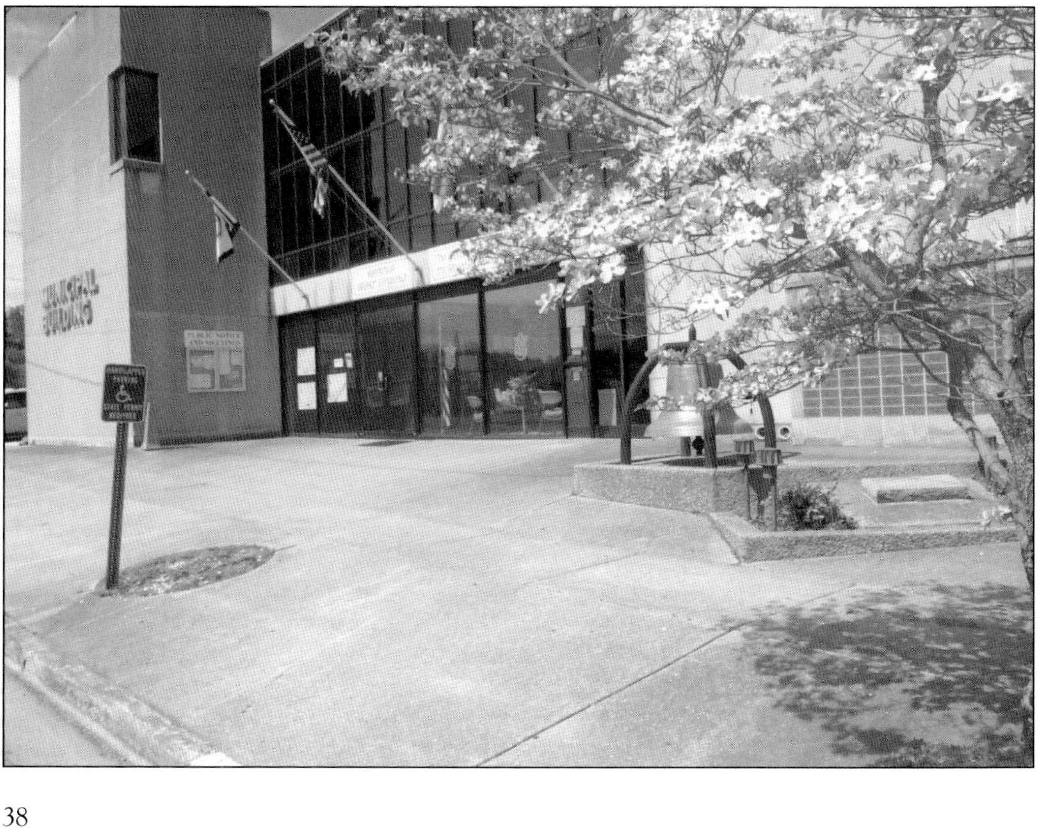

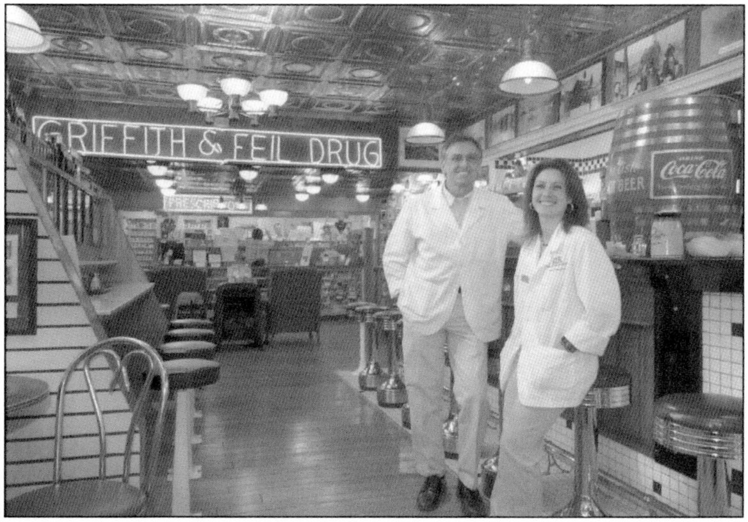

Griffith & Fiel is partly a working drugstore and partly a museum, with a stamped tin ceiling, vintage photographs, and a working 1929 soda fountain. Kenova mayor Ric Griffith and his daughter Heidi Griffith Romero stand in the family drugstore, where generations of Ceredo and Kenova residents have come for a prescription and stayed for a soda. (Courtesy of *HQ*.)

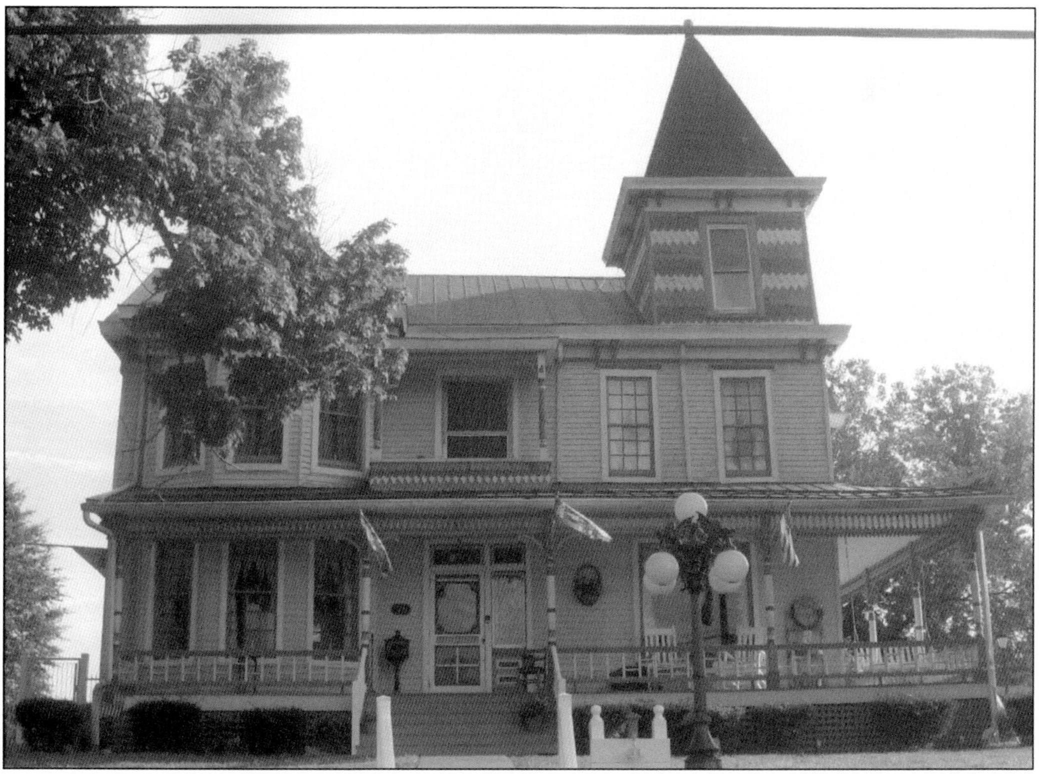

Mayor Ric Griffith also has faithfully restored this Queen Anne house that stands on Kenova's Beech Street, overlooking the Ohio River. The house, known as the Beeches, was built in 1891 for Joseph S. Miller, a local entrepreneur who was commissioner of the IRS under Pres. Grover Cleveland. The unincorporated Wayne County community of Lavalette, located at the intersection of West Virginia Routes 152 and 75, about eight miles south of Huntington, is named for Miller's daughter. (Courtesy of *H-D*.)

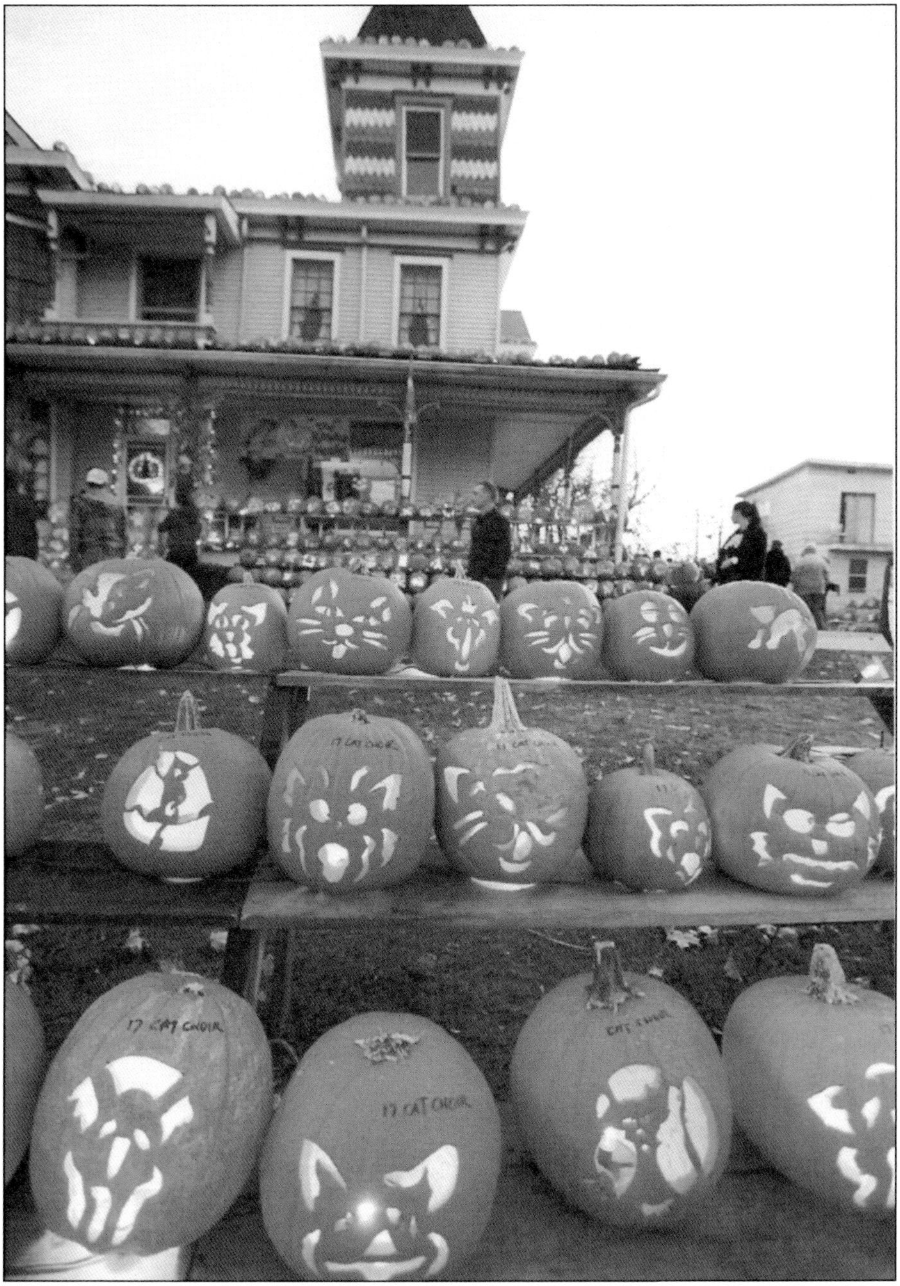

Kenova's famous Pumpkin House is a major tourist attraction, attracting thousands of visitors every year at Halloween time. It all started back in 1978 when Ric Griffith carved a half dozen jack-o'-lanterns and put them on display at his historic Beech Street house. At the urging of family and friends, he added more carved pumpkins each year after that. The total kept growing, first into the hundreds and then the thousands. Today, 3,000 lighted jack-o'-lanterns are perched on the house and lawn and fill a network of scaffolding and shelves that surround the property. What was once simple family fun has exploded into a community-wide festival, with a small army of volunteers reporting to the house each year, weeks before Halloween, to start the mammoth task of carving the many colorful pumpkins. (Courtesy of *H-D*.)

Four

Recreation Mecca

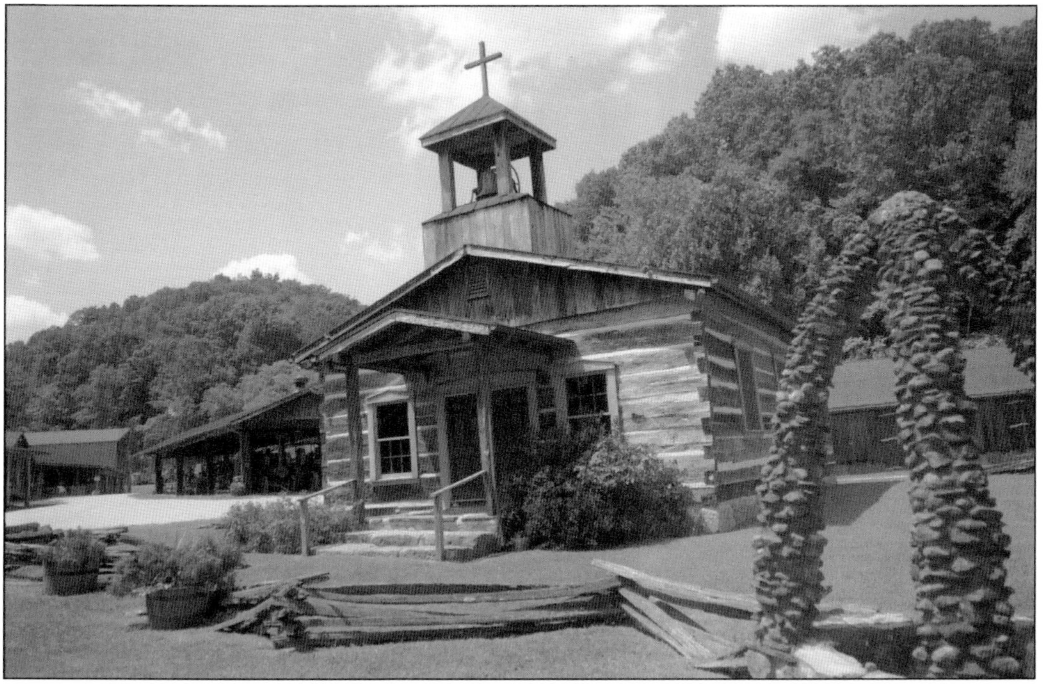

As antique lovers Mike Perry and his wife, Henriella, added items by the dozen to their collection, they soon ran out of room at their Wayne County home, so they filled their barn. Then they started buying log buildings, disassembling them, and moving them to their 500-acre farm. Today, Heritage Farm Museum and Village is a major tourist attraction that features 16 exhibit-filled buildings, including this historic church. (Courtesy of *HQ*.)

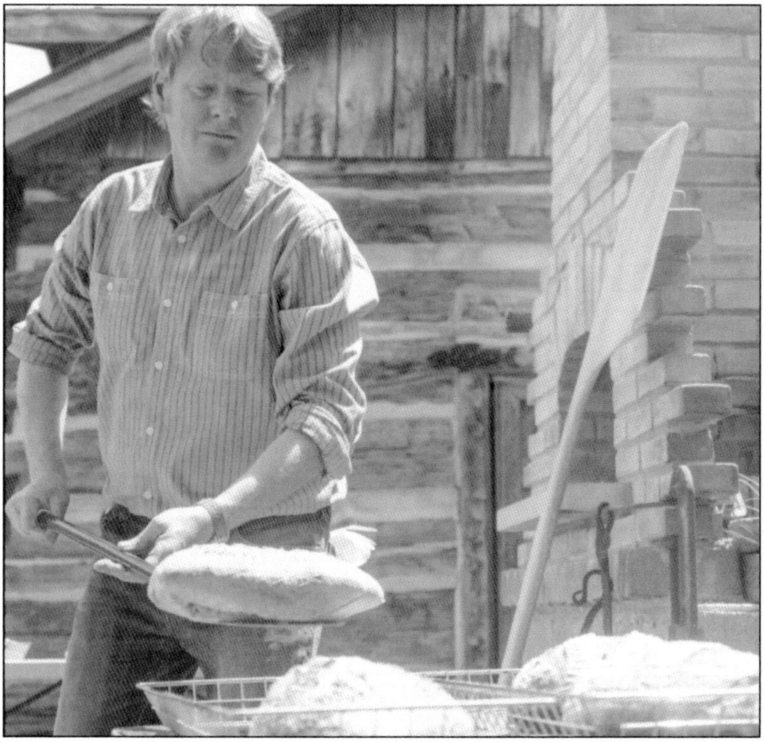

Each year, Heritage Farm attracts thousands of visitors who get a glimpse of what daily life was like in pioneer days. As the late Mike Perry frequently reminded the farm's visitors, the region's early settlers "couldn't run out to the store if they found they were out of bread. They were strictly on their own. They had to be resourceful and self-reliant." Here, Rory Perry pulls loaves of freshly baked sourdough bread out of the farm's newly operational brick oven. (Courtesy of *H-D*.)

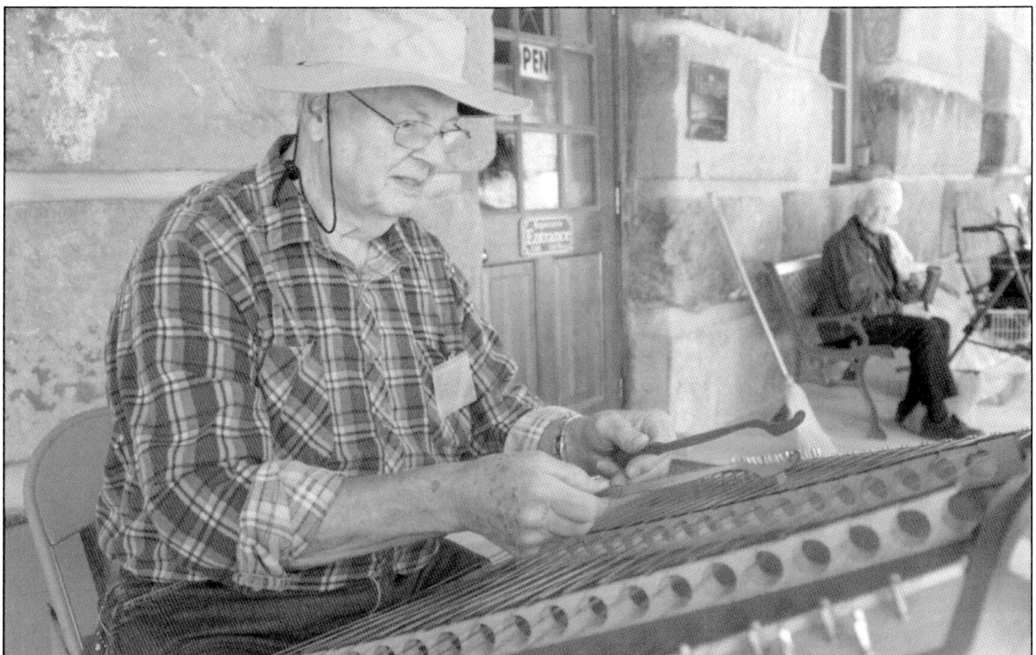

Wayne County musician Neal Koch plays the hammered dulcimer at the farm's 2015 spring festival, its largest annual event. It takes 200 musicians, craftspeople, reenactors, and other volunteers to bring the farm to life for the festival. Other, smaller weekend events are staged year-round, and the farm offers daily guided tours. (Courtesy of *H-D*.)

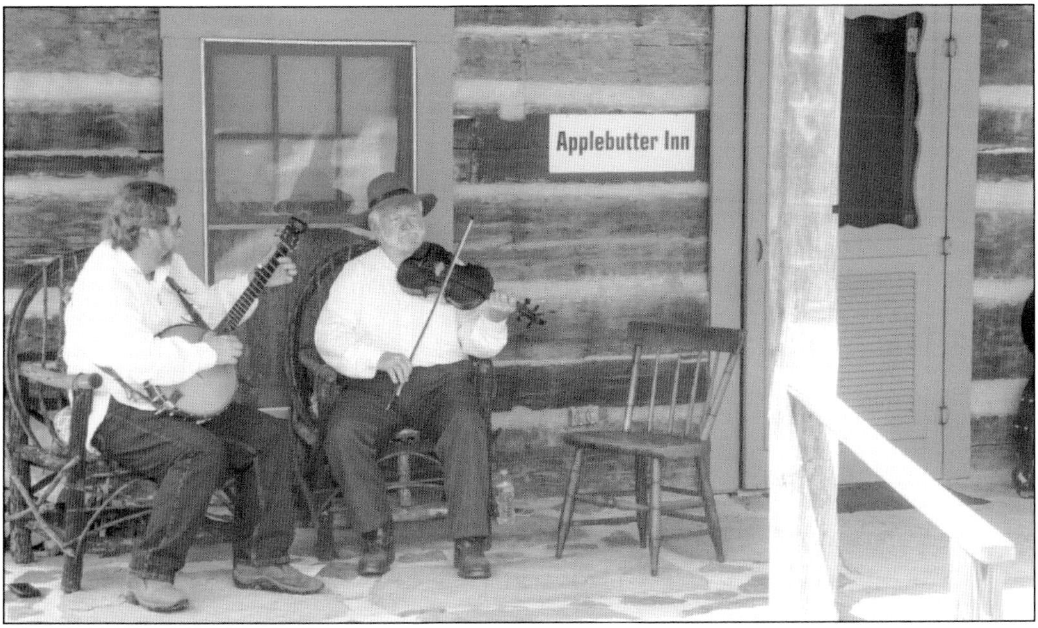

Heritage Farm offers overnight lodging at five small rustic inns, including the Applebutter Inn. It is country-style living with all the modern amenities. An original dairy barn built in the 1800s has been converted into a retreat center, suitable for corporate gatherings or family reunions. The barn has seven meeting rooms, four restrooms, a fully equipped kitchen, air-conditioning, cable television, and Wi-Fi. (Courtesy of *H-D.*)

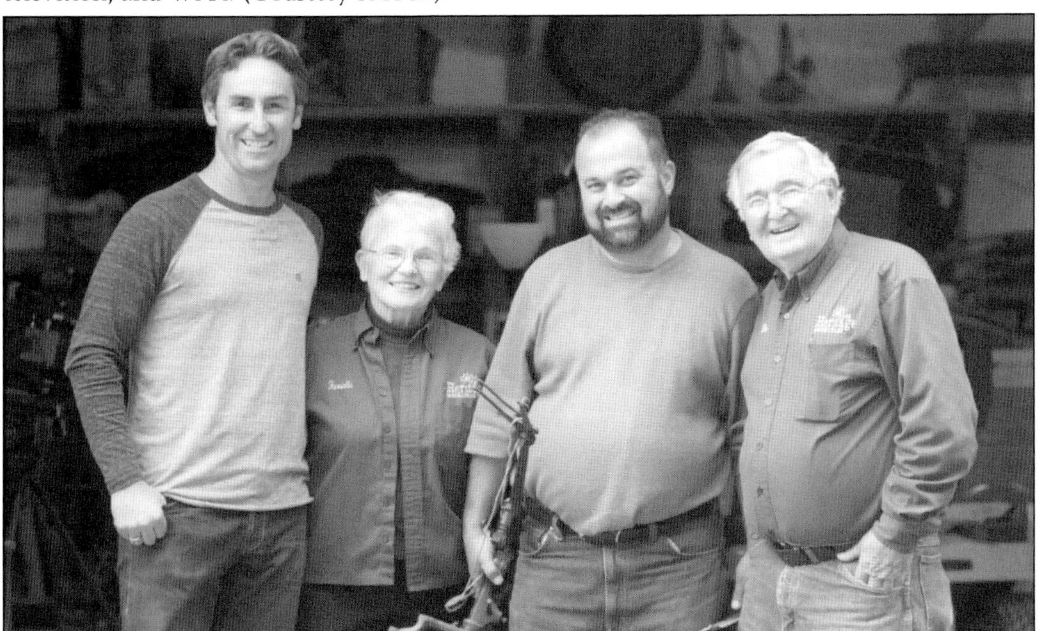

On October 4, 2011, the popular History Channel television show *American Pickers* taped a visit to Heritage Farm. The show was broadcast the following December and is still aired from time to time in reruns. Posing for the camera are, from left to right, show cohost Mike Wolfe, Henriella Perry, cohost Frank Fritz, and Mike Perry. (Courtesy of *H-D.*)

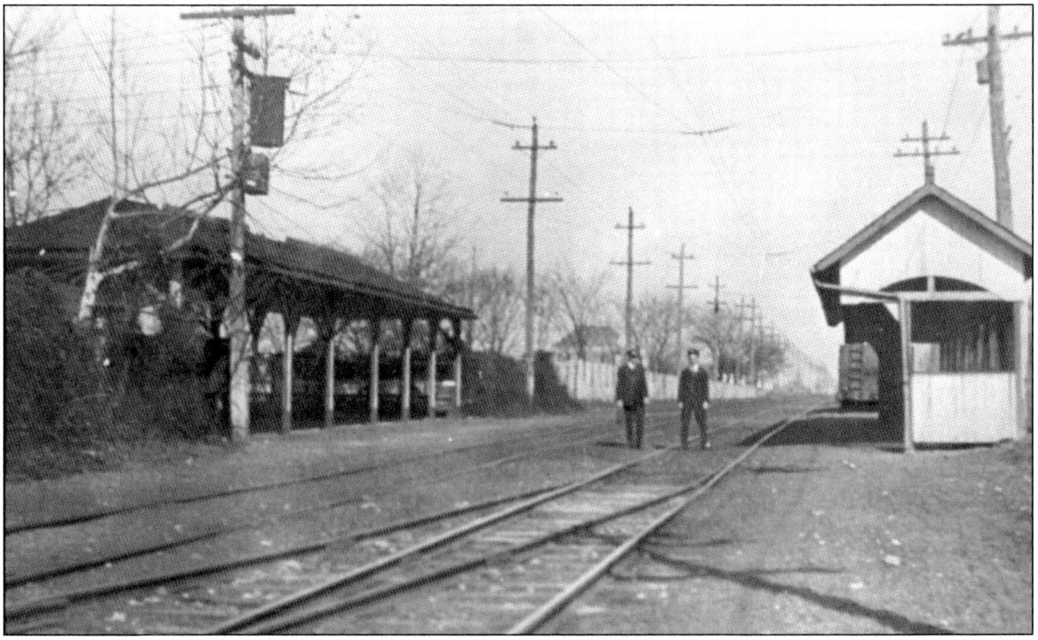

By the early 1900s, almost every large town in America had streetcars, and many had streetcar parks to boost weekend and holiday traffic. Camden Park, located five miles west of Huntington and just outside Ceredo on US 60, was originally developed as a picnic area by the Camden Interstate Railway in 1903. This rare 1918 photograph shows the Camden Park streetcar station. (Courtesy of Bob Withers.)

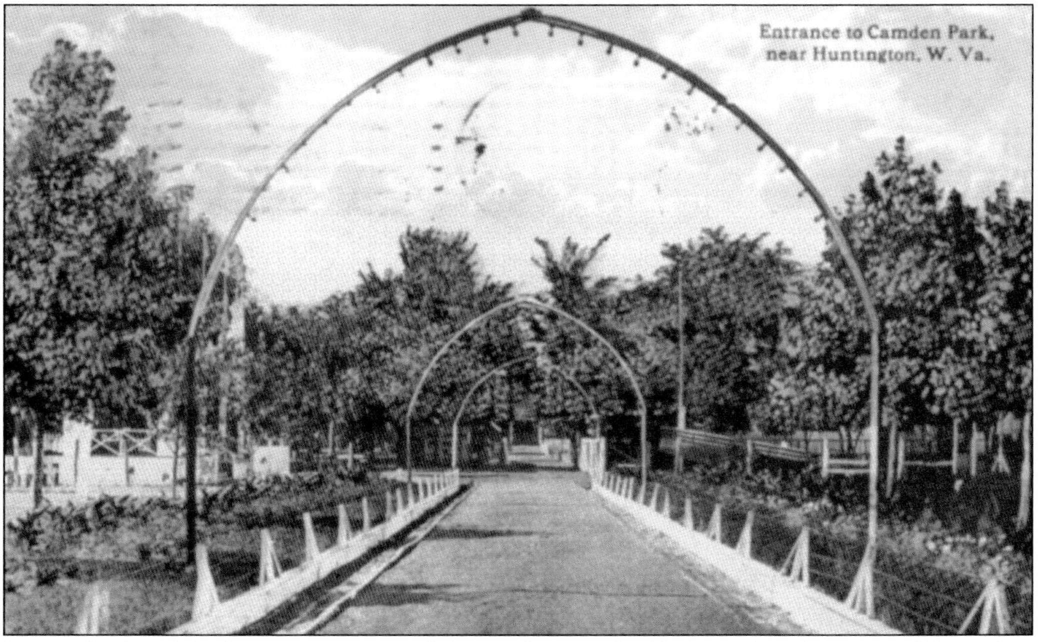

Postmarked in 1915, this vintage postcard depicts Camden Park's flower-lined entrance. The arches overhead provided electric lights to illuminate the pathway after dark. In 1919, the nation had more than 1,500 trolley parks. The handful still open have been able to do so because, like Camden Park, they have grown from picnic groves to full-fledged amusement parks. (Author's collection.)

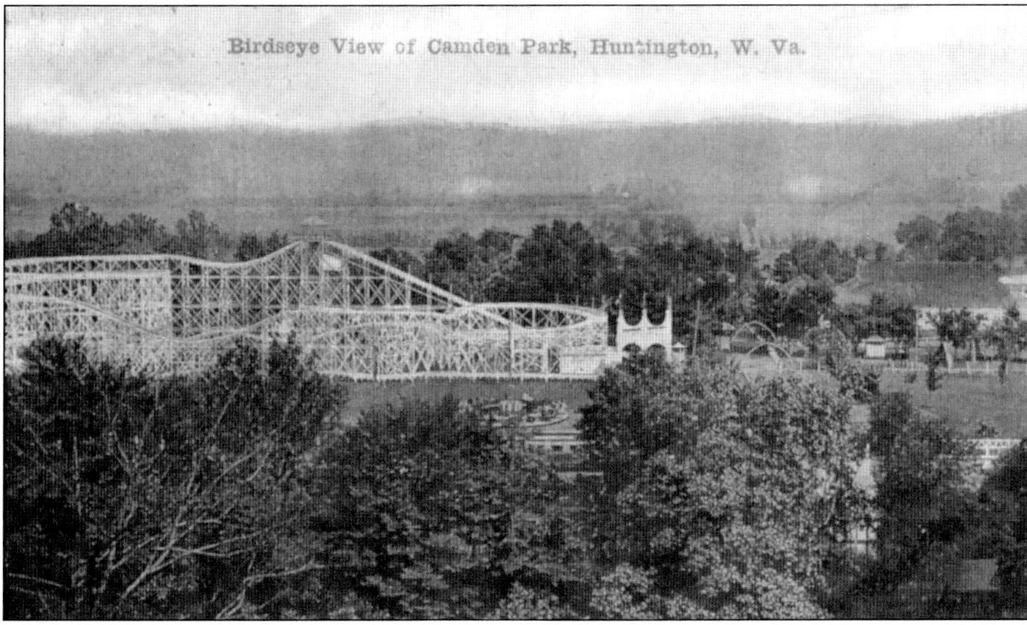

The first park ride installed at Camden Park was a carousel. It is still in use but has fiberglass horses rather than its original wooden ones. About 1912, the park's first roller coaster was added. It thrilled riders for decades before it was finally dismantled in 1957 and replaced with a new coaster the following year. (Author's collection.)

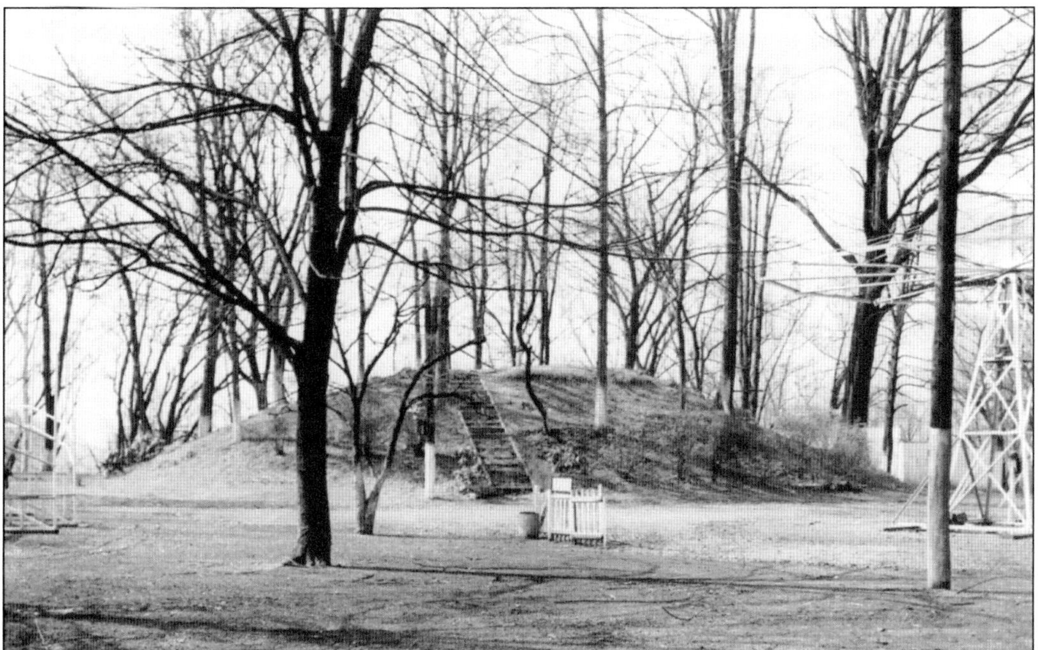

A flat-topped conical Indian burial mound located at Camden Park is the largest mound in the Huntington area and one of the largest in West Virginia. Never excavated, it was probably built by the Adena people between 1000 and 200 BC. The mound was used as a bandstand during the park's early years. (Courtesy of *H-D*.)

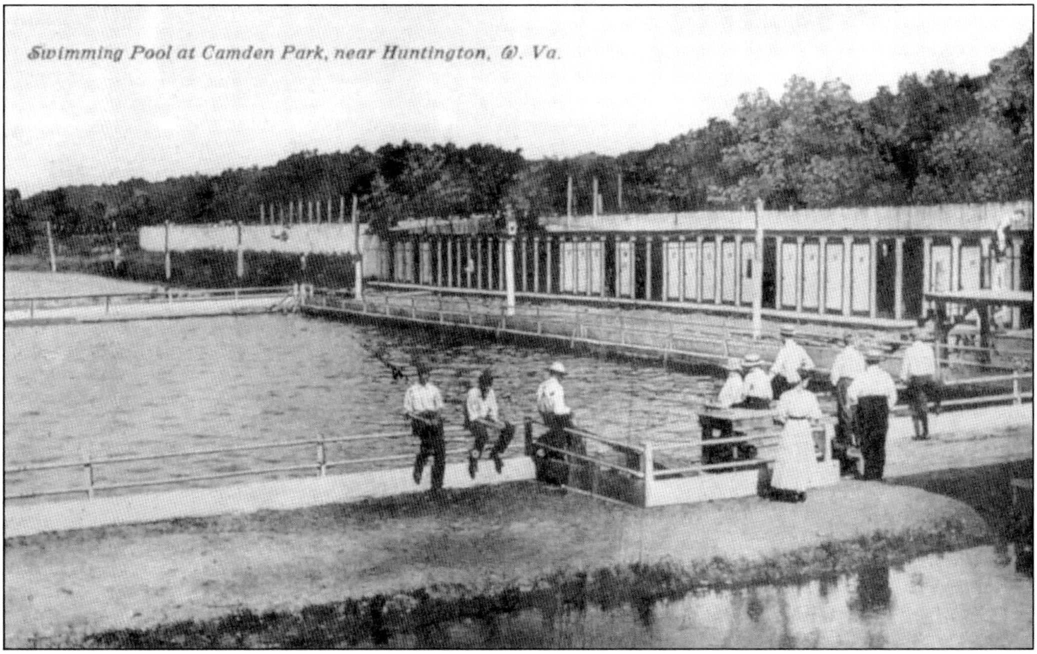

Until Dreamland Pool opened in Kenova in 1925, Camden Park had the only public pool in the region, shown here in a postcard mailed in 1911. The park had its own well and pump. The doors seen lining one side of the pool were entrances to individual dressing rooms. The pool was drained and demolished in 1949. (Author's collection.)

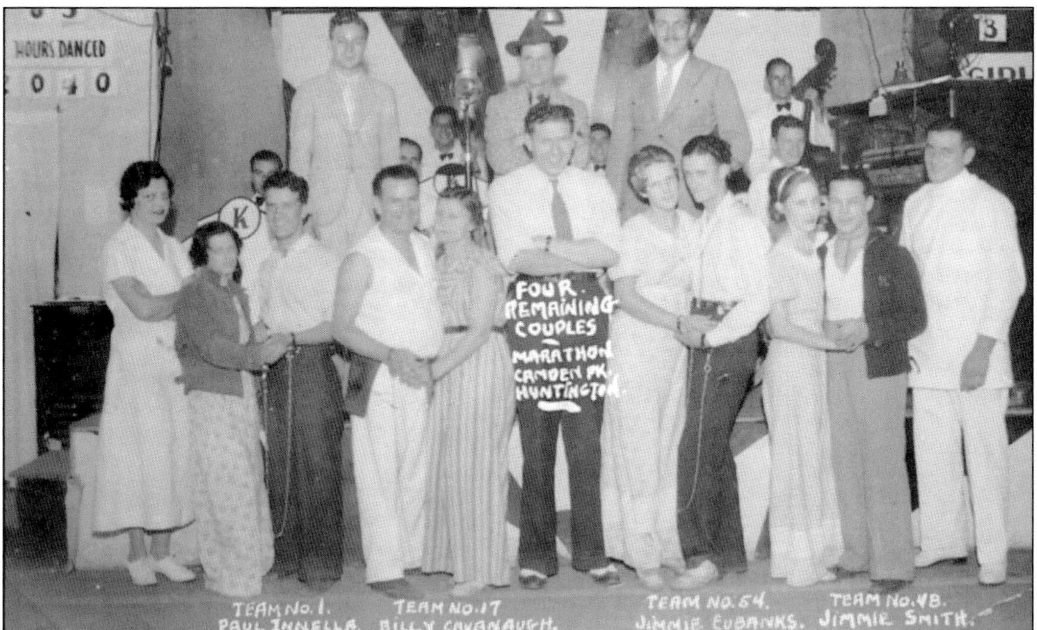

Around 1910, E.G. Via was hired to manage Camden Park. In 1916, he bought the park from the streetcar company and ran it until his death in 1946. Via staged an almost bewildering list of events and activities at the park, everything from baseball games and prize fights to hot-air balloon rides and, as shown in this undated photograph, marathon dance contests. (Author's collection.)

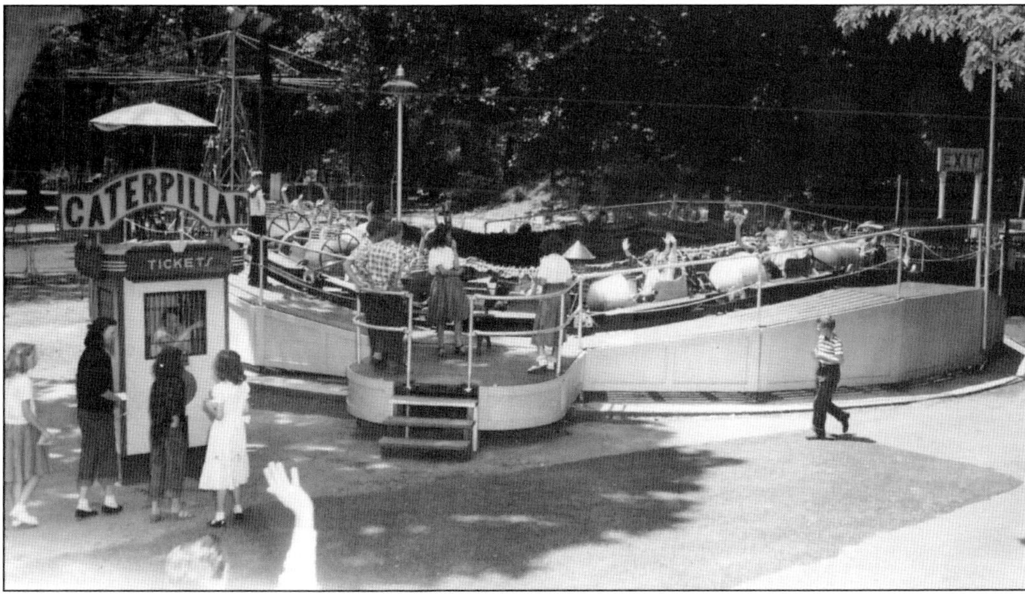

E.G. Via's heirs sold Camden Park to James Boylin, who enlisted Harry Nudd as his partner. Over the years, the park had become badly run down. The new management began cleaning, repairing, and rebuilding. The first ride they bought was the Caterpillar, a classic amusement park ride with cars that follow an undulating circular track. Long since replaced, it was the first of several secondhand rides the park was able to purchase from the old Coney Island park in Cincinnati. (Courtesy of *H-D*.)

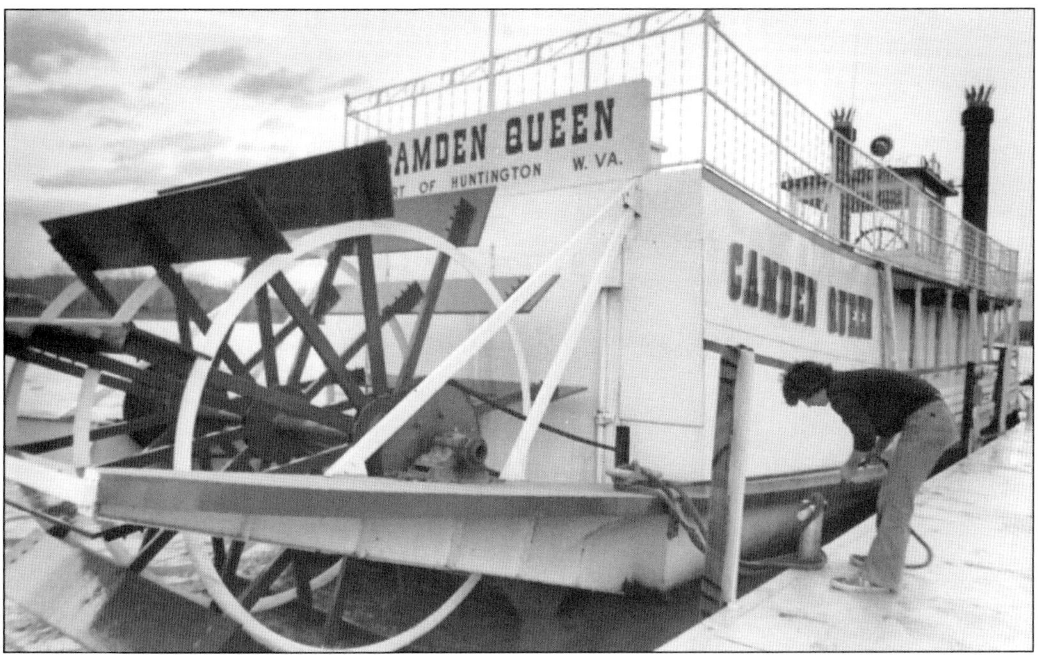

In 1978, the stern-wheeler *Camden Queen* was added to the park's attractions. A small reproduction of an Ohio River packet boat from the 1880s, the *Queen* gave passengers a 45-minute ride from the park's landing on Twelve Pole Creek. The boat was owned and operated by Capt. Gene Lister. (Courtesy of *H-D*.)

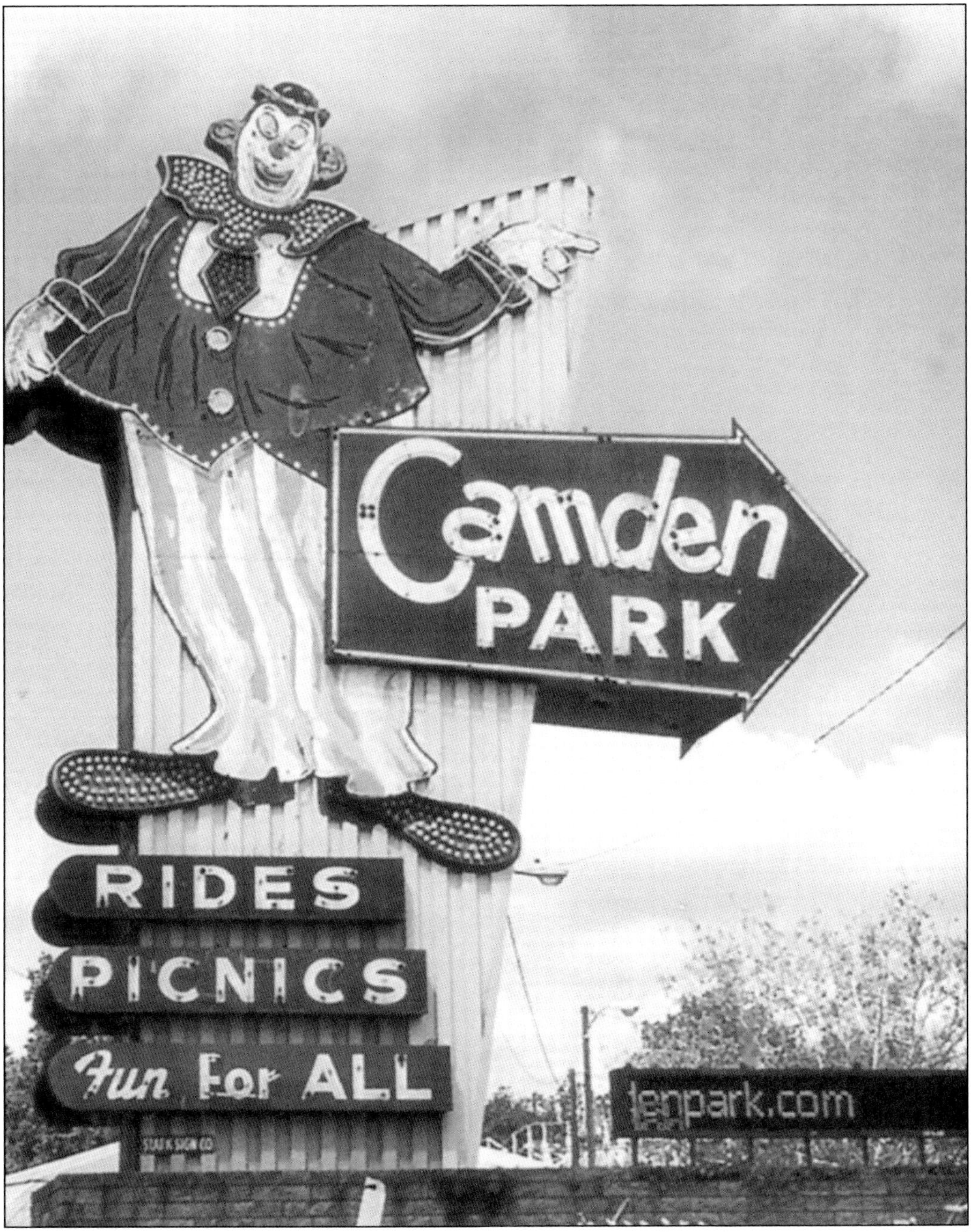

In 1980, the Boylin family sold Camden Park to out-of-town ownership. The new owners neglected essential park maintenance and when they found themselves deeply in debt even sold off the hand-carved wooden horses that once graced the park's vintage carousel. By 1994, the park owners owed $2 million to their creditors, including the Boylin family. The following year, the Boylins reclaimed the park. Since then, Jack Boylin and his mother, Jane, have worked hard to bring the park back from the brink, catching up on long-delayed maintenance projects and adding new attractions. Today, the giant neon sign at the park's entrance welcomes fun seekers to a park that has regained much of its once-tarnished luster. (Author's collection.)

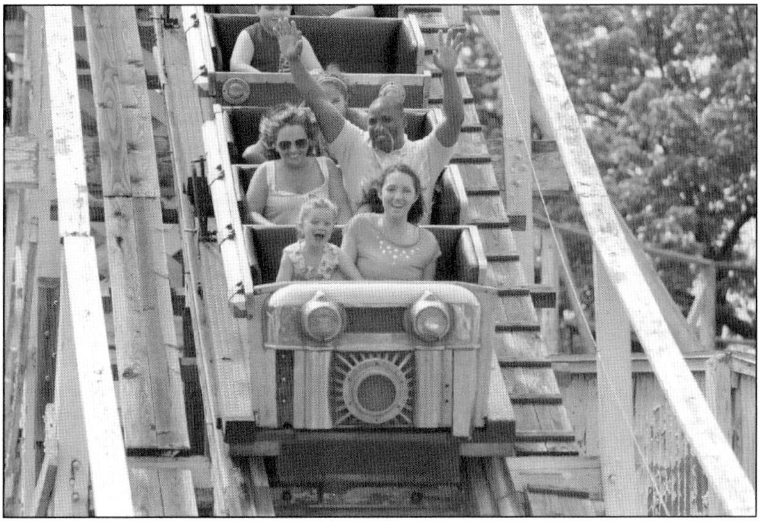

Every summer sees roller coaster fans from across the nation visiting Camden Park to ride the Big Dipper, the roller coaster that replaced the park's original coaster in 1958. The Big Dipper, a traditional wooden coaster, features original Century Flyer cars with working headlights and a classic figure-eight track design. (Courtesy of *H-D*.)

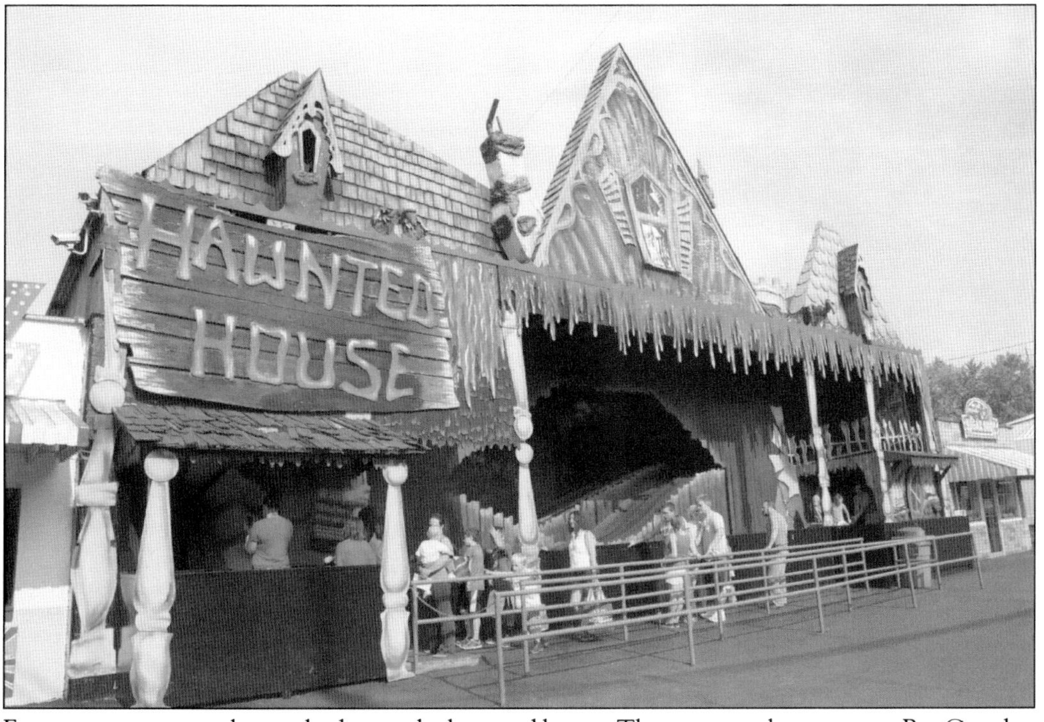

Every amusement park once had a spooky haunted house. They are mostly gone now. But Camden Park's recently refurbished haunted house is still one of the park's most popular attractions. The house offers a dark ride inspired by ghost stories, monster movies, and mad scientists. The narrow winding corridors feature sudden lights and noises, luminescent paint and models, animated props, and lots of frightening fun. (Courtesy of *H-D*.)

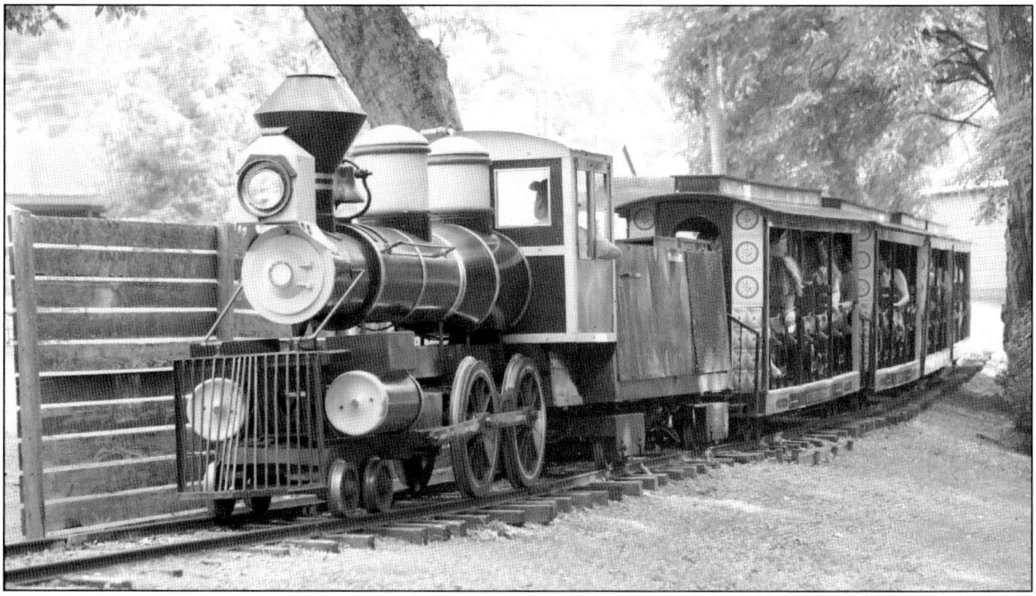

What is an amusement park without a miniature train? Camden Park's train features a replica steam locomotive and four cars with wooden bench seats. The ride begins near the park midway and circles the northeastern portion of the park, then passes through a covered bridge before heading for home. (Courtesy of *H-D*.)

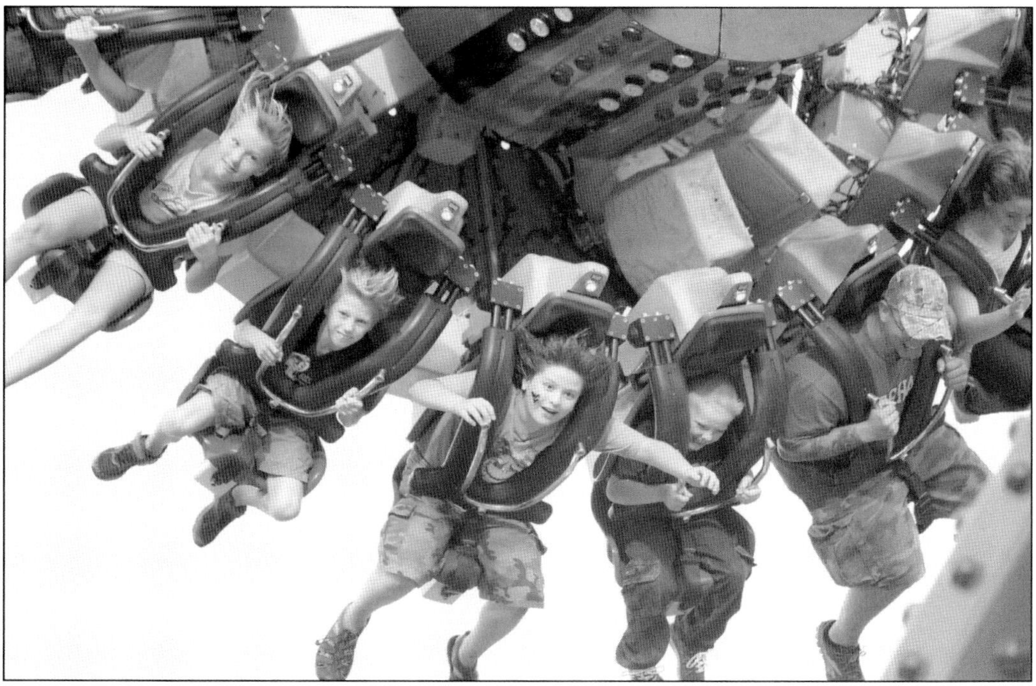

Fans of Camden Park's vintage Ferris wheel are still lamenting that it is dismantled and gone, a victim of old age. But it has been replaced by the park's newest attraction, the Rattler, a pendulum ride that sends 16 riders head over heels through dual swinging and spinning motions. It is suggested that one climb aboard the ride before that hotdog lunch rather than afterward. (Courtesy of *H-D*.)

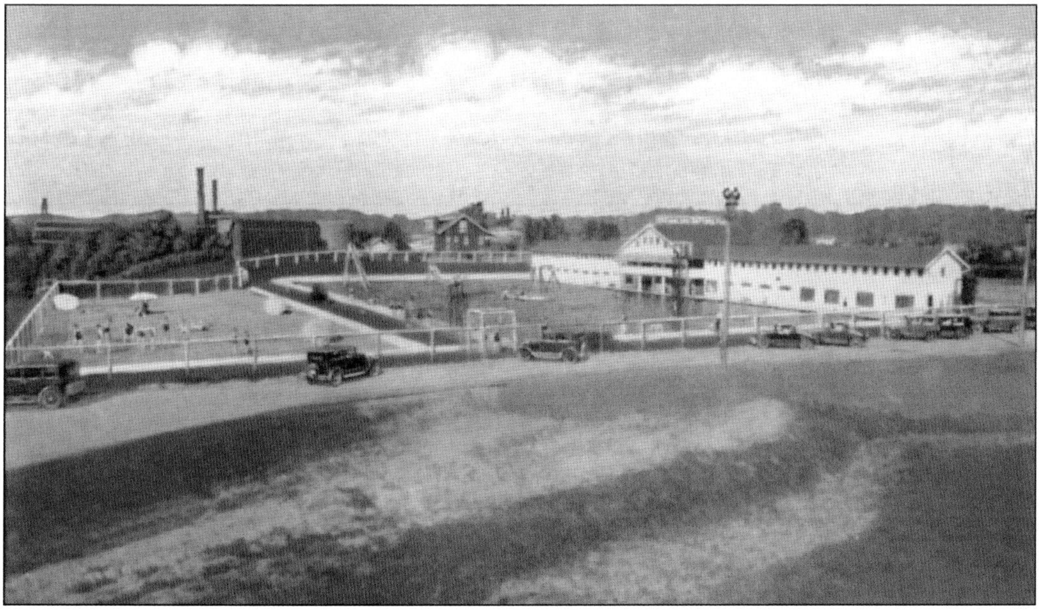

Opened as a private business in 1925, Dreamland Pool has been operated by the City of Kenova since 1974. This vintage postcard is not dated, but judging from the cars parked on the lot, it must show the pool as it looked shortly after it was built. (Author's collection.)

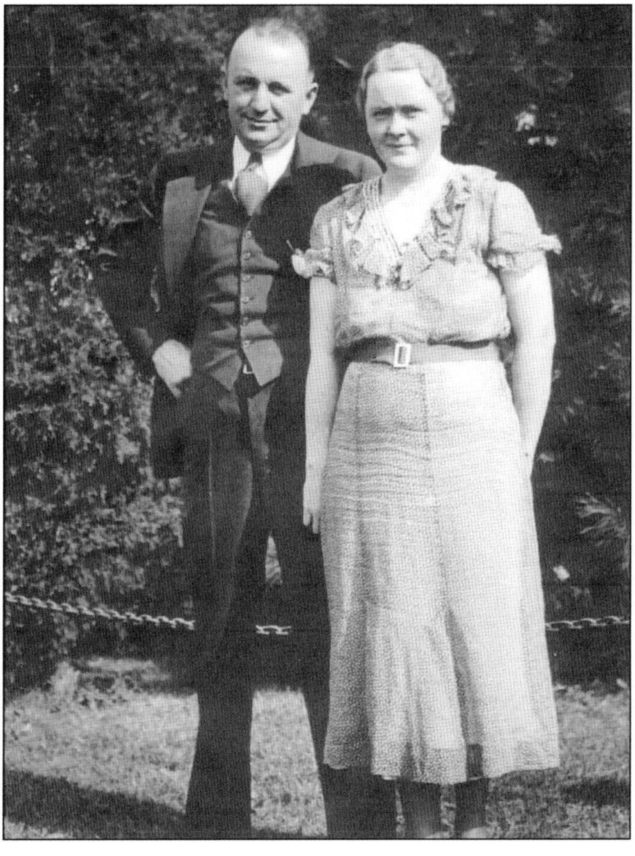

Grocer J.D. Booth of Kenova operated an ice business and had water wells for his icehouse. Thinking about other businesses that used water, he came up with the idea of a pool, which he built on the edge of the Big Sandy River where US 60 crosses into Kentucky. After Booth's death, his son Alex—shown here with his wife, Roxanna—ran the pool until the end of World War II. (Courtesy of the Kenova Historical Society.)

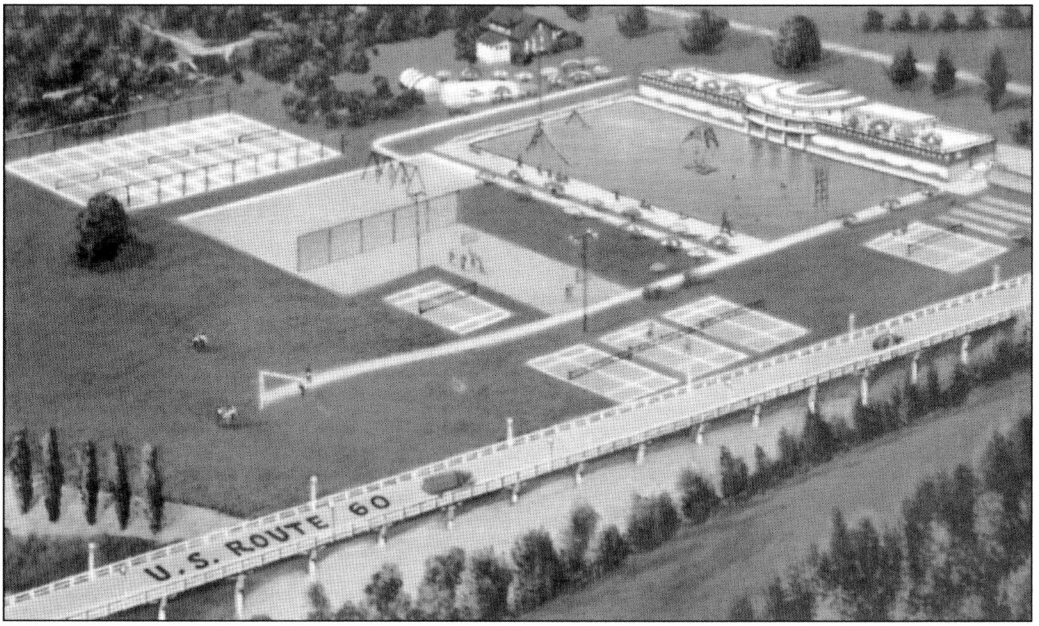

Dreamland Pool was constructed on an imposing scale—125 feet by 250 feet—and graduated from only a few inches at its shallow end to a depth of nine feet at the other. The pool's location proved ideal, drawing people from miles away in West Virginia, Kentucky, and Ohio. (Author's collection.)

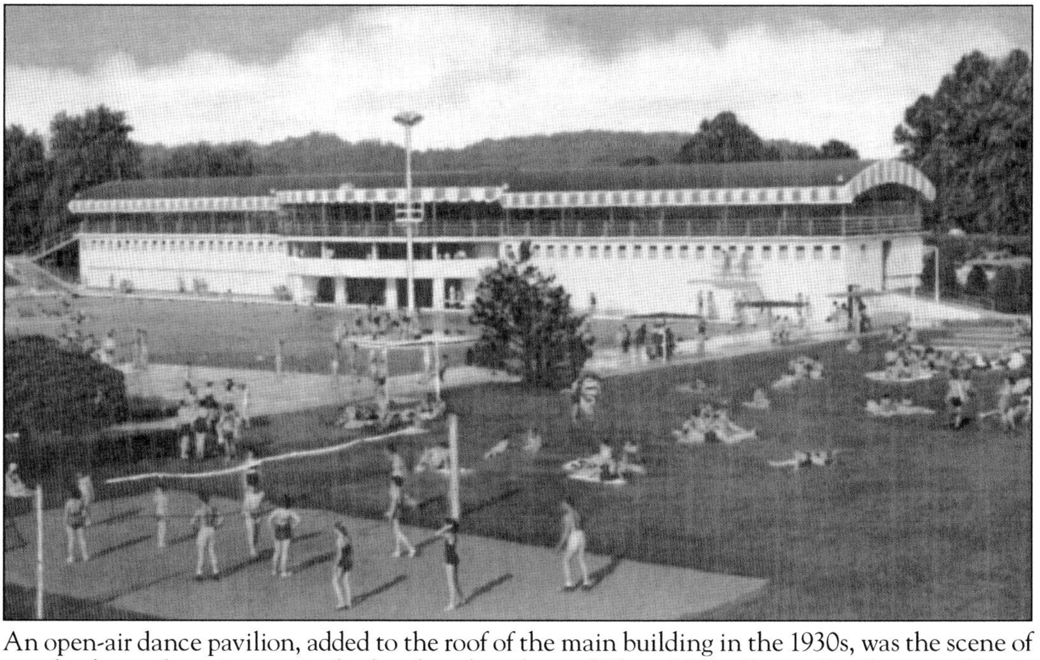

An open-air dance pavilion, added to the roof of the main building in the 1930s, was the scene of popular dances featuring touring big bands such as those of Glenn Miller, Benny Goodman, and Louis Armstrong. When Armstrong's group could not find hotel rooms in still-segregated Huntington, the Booths invited the musicians to stay at their nearby home. (Author's collection.)

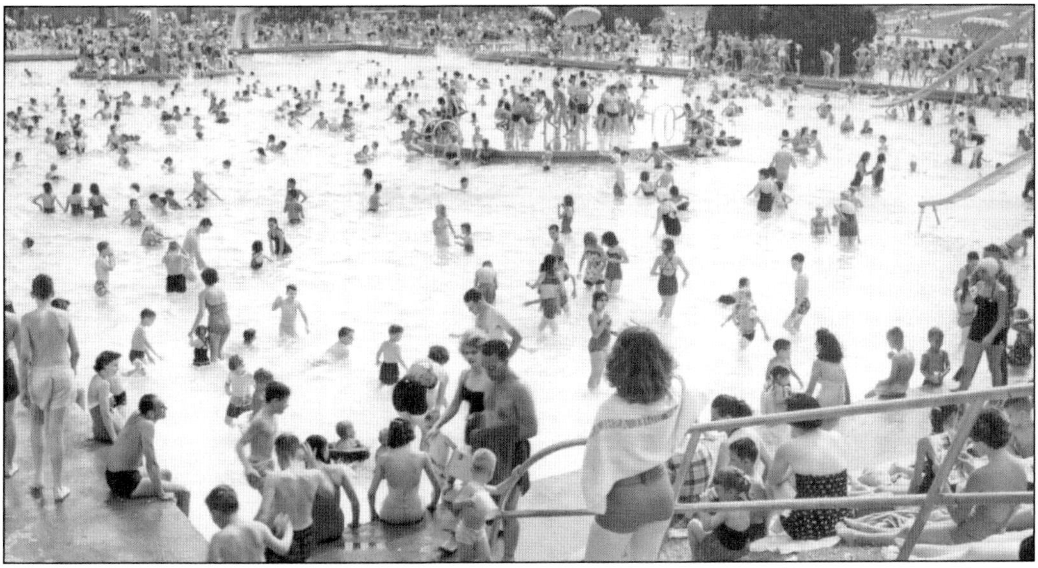

In 1949, the Booth family sold Dreamland to a group of Huntington businessmen, including Fred Salem, who later became the pool's sole owner. Summer days in the 1950s always found a big crowd at Dreamland, even after the City of Huntington opened its Olympic Pool in 1954. In addition to swimming, Dreamland offered tennis, volleyball, handball, and shuffleboard, along with picnic facilities. (Courtesy of *H-D*.)

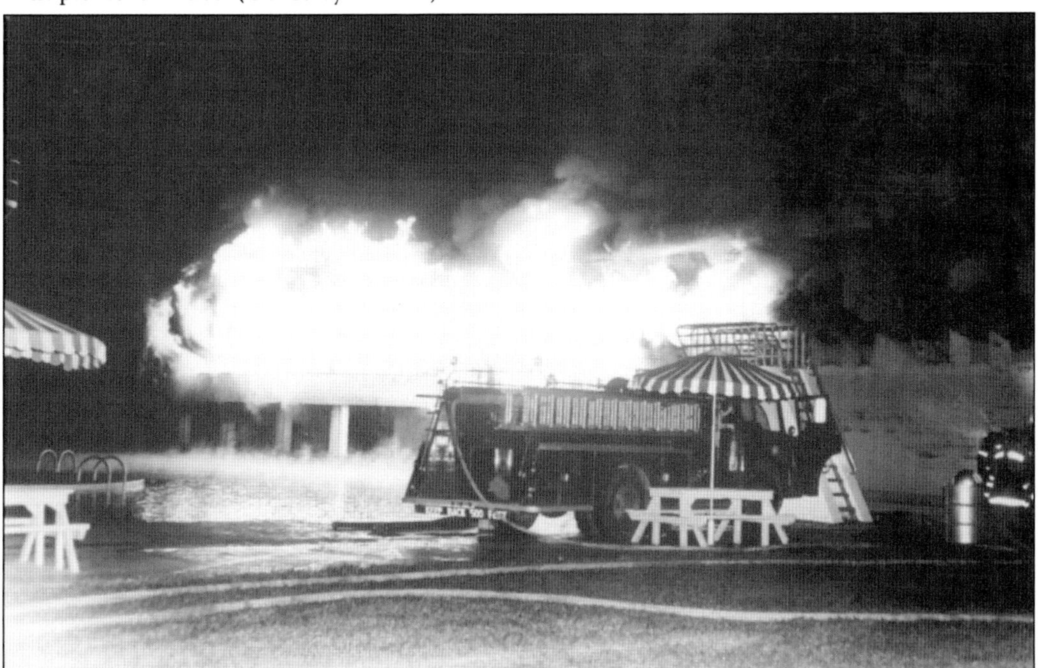

In 1973, as Fred Salem was negotiating to sell the pool to the City of Kenova, a fire destroyed the three-story building topped by the dance pavilion. After a lengthy investigation, three Kenova teenagers were charged with arson in connection with the blaze. Despite the fire, Kenova's purchase was completed, and the pool opened in May 1974 for its first season under municipal ownership. (Courtesy of *H-D*.)

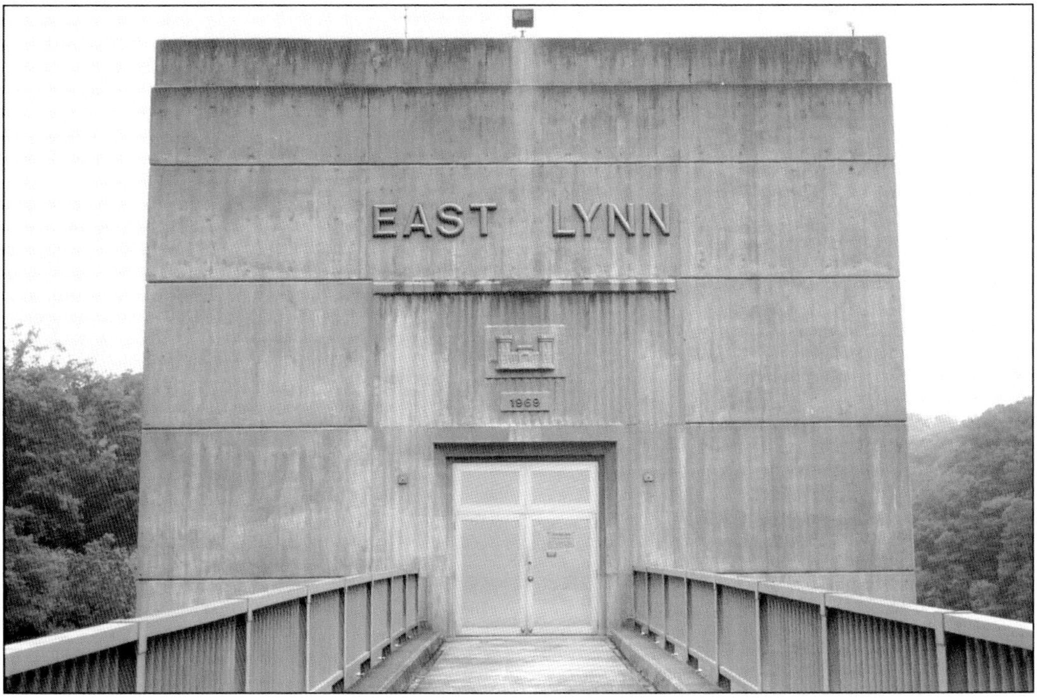

East Lynn Lake is a 1,005-acre reservoir on the East Fork of Twelve Pole Creek in Wayne County. It is operated by the US Army Corps of Engineers for combined flood control, recreation, and wildlife management purposes. The reservoir was first proposed in the wake of the record-setting Ohio River flood of 1937 but was not built until the 1960s. Construction of the dam and reservoir forced many families from their longtime homes. (Courtesy of *H-D*.)

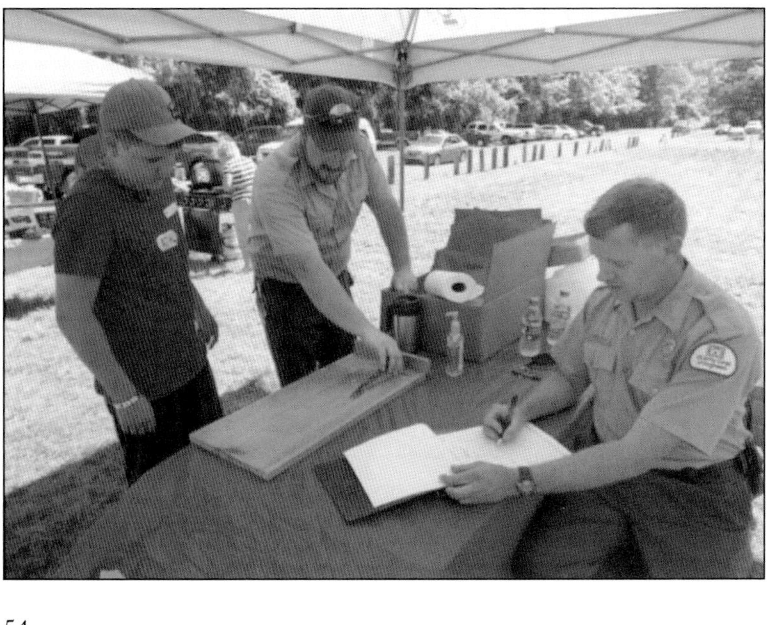

East Lynn Lake is home to more than two dozen species of fish indigenous to southern West Virginia as well as carp and other nonnative species. Here, park ranger Michael Rakes (center) and Jay Davis (right) measure a fish caught by a youngster in an East Lynn fishing tournament. (Courtesy of the US Army Corps of Engineers.)

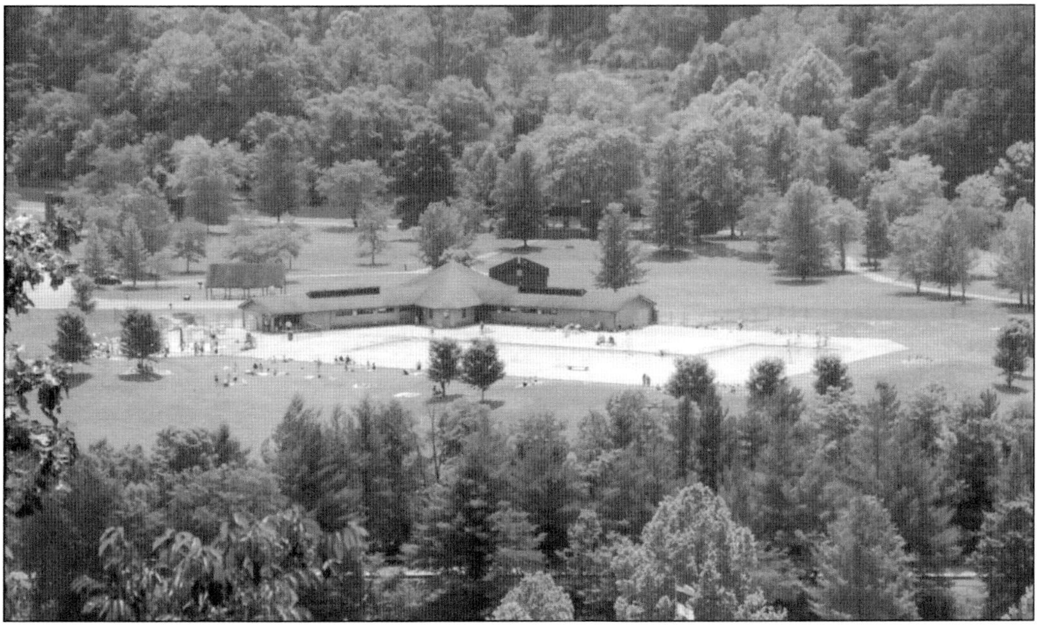

Beech Fork State Park offers 3,144 acres of some of prime recreation experience in the southwestern section of West Virginia. It is located 12 miles south of Huntington and Barboursville, just a short drive from Charleston, West Virginia; Cincinnati, Ohio; and Lexington, Kentucky. Developed by the US Army Corps of Engineers in the mid-1970s, Beech Fork Lake is popular for boating, fishing, and wildlife watching. (Courtesy of the West Virginia Department of Commerce.)

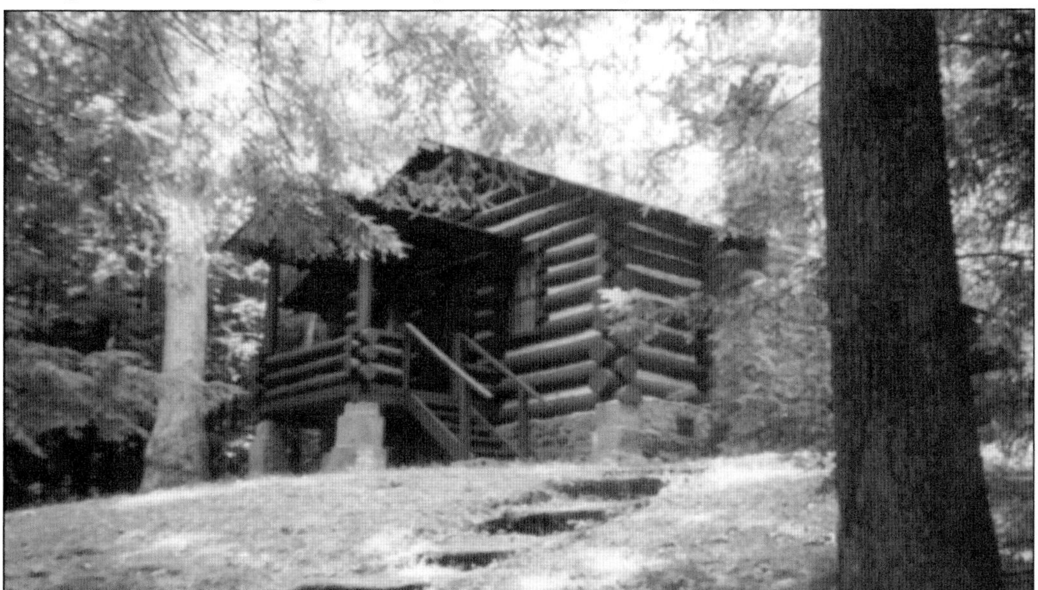

Cabwaylingo State Forest is located on 8,123 heavily forested acres in the heart of southern West Virginia. Cabwaylingo is steeped in the history of the Civilian Conservation Corps of the 1930s and 1940s. The CCC camps, including Cabwaylingo, were established to rebuild forested acres, which in turn marked the beginnings of the West Virginia State Park system. (Courtesy of the West Virginia Department of Commerce.)

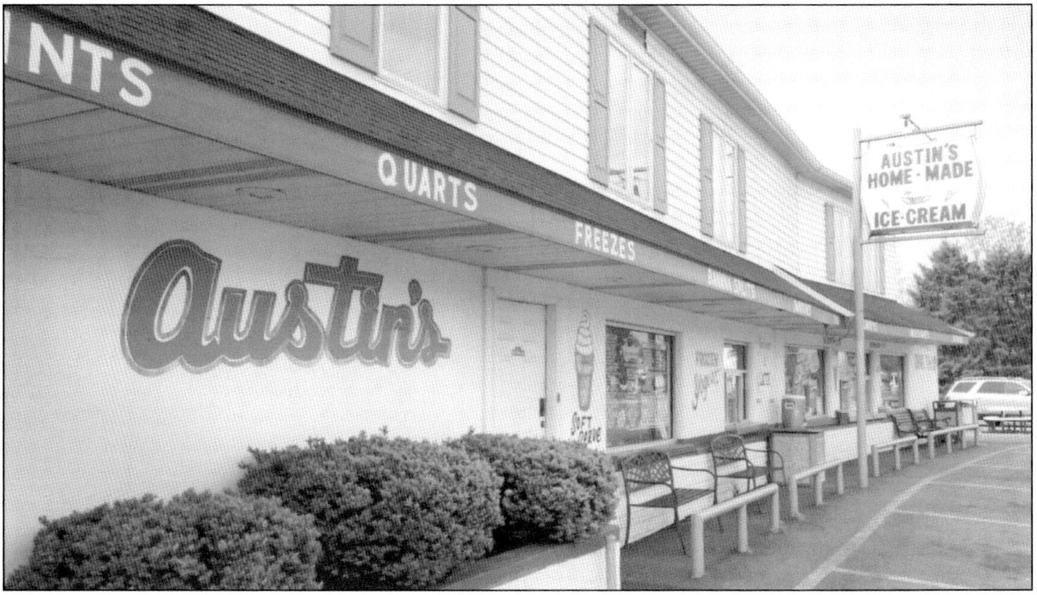

The opening of Austin's Home-Made Ice Cream in Ceredo each year is a sure sign of spring. When Joyce Snyder retired from her job at the Ceredo Bank, she saw the ice cream stand was for sale, so she bought it. Before working for the bank, she had run a Dairy Queen franchise, so she knew a thing or two about ice cream. When Snyder bought the shop, it offered only 12 flavors. After a lot of experimenting, she increased that to 30. She also expanded the building three times and put in a drive-in window. (Courtesy of HQ.)

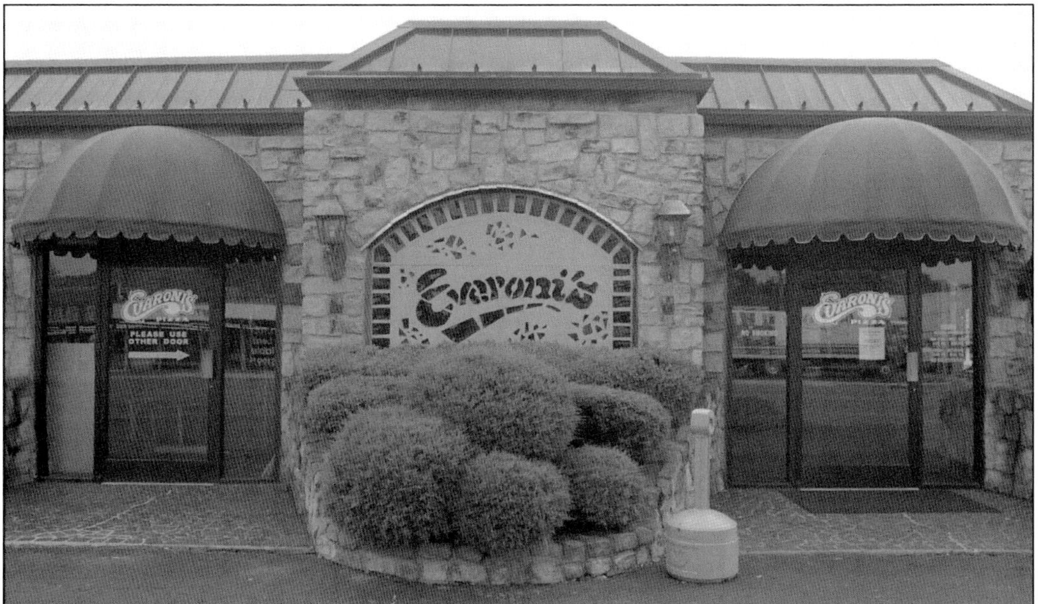

The big sign outside says it all: "In all the world there's only one Evaroni's." Kenova residents have been enjoying the pizzeria run by William and Jean Evans since 1968. The restaurant's home on Oak Street was once a glass factory. Over the years, the eatery has expanded to include a fireside dining room, banquet room, stained-glass windows, and the family's growing collection of Marshall University memorabilia. (Author's collection.)

Five

Getting from Here to There

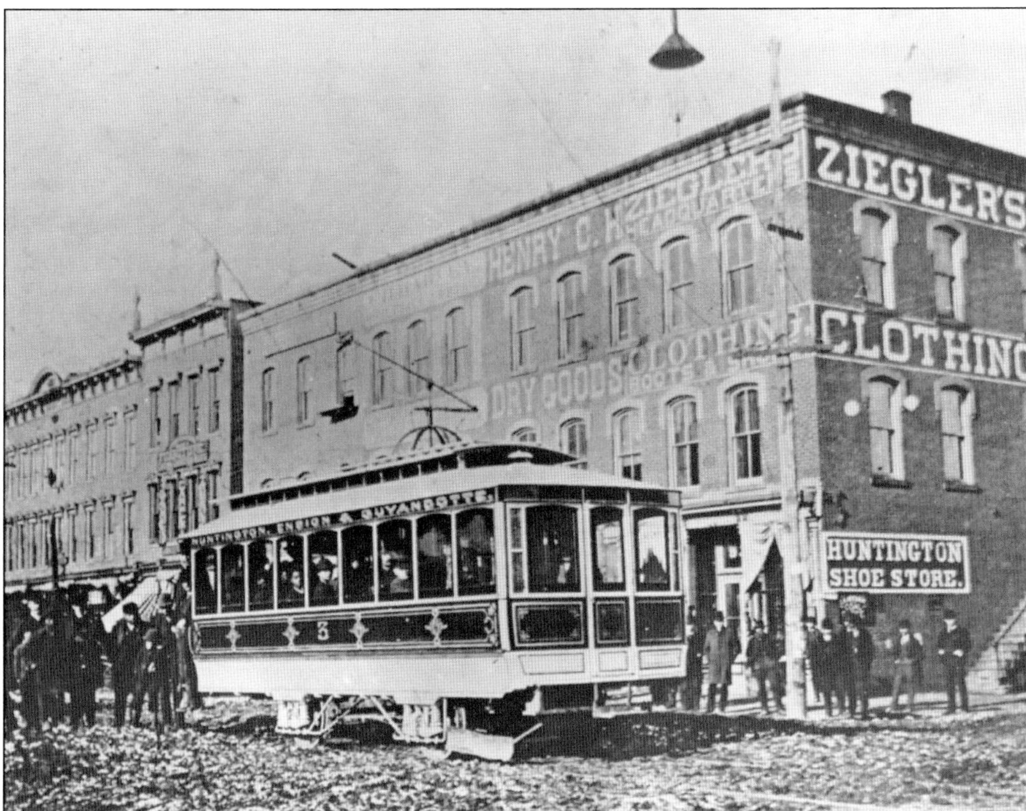

In an era before paved roadways, streetcars were a transportation mainstay. The first streetcars traveled on rails but were drawn by horses. Richmond, Virginia, was the first city to put its horses out to pasture, replacing them with electricity drawn from an overhead wire. That was in February 1888. In December of the same year, Huntington debuted it own electric streetcar, shown here. Local lore says Huntington was the nation's second city to have an electric streetcar line. (Courtesy of MU.)

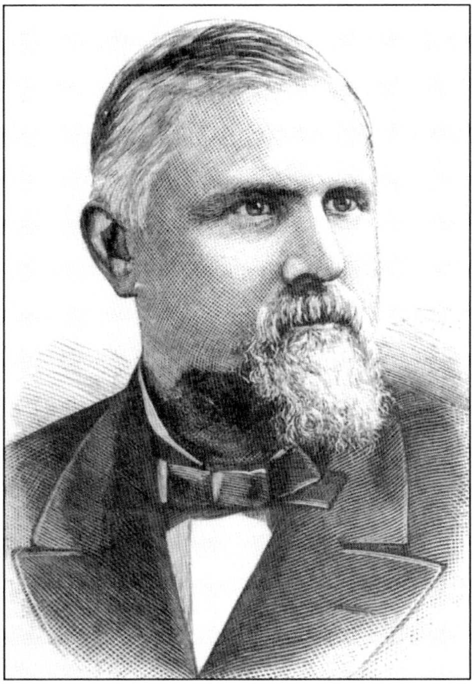

At the turn of the 20th century, separate streetcar lines in Huntington and the nearby Kentucky communities of Catlettsburg and Ashland had something in common—all were running in the red. Huntington businessman Z.T. Vinson had the idea of combining the separate lines and linking the towns. To finance his idea, he turned to this man, Johnson N. Camden, a successful oilman and member of the US Senate. (Author's collection.)

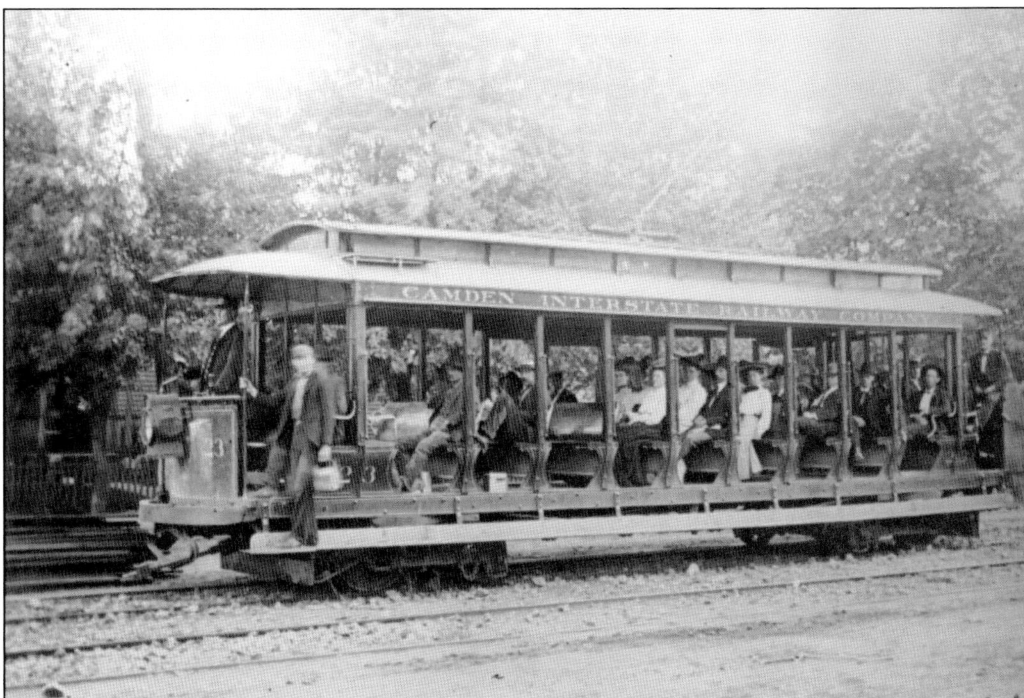

With the infusion of Camden's cash, Huntington's Consolidated Light and Railway Company became the Camden Interstate Railway Company, linking Huntington, Ceredo, and Kenova in West Virginia; Catlettsburg and Ashland in Kentucky; and (by ferry boat) Ironton in Ohio. Passengers flocked to the new system, which generally operated from 5:00 a.m. to 12:00 a.m. (Courtesy of MU.)

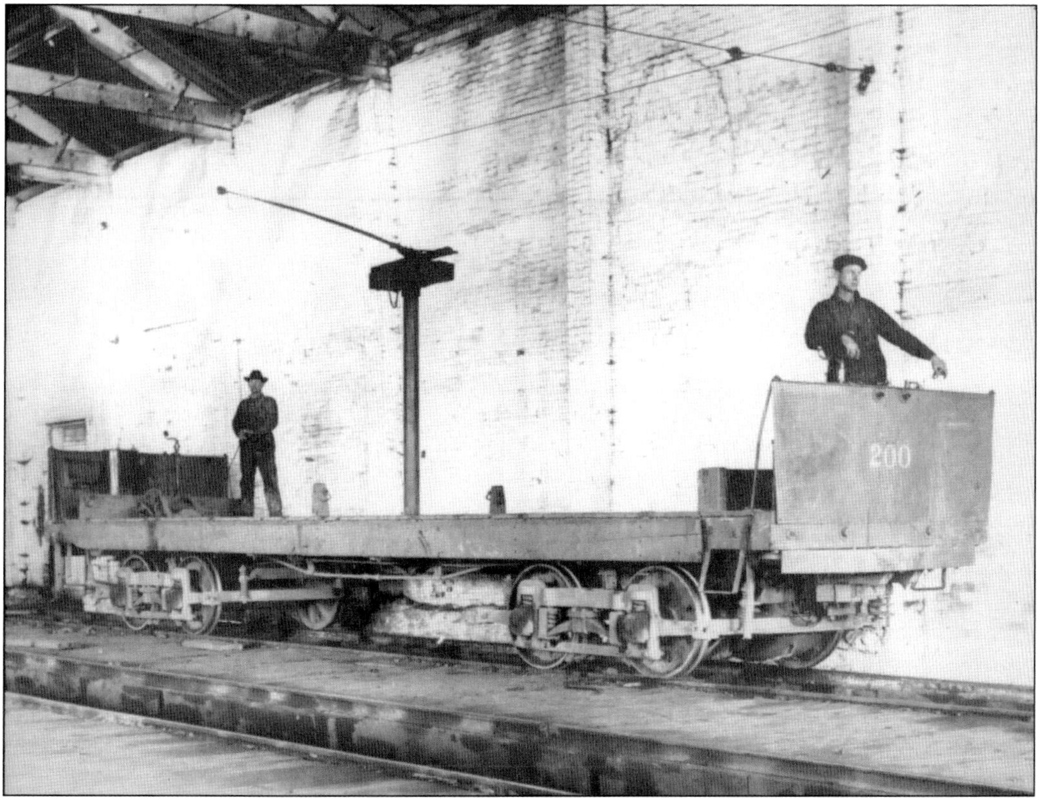

When one thinks of streetcars, generally passengers come to mind, but the Camden Interstate Railway did a booming business hauling freight on specially designed cars such as the one shown in this undated photograph. Cars such as this were also used to haul workers, tools, and supplies used to maintain the system's track. (Courtesy of MU.)

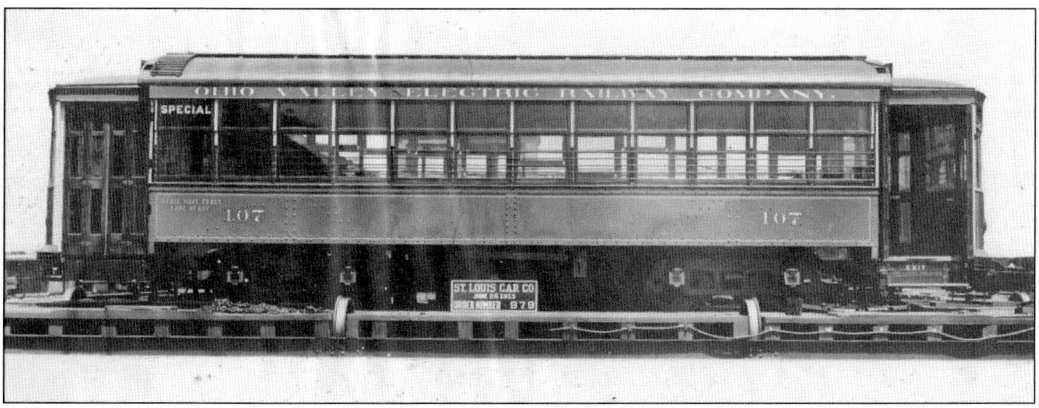

Camden died in 1907, and with his death, the streetcar line changed its name again, this time to the Ohio Valley Electric Railway Company. The streetcar above, looking more like a railroad coach than a trolley, was one of 10 all-steel cars built for the line by the St. Louis Car Company in 1913. The system began replacing streetcars with buses in 1925, with the last streetcar taken out of service in 1937. (Author's collection.)

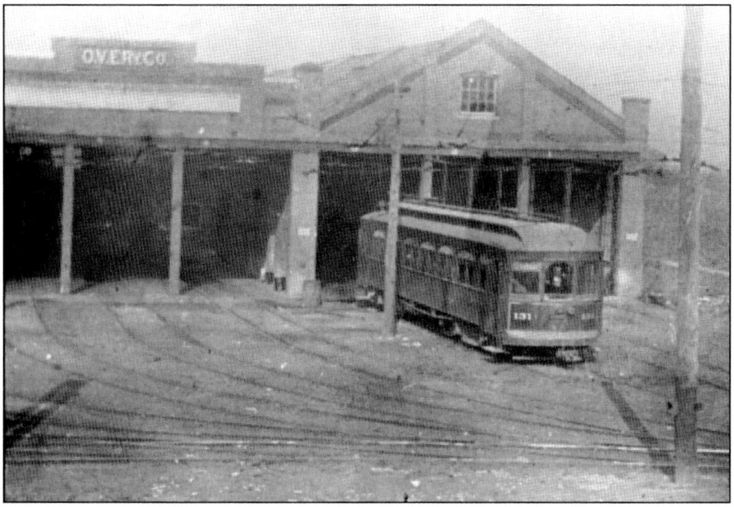

This 1913 shot of the Ohio Valley Electric Railway carbarn at West Eighteenth Street in Huntington shows car No. 131, a heavy wood interurban, rolling out for its early-morning run. The old carbarn later housed the Ohio Valley Bus Company and its fleet. Later, it was home to a flea market and then demolished to make way for a new convenience store. (Author's collection.)

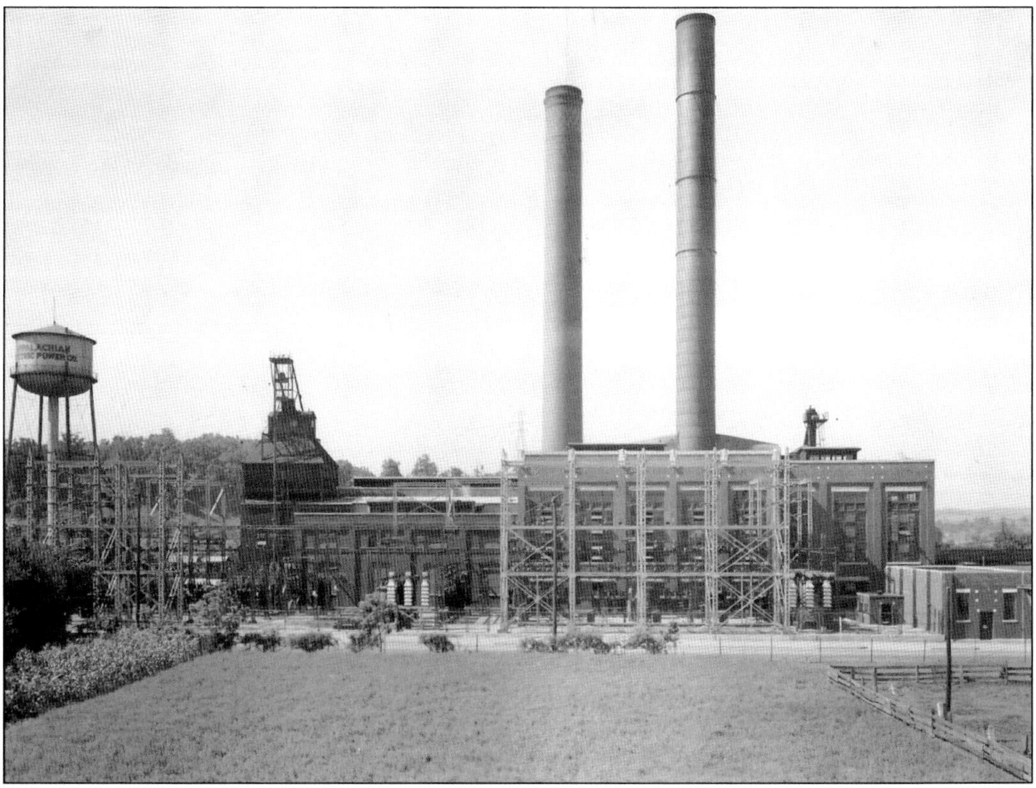

Electricity to propel the system's streetcars was generated at a power station built in Kenova in 1903. In 1915, the station was sold to the Consolidated Light, Heat, and Power Company. Later, Appalachian Power Company absorbed the Consolidated company and set about enlarging the station. Long a Kenova landmark, the station was closed in 1962 and demolished in 1966. (Courtesy of *H-D*.)

The Big Sandy River marks the border between Wayne County and Kentucky from Fort Gay to the Ohio River. In 1874, Congress authorized a survey of the Big Sandy to determine the feasibility of building locks and dams. As a result, three locks and dams were built, making the river navigable. Here, workers at a Fort Gay stone yard prepare blocks to construct Lock and Dam No. 1 (Courtesy of the Library of Congress.)

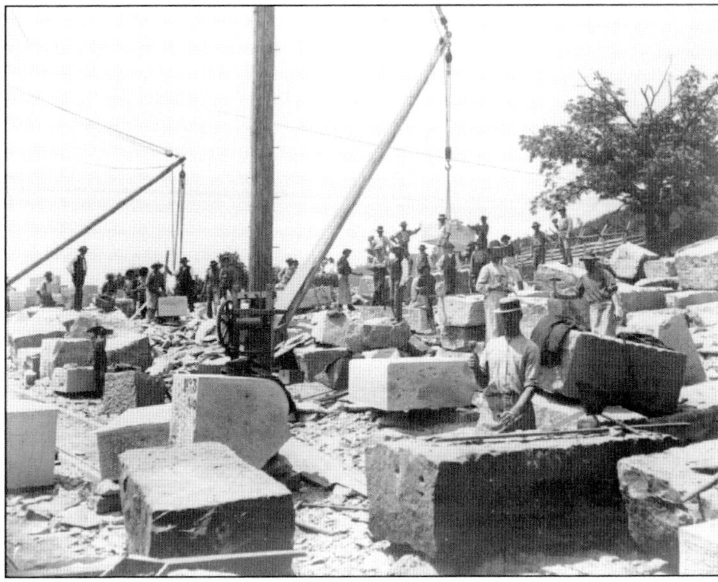

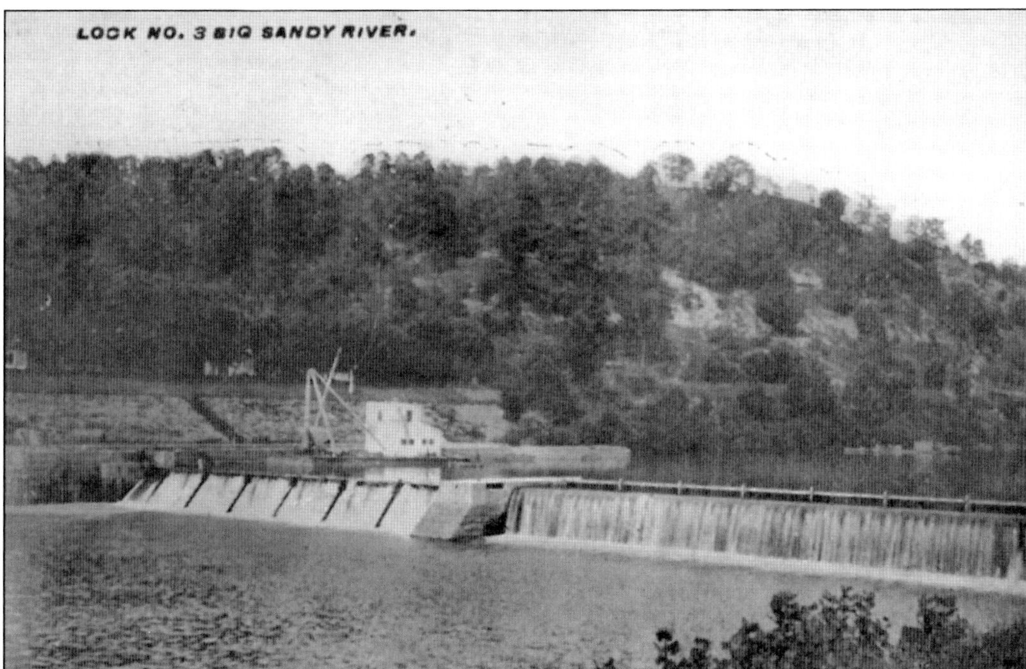

With the railroads steadily reducing river traffic on the Big Sandy River, operations at Lock and Dams No. 2 and 3 (shown here) were discontinued in 1947. Lock and Dam No. 1 was closed in 1952. Today, the Big Sandy River is navigable for only a distance of approximately nine miles upstream from the Ohio River. (Author's collection.)

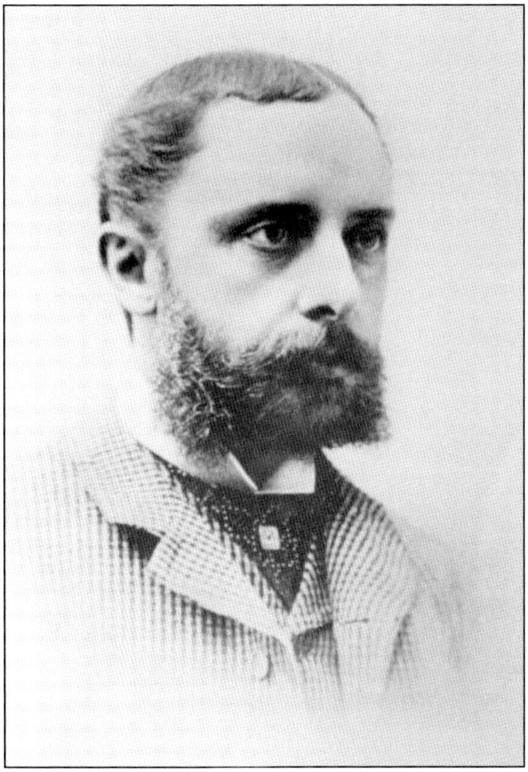

Becoming president of the Norfolk & Western Railway in 1883, Frederick J. Kimble became the driving force behind laying a route from West Virginia's southern coalfields to the Ohio River, a decision that would bring the N&W to Wayne County and give birth to the town of Kenova. (Courtesy of the West Virginia State Archives.)

The N&W's initial route through Wayne County followed along Twelve Pole Creek. Known by locals as the "Tadpole Line," the track traveled through desolate countryside, where the population was sparse and the terrain challenging. In 1891, the N&W constructed what it described as a first-class station at Lavalette, the first station built on the line. The station was demolished years ago, leaving only this wooden shack. (Courtesy of Jack Dickinson.)

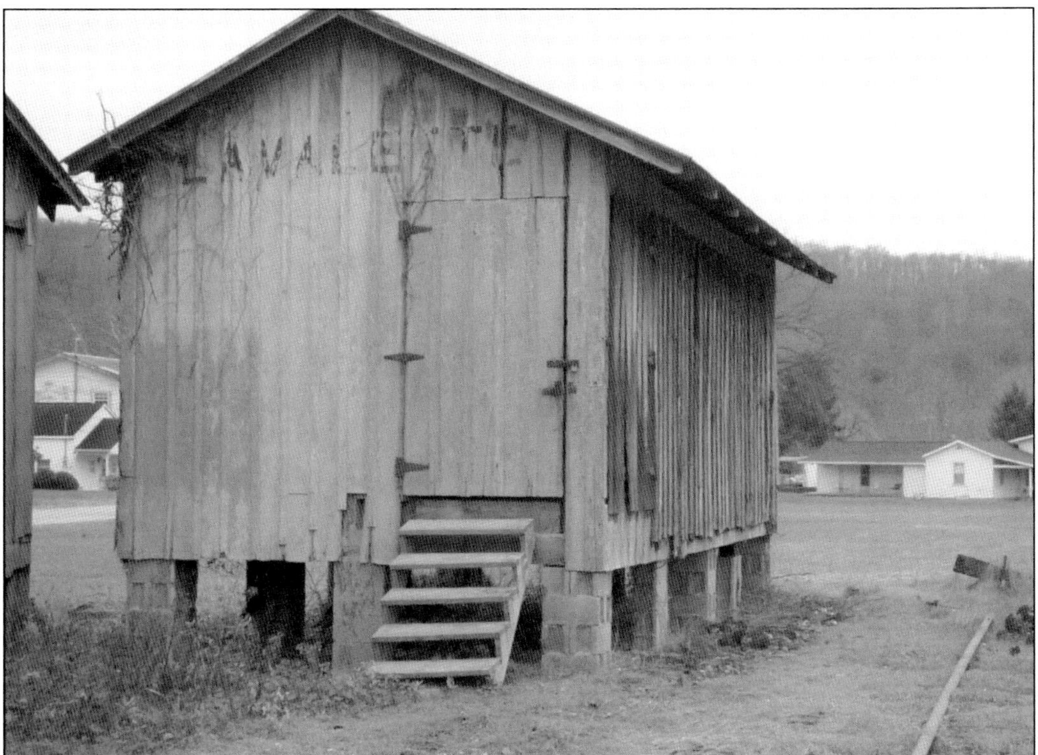

Disappointed in the low level of traffic generated on the Tadpole Line, the N&W decided to build a second route into Wayne County, one that would roughly follow the Big Sandy River and West Virginia's border with Kentucky. This second route would prove to be far more profitable and would keep the railroad's men and equipment busy—but not too busy to take a break for this 1910 photograph. (Courtesy of MU.)

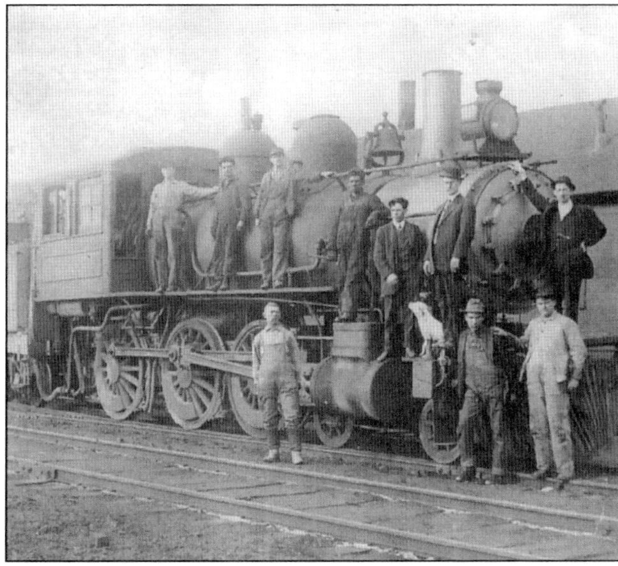

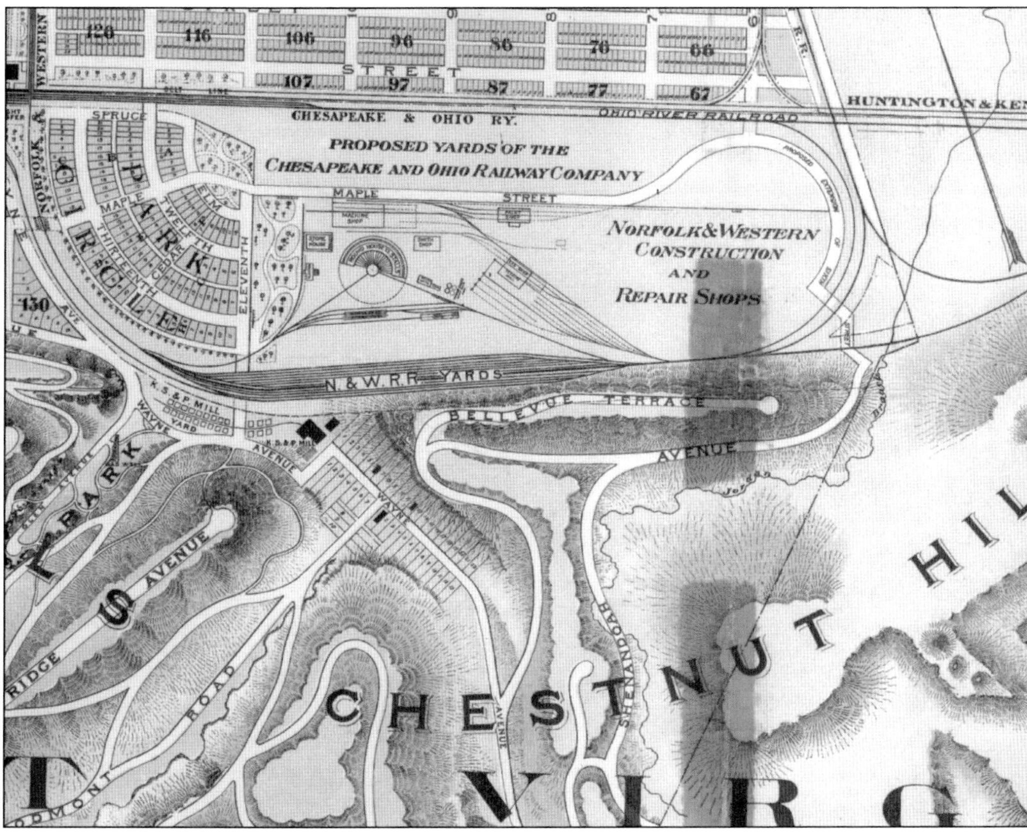

Once the N&W had decided where its track would reach and cross the Ohio River, a small army of workers descended on the site to begin construction of the new bridge and the long trestle leading to it, along with the rail yards, roundhouse, and other facilities. Streets for the new community of Kenova were laid out, and it quickly became a boomtown, attracting businesses and industries. (Courtesy of MU.)

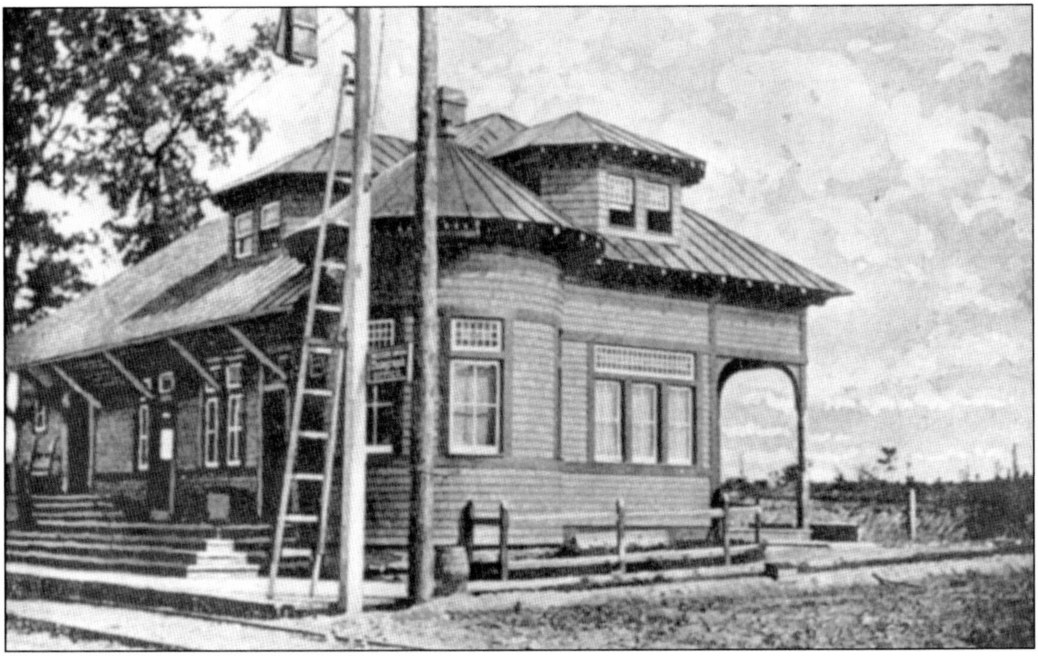

From the outset of its plans for Kenova, the N&W envisioned construction of a large two-level passenger depot. While that ambitious project was under construction—a process that took three years—this temporary station was erected. It opened in 1891 and was closed and demolished when the completed Union Station opened in 1894. (Courtesy of MU.)

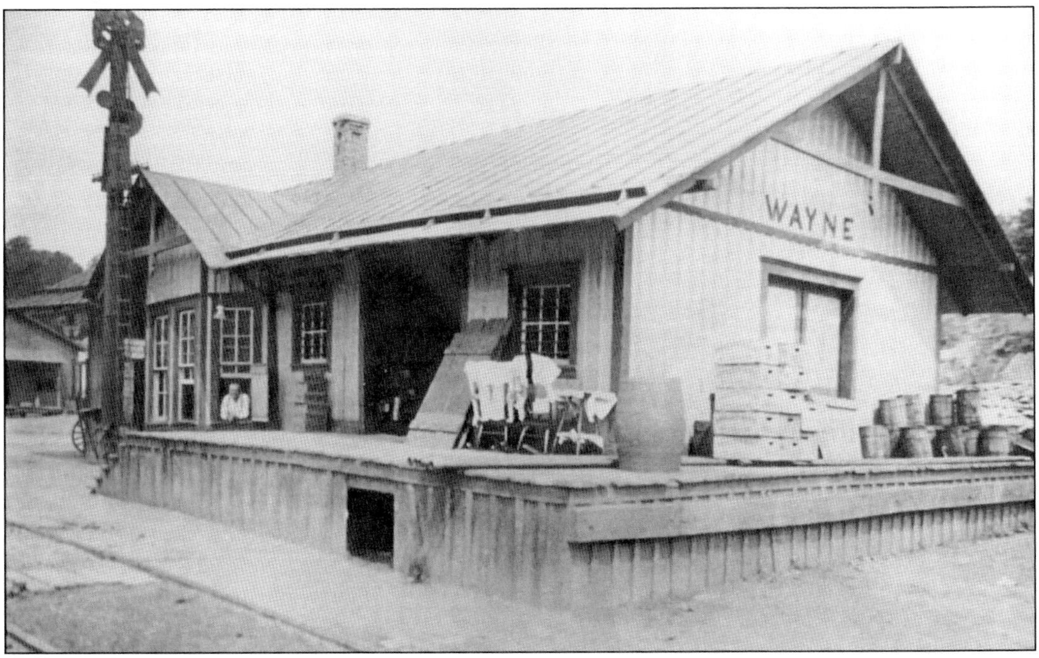

The N&W's services to Wayne residents were provided at this local combination freight and passenger station, where the fellow in the bay window was everything to everybody. He was a telegraph operator, freight agent, and ticket seller. The building, seen here around 1920, most likely dated from the original main lines opening in November 1892. (Courtesy of Bob Withers.)

Engineer Ephraim Rogers (right) and fireman E.E. Davis pose for a photographer on the rear of N&W passenger GP9 515 before taking the Norfolk-Cincinnati Train 25, the *Powhatan Arrow*, out of Kenova for the last time at 2:15 p.m. on Friday, May 23, 1969. (Courtesy of Bob Withers.)

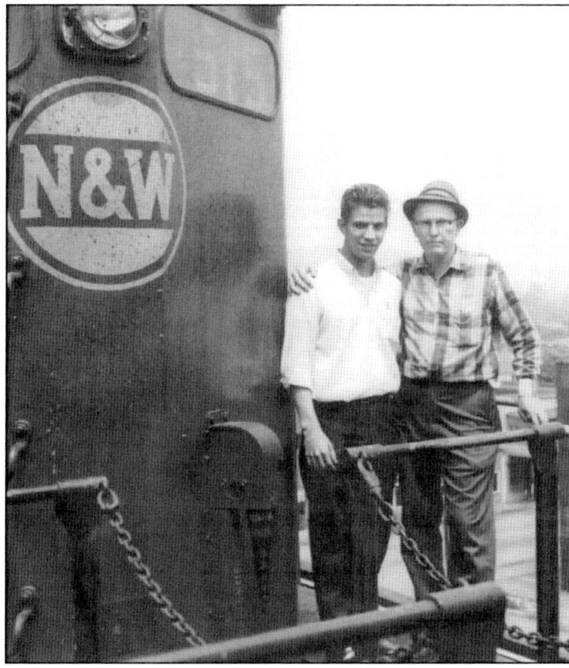

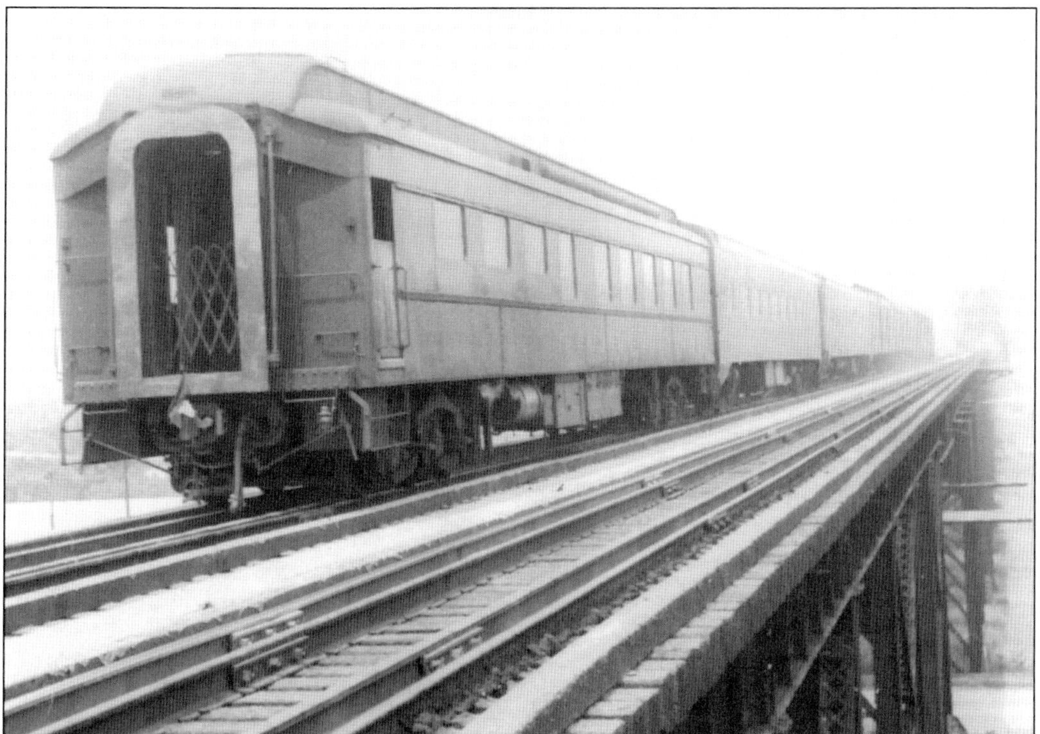

Westbound Norfolk-Cincinnati Train 25, the *Powhatan Arrow*, departs Kenova for the last time at 2:18 p.m., three minutes late, on Friday, May 23, 1969. This left N&W's *Pocahontas* as its only remaining passenger train. It would last until Amtrak's takeover of most US intercity rail travel on May 1, 1971. (Courtesy of Bob Withers.)

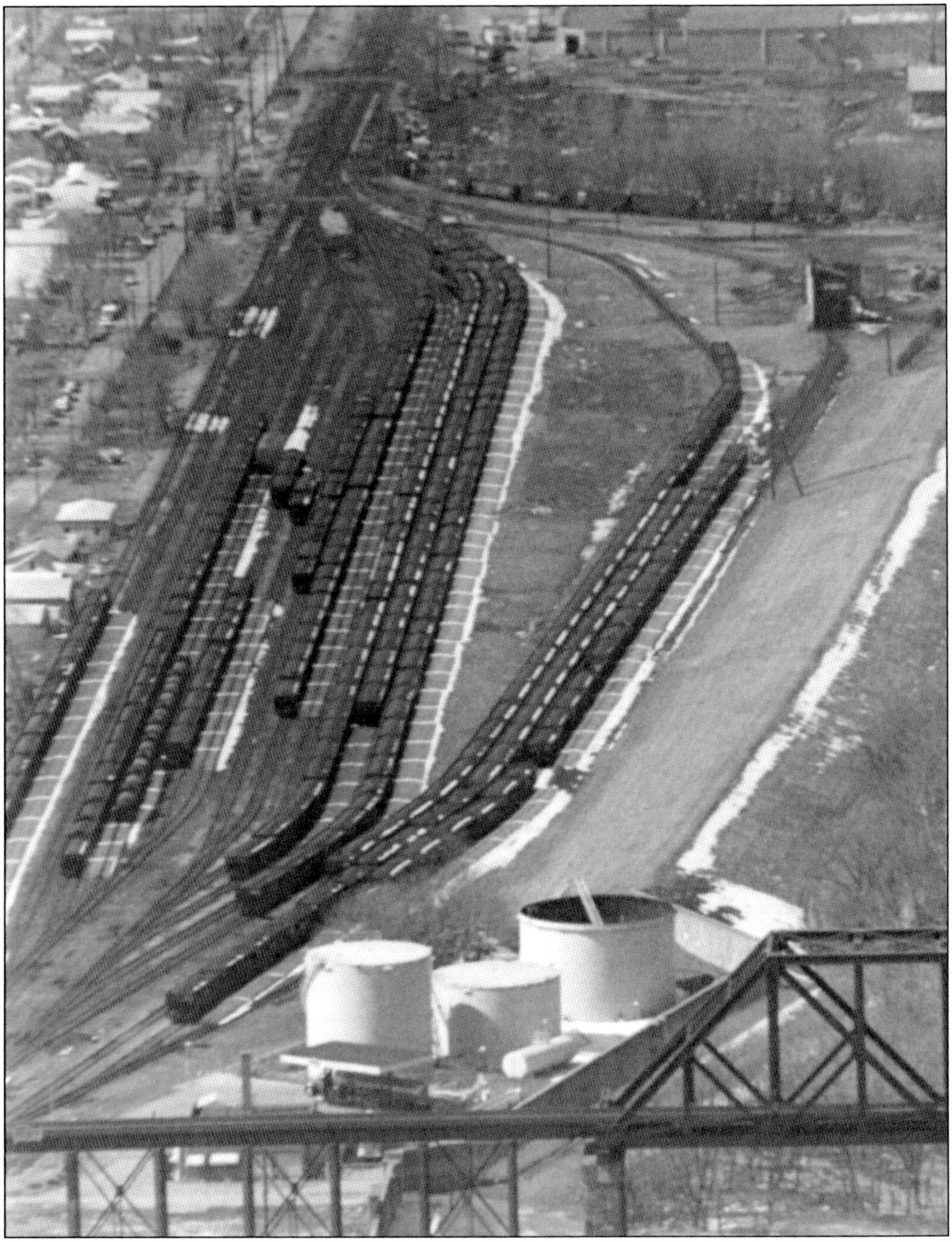

Coal was the lifeblood of the Norfolk & Western. At its founding, the railroad primarily transported agricultural products. Frederick Kimball, who had a strong interest in geology, led the railroad's efforts to open the Pocahontas coalfields in western Virginia and southern West Virginia. As more and more mines opened, the N&W hauled steadily larger amounts of coal each year. Later construction of the railroad's Big Sandy route dramatically increased each year's annual tonnage of coal. This 1978 aerial view of the N&W storage tracks at Kenova offers graphic evidence of coal's importance to the railroad, with long strings of loaded coal cars awaiting shipment to steel mills and power plants everywhere. Today, despite a recent downturn in the coal industry, Norfolk Southern, the corporate successor to the old N&W, operates a fleet of more than 23,000 coal cars and continues to haul vast quantities of coal each year. (Courtesy of *H-D*.)

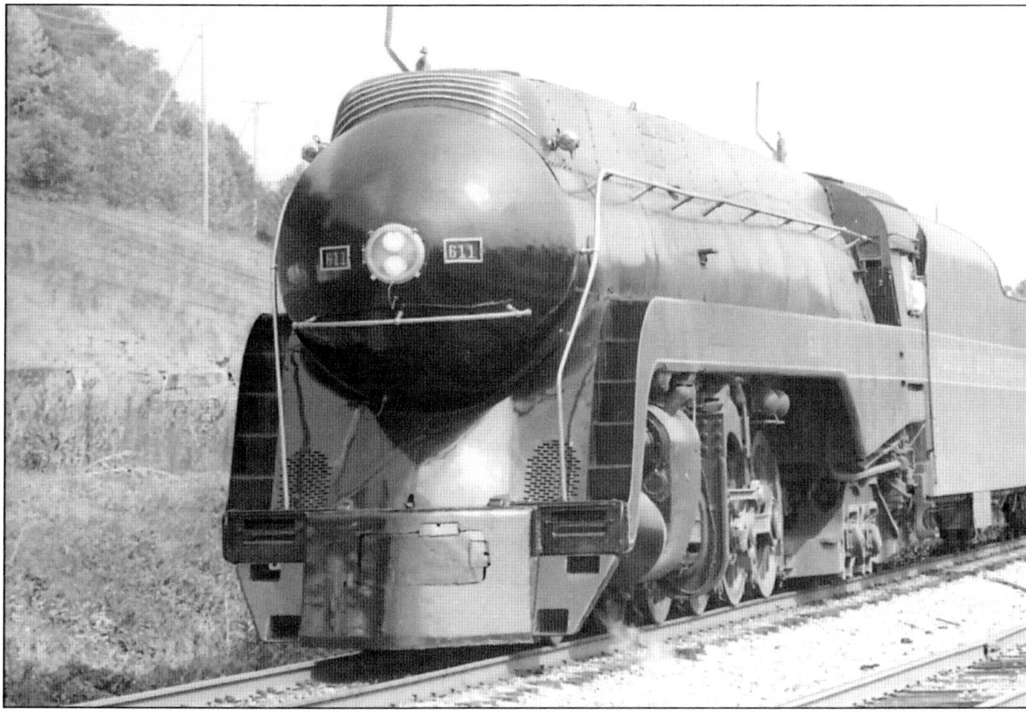

In the years after World War II, America's railroads one by one retired their coal-fired steam locomotives, replacing them with diesels, which were cheaper to run. Yet the N&W stubbornly clung to steam. This steam-powered Class J locomotive, No. 611, was designed and built at the N&W shops in Roanoke, Virginia, in 1956, when the nation's other railroads were well on their way to dieselization. The 611 became a museum piece but now has been restored to operating order for excursion runs. (Courtesy of *H-D*.)

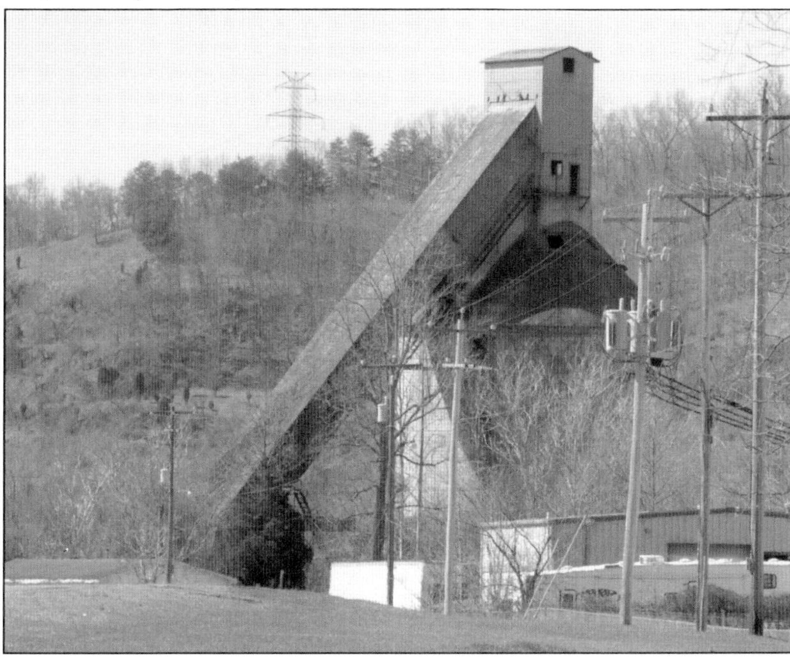

Perhaps it was not surprising that the N&W was reluctant to switch to diesels given that hauling coal was an important source of revenue for the railroad. Finally, in 1960, the N&W switched to diesel power, leaving coal tipples such as this one at Prichard in Wayne County as abandoned relics. (Courtesy of Jim Ross.)

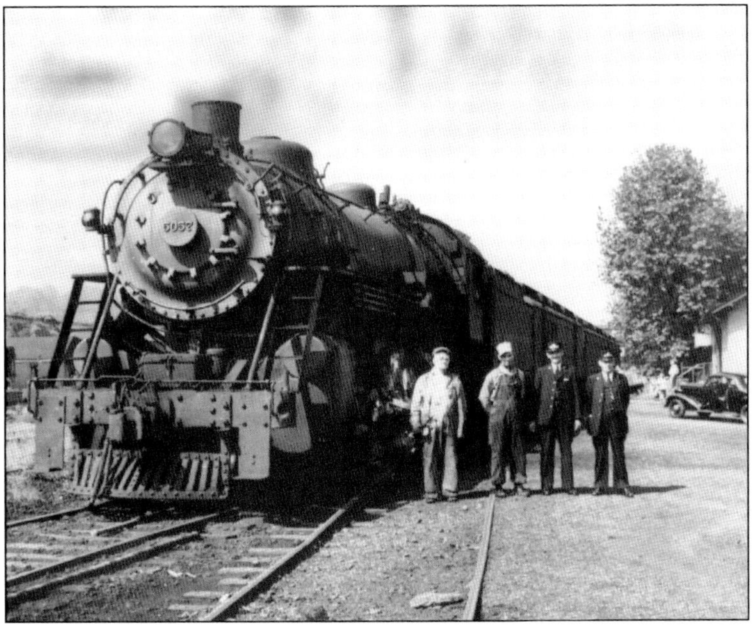

The crew of Baltimore & Ohio Kenova-Pittsburgh passenger Train 72 poses beside engine 5057 before departing the Kenova station at 11:10 a.m. on Thursday, May 12, 1949. From left to right, the crew includes engineer Les Dyke, fireman Johnny Lightner, flagman Bob Cariens, and conductor John P. Hill. The baggage handler/brakeman must have been attending to duties elsewhere. (Courtesy of Bob Withers.)

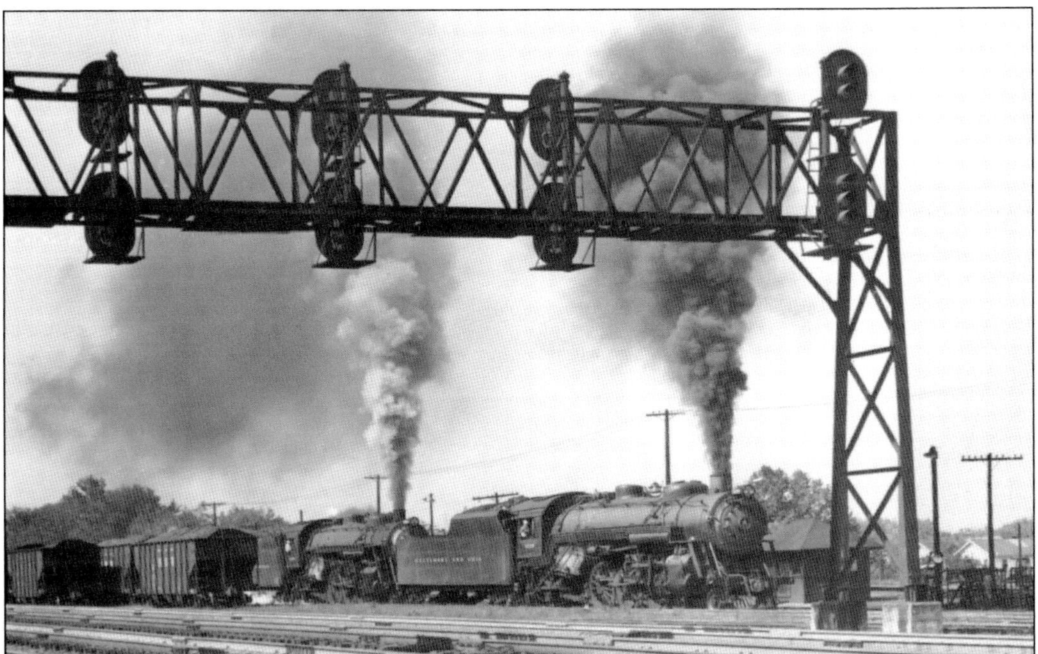

Baltimore & Ohio Railroad Class P-5a Pacific 5229 and Class P-5 Pacific 5209 take a nine-car Train 72 out of Kenova for Wheeling at 1:05 p.m. on Sunday, September 27, 1953. A double-headed passenger train on the B&O's Ohio River branch line was extremely rare, but this one was occasioned not by good business but by the fact the extra locomotive and six extra cars were deadheading back up the Ohio River. (Courtesy of Bob Withers.)

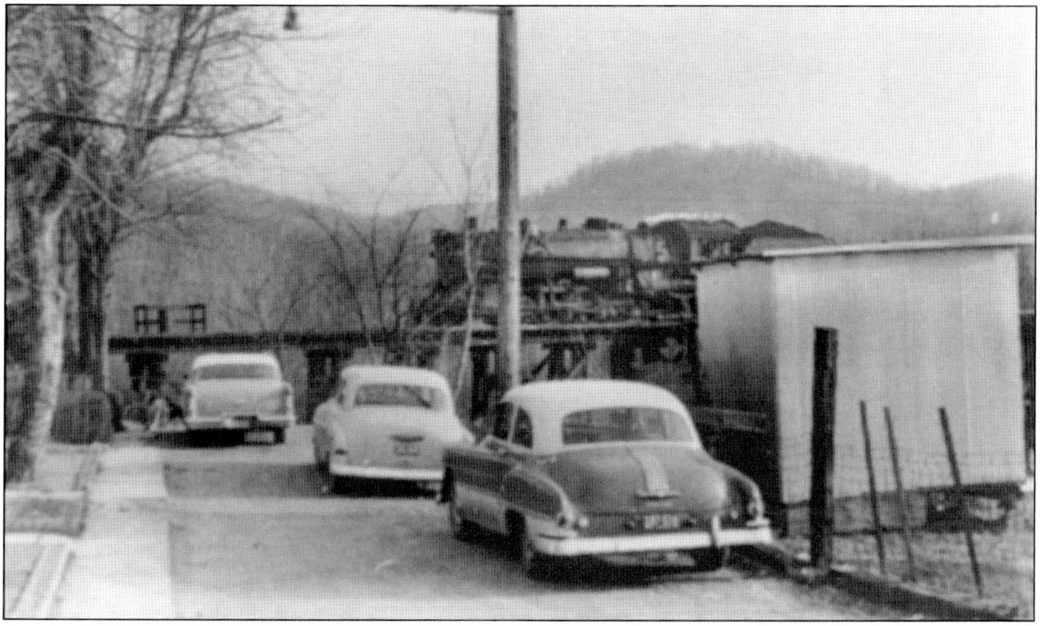

A B&O Class Q-3 Mikado locomotive crosses the Four Pole Creek pile trestle between Kenova and West Huntington in the winter of 1955 or 1956. In those days, B&O eastbound freight engines ran light, or by themselves, from Kenova, where coaling, watering, and turning facilities were available, to Huntington, where they picked up their freight trains and continued on to Parkersburg. (Courtesy of Bob Withers.)

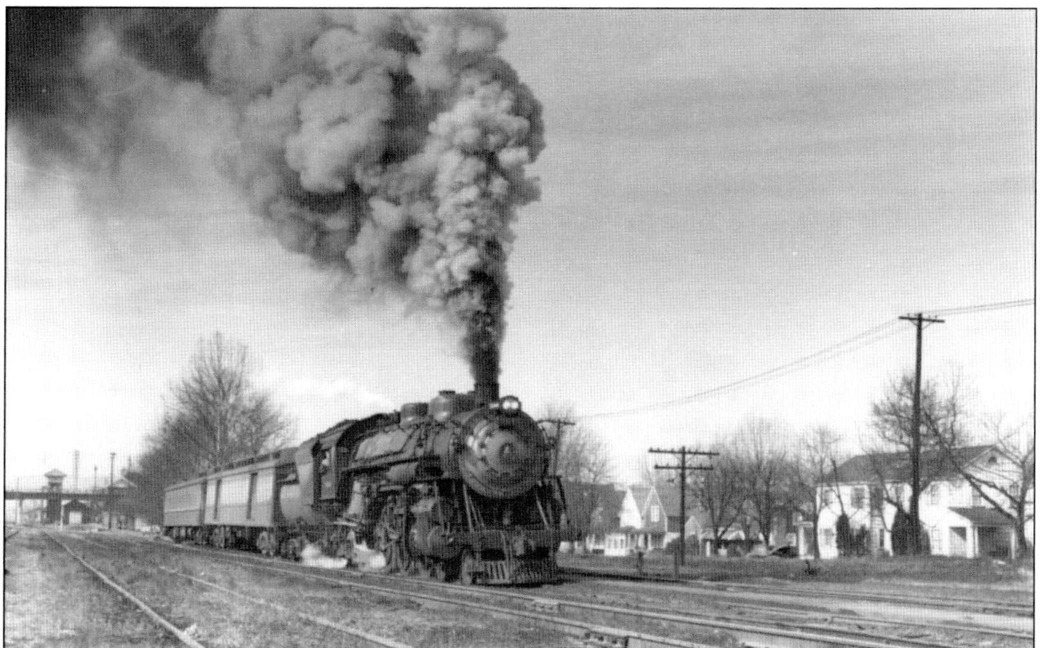

B&O passenger Train 72 departs Kenova at 1:05 p.m. for Wheeling in February 1956. Locomotive 5244 is a Class P-6a Pacific built in 1922. The train includes only an express/baggage car and a coach and will be discontinued in less than a year. (Courtesy of Bob Withers.)

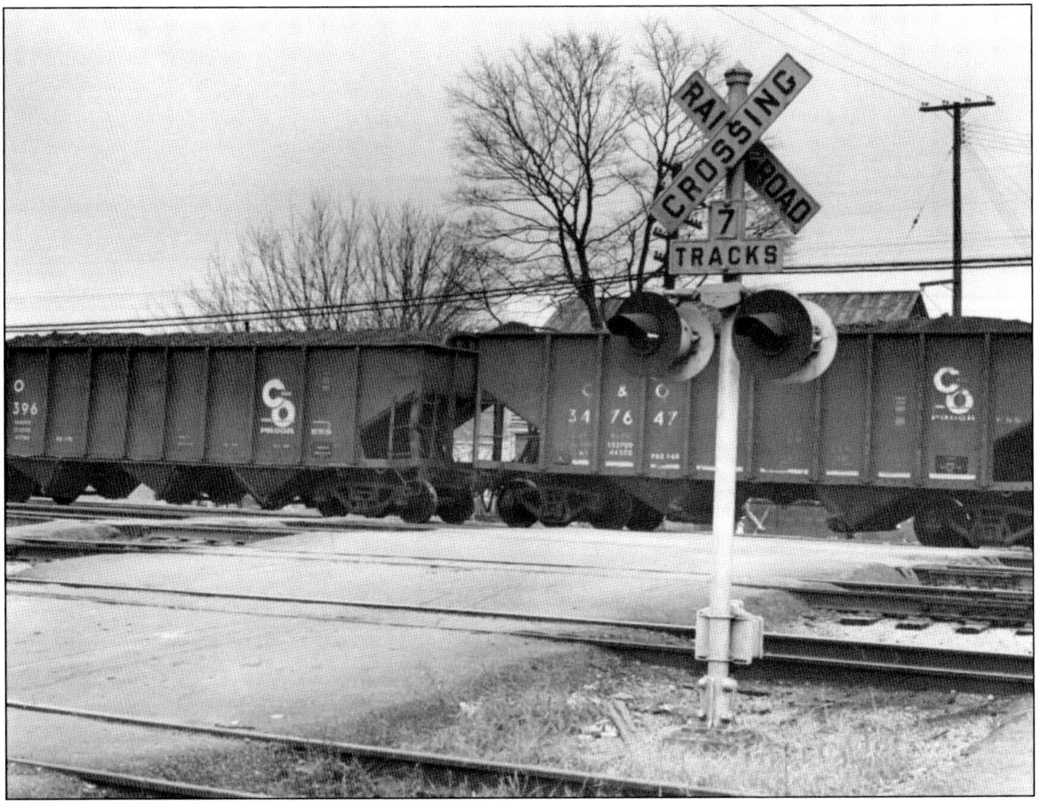

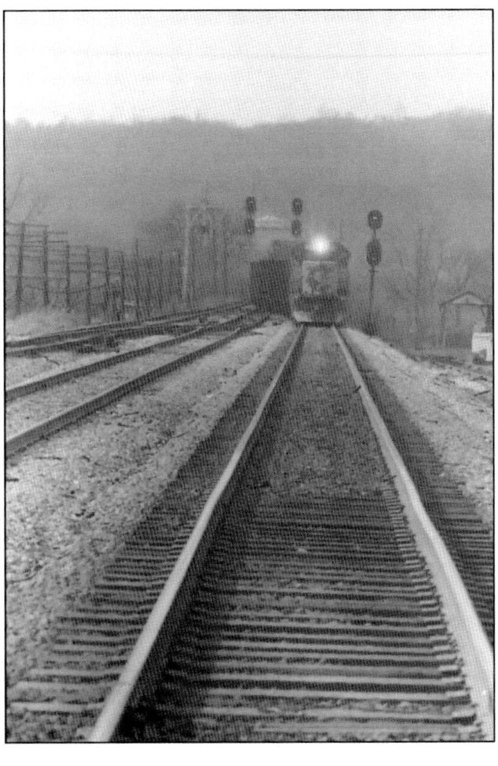

When railroad mogul Collis P. Huntington pushed the tracks of his Chesapeake & Ohio Railway westward across West Virginia from its birthplace in Virginia, the first train from Richmond arrived in the new city of Huntington in 1873. A century later, in 1973, these loaded coal cars photographed at a Kenova grade crossing still carried the C&O name. Not one but two name changes lay ahead for the railroad. (Courtesy of *H-D.*)

After the C&O and the B&O merged in 1963, the combined railroad was renamed the Chessie System, adopting the name of the C&O's longtime kitten mascot. In 1980, the name changed again, this time to CSX Transportation. Today, the CSX main line still traverses Wayne County, traveling east-west along the Ohio River. (Courtesy of *H-D.*)

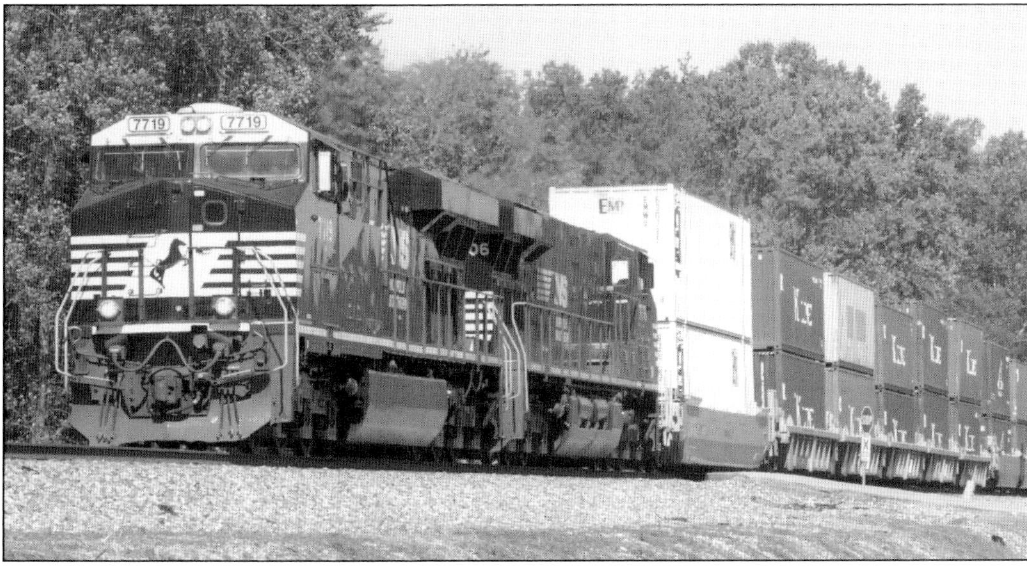

Enlarged railroad tunnels now permit Norfolk Southern to ship double-stack freight containers from Norfolk, Virginia, across southern West Virginia to Midwest destinations. Taking advantage of that, the West Virginia Public Port Authority is developing a major intermodal freight facility at Prichard in Wayne County. (Courtesy of Jim Ross.)

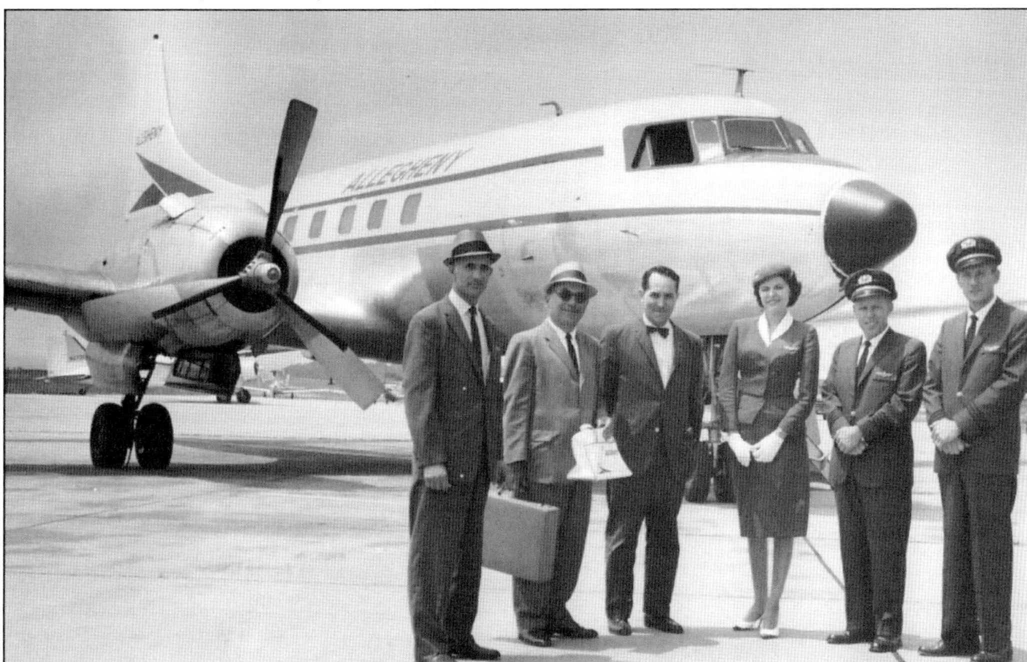

Carved from a Wayne County hilltop, Tri-State Airport offers airline service to West Virginia, Kentucky, and Ohio. Opened in 1952, Tri-State was served in its early years by Eastern, Piedmont, and Allegheny Airlines. This photograph was taken on July 31, 1962, to mark the first flight to Tri-State by a new Allegheny airliner, the Martin 404. Posing with the plane's crew and an airline official are, at far left, Denvil Chandler, president of the Airport Authority, and airport manager A.O. "Pete" Cappadony. (Courtesy of *H-D*.)

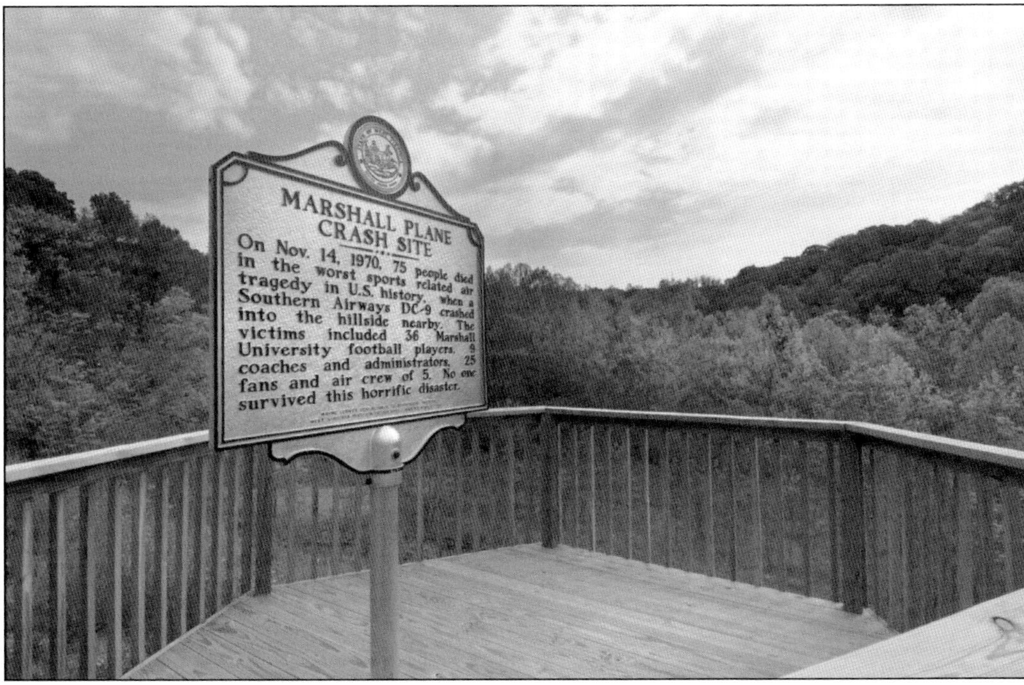

An historical marker stands at the spot where on November 14, 1970, a chartered airliner crashed into a hillside at Tri-State Airport, killing all 75 people aboard, including nearly the entire roster of the Marshall University football team, their coaches, the plane's crew, and a number of leading community members who were traveling with the team. The crash and subsequent rebirth of the MU football program were recounted in the film *We Are Marshall*. (Courtesy of *H-D*.)

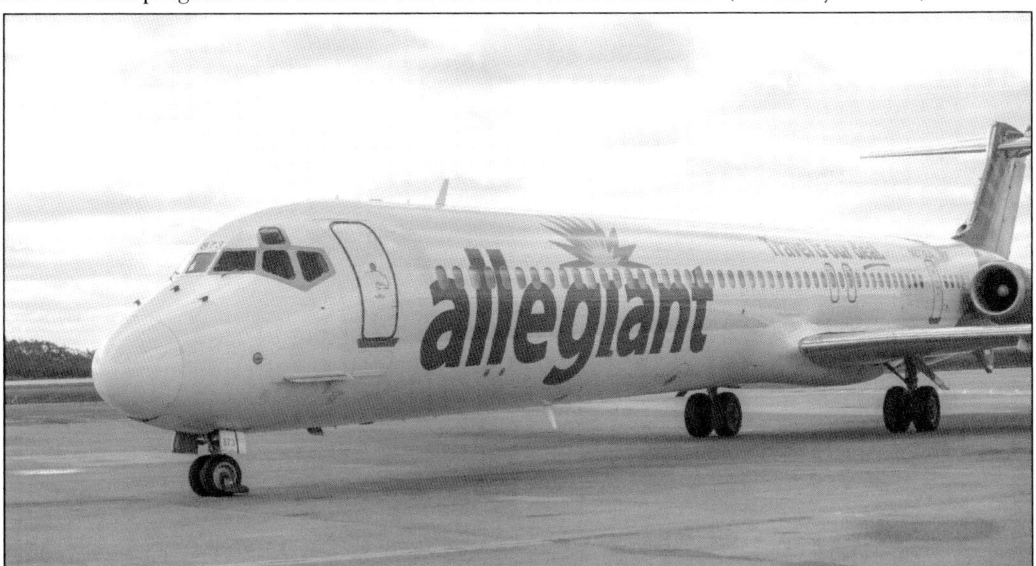

Today, Tri-State Airport is served by Allegiant Air and US Airways. Allegiant offers nonstop service to three Florida destinations—Orlando, Tampa Bay/St. Petersburg, and Fort Myers/Punta Gorda—along with seasonal service to Myrtle Beach, South Carolina. US Airways operates nonstop service to Charlotte, North Carolina. (Courtesy of *H-D*.)

Six

Around the County

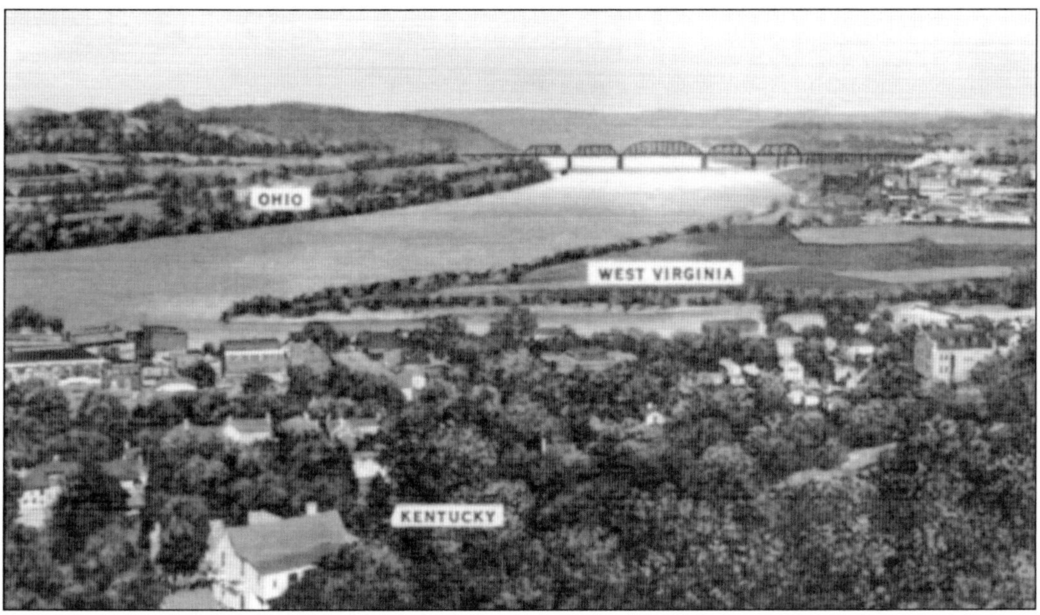

The helpful labels affixed to this postcard show where the Big Sandy River flows into the Ohio River and give a good view of the lay of the land. That is the state of Ohio on the northern bank of the Ohio River. Note the Norfolk Southern bridge crossing the river a bit upstream. Catlettsburg, Kentucky, stretches across the bottom half of the card, and Kenova occupies the card's middle portion. (Courtesy of *H-D*.)

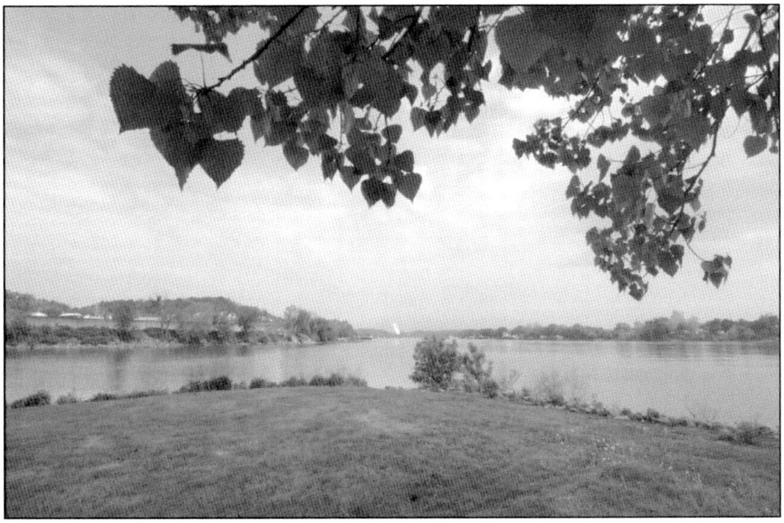

Virginia Point Park, the most westerly spot in West Virginia, presents visitors this eye-catching view of the Ohio and Big Sandy Rivers and neighboring Ohio and Kentucky. The park offers overnight campgrounds, a boat ramp, and a large picnic shelter. (Courtesy of *H-D*.)

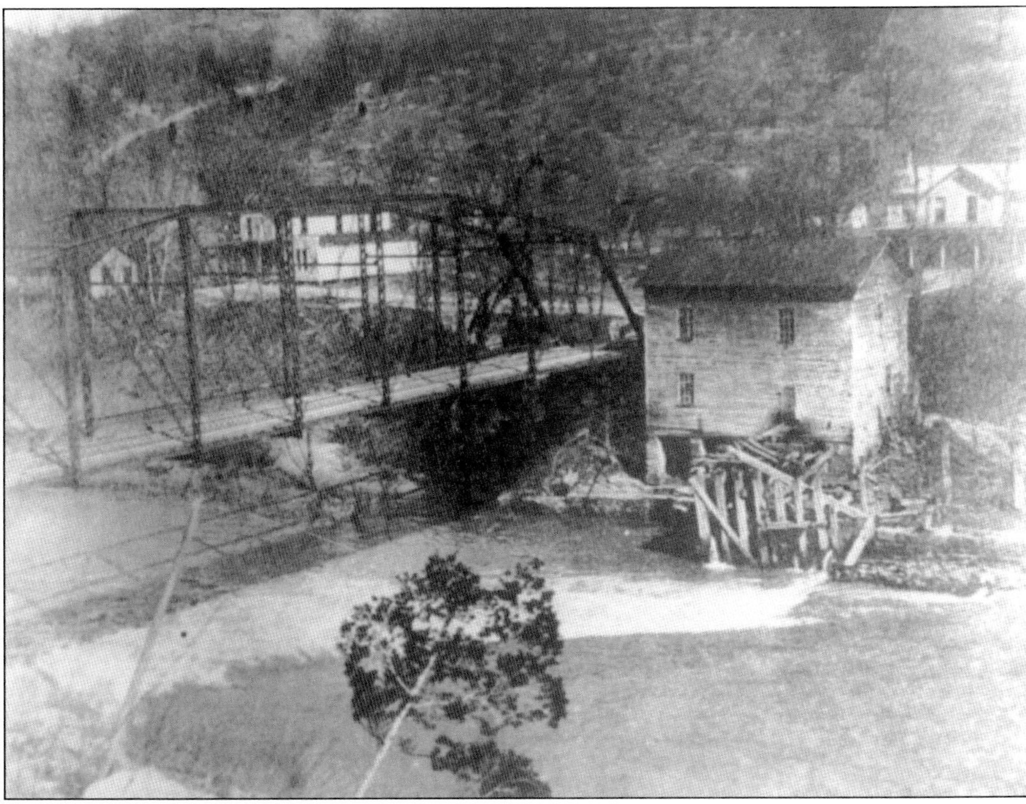

Early American farmers needed mills to grind their grain. The falls at Dixon on Twelve Pole Creek became the site of the region's first dam and gristmill in the early 1800s. Chester Howell was the builder. Later, it would be operated by Stephen Spurlock and still later by his son Jesse. The need for mills faded, but the Dickson mill became a popular spot for tourists (and late-night partiers). A bridge constructed at the mill in 1920 collapsed in 2006 and was not rebuilt. (Author's collection.)

Chimney Rock, an unusual rock formation in Wayne County south of Kenova, fascinated local residents for decades. The chimney-shaped rock stood 25 feet tall. This vintage postcard featuring the odd-shaped rock was mailed in 1908. Chimney Rock was leveled during the construction of Interstate 64 in the 1960s. (Author's collection.)

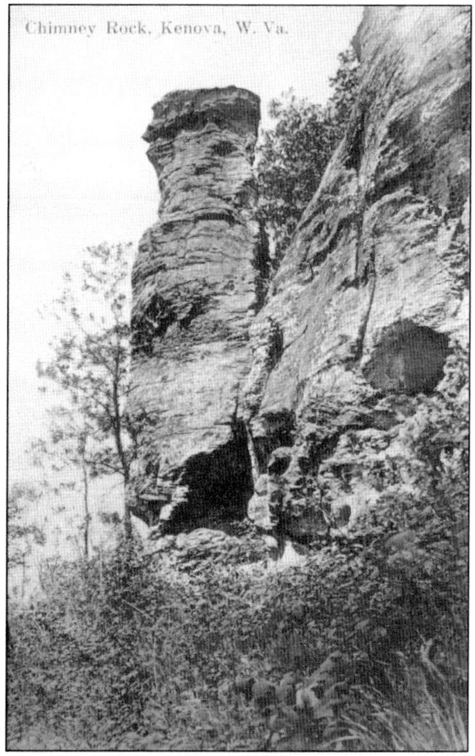

This vintage photograph features a family gathering at the Hoback home on White's Creek in Wayne County about 1896. From left to right are Helen Pyles Hoback, Jesse Lawrence Hoback, John Frank Hoback, Charles Clinton Hoback, and John Franklin Hoback. Jesse Hoback was the father of Dr. John Holland Hoback, a chemistry professor at Marshall University, and Karl Hoback, a patent attorney in Alexandria, Virginia. Charles Clinton Hoback was the father of Mike Hoback, onetime editor of the *Wayne County News*. (Courtesy of Mike Hoback.)

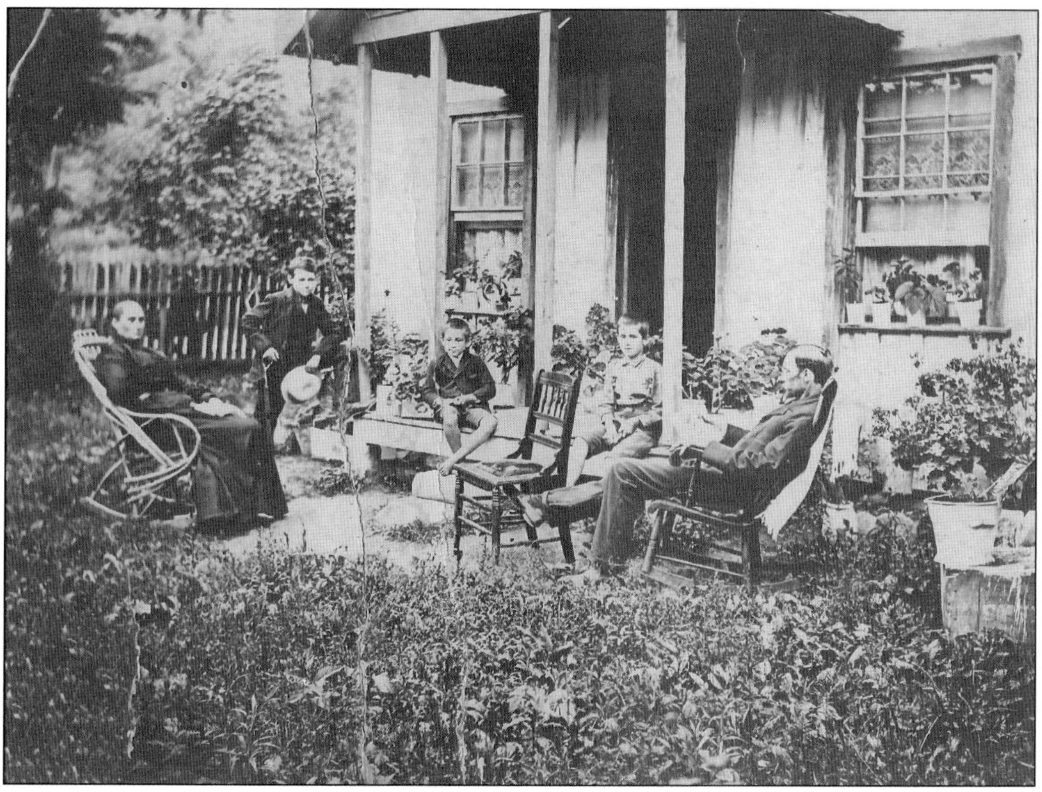

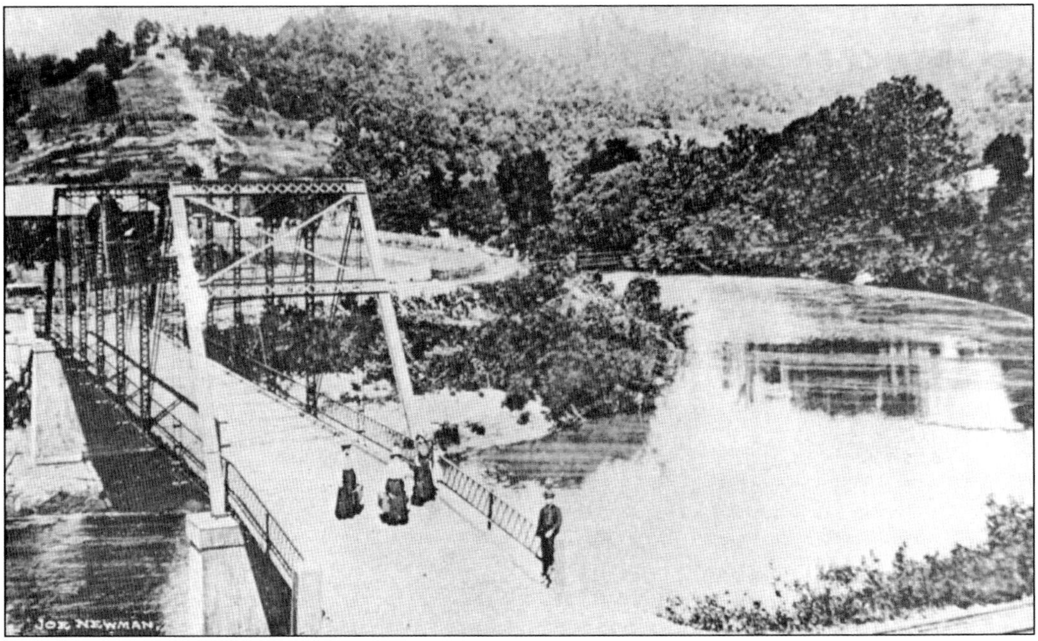

In 1907, a bridge was built across Twelve Pole Creek on the northern edge of the town of Wayne. At first people called the simple steel-truss bridge the New County Bridge, but because it connected Wayne with a farm owned by Robert Scott Sansom, it became known as the Sansom Bridge. In 1960, David Brinkley would make the little bridge famous. (Author's collection.)

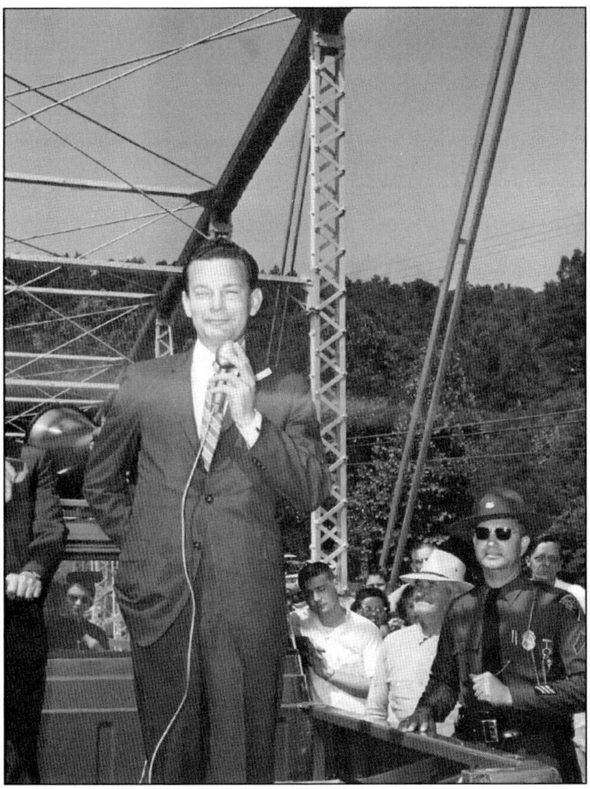

Visiting Wayne County during the 1960 presidential campaign, NBC's David Brinkley did a news report from the old bridge across Twelve Pole Creek. Brinkley held the microphone down so viewers could hear the bridge's floorboards pop and groan as vehicles rumbled across it. Stung by Brinkley's report, the state did a rush repair job on the rickety bridge and then invited Brinkley to attend its reopening. (Courtesy of *H-D*.)

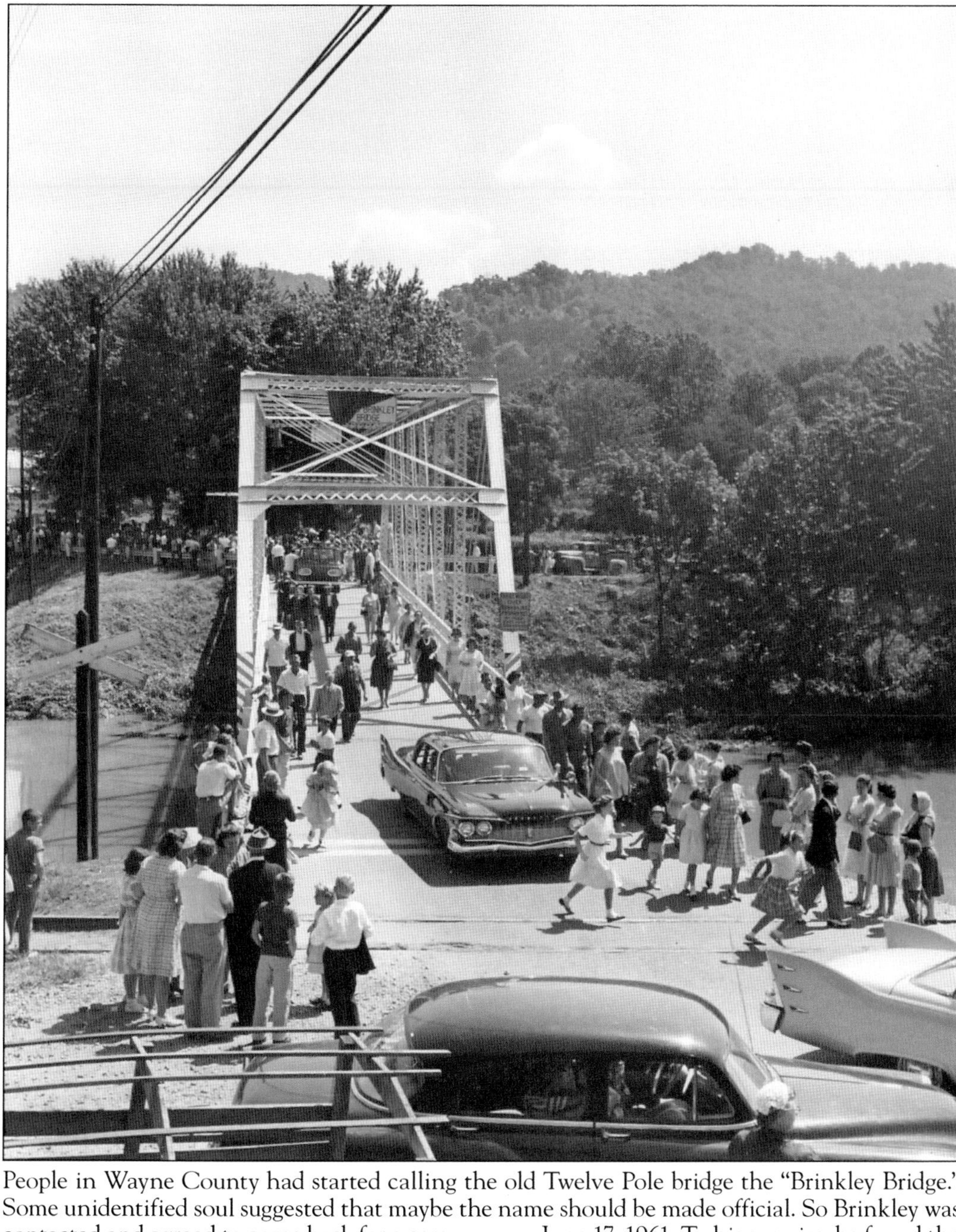

People in Wayne County had started calling the old Twelve Pole bridge the "Brinkley Bridge." Some unidentified soul suggested that maybe the name should be made official. So Brinkley was contacted and agreed to come back for a ceremony on June 17, 1961. To his surprise, he found the bridge was being named for him. He made brief remarks, then cut the obligatory ribbon, allowing a motorcade—and a crowd of curious spectators—to cross the span. But that is not the end of the story. By 1970, the old bridge was again in bad shape, and on September 22 of that year, it collapsed under the weight of an overloaded truck. The following year, a new replacement bridge was opened, minus the famous newsman's name. The Brinkley Bridge was no more. After the famed newsman's death in 2003, the bridge sign with his name on it reportedly was found in his family garage. (Courtesy of *H-D*.)

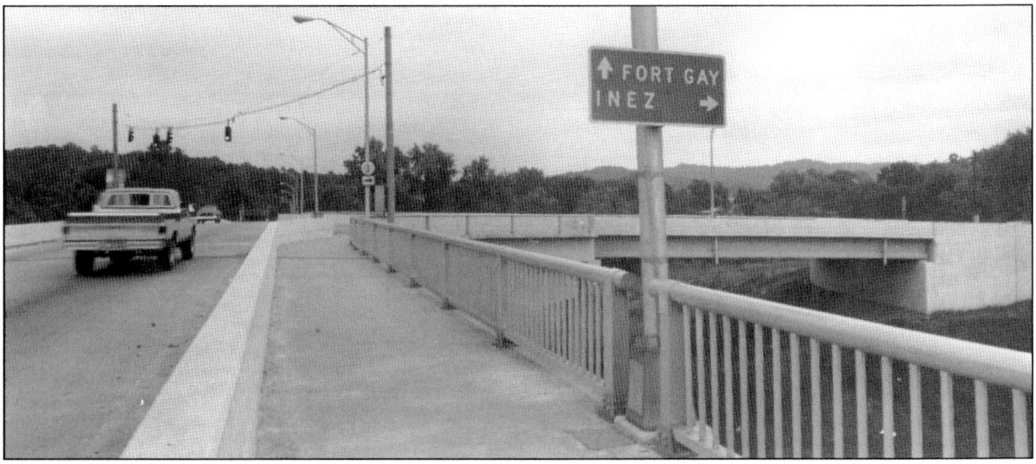

The T-shaped bridge connecting Fort Gay, West Virginia, with Louisa, Kentucky, is said to be the only US bridge that connects two states, two counties, and two cities; runs over three rivers; connects three land masses; and has a turn in the middle. A common local joke in giving directions is to tell motorists to "Drive to the center of the bridge and turn right." An old toll bridge has been replaced by a new span, but as this photograph shows, the joke still fits. (Courtesy of *H-D*.)

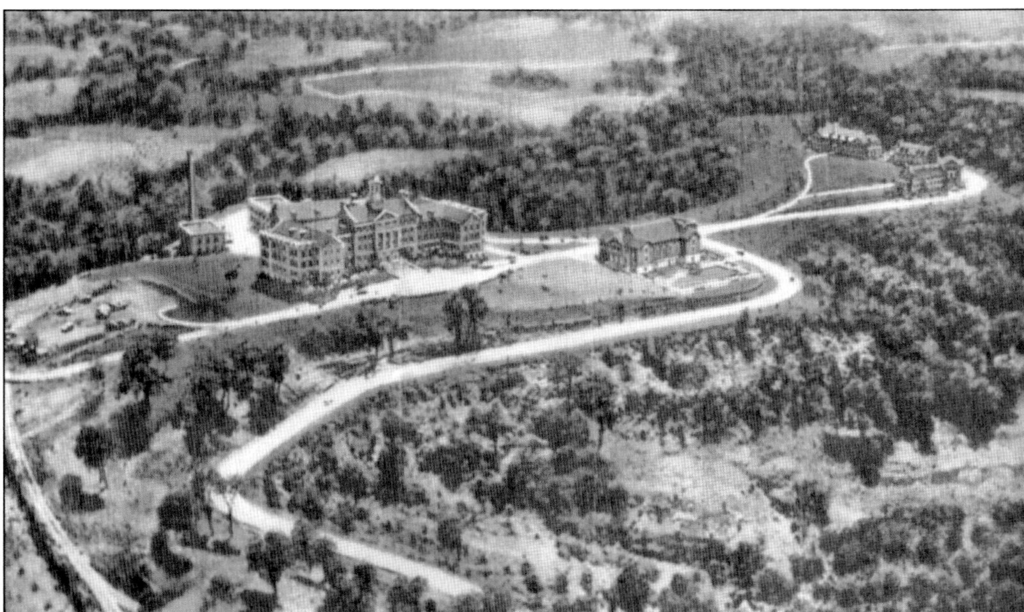

The Huntington Veterans Administration Hospital finally opened in 1932. Today, it is called the Huntington VA Regional Medical Center. But no matter what one calls it, the facility is not in Huntington. It is on a wooded hillside in the Spring Valley section of Wayne County. (Author's collection.)

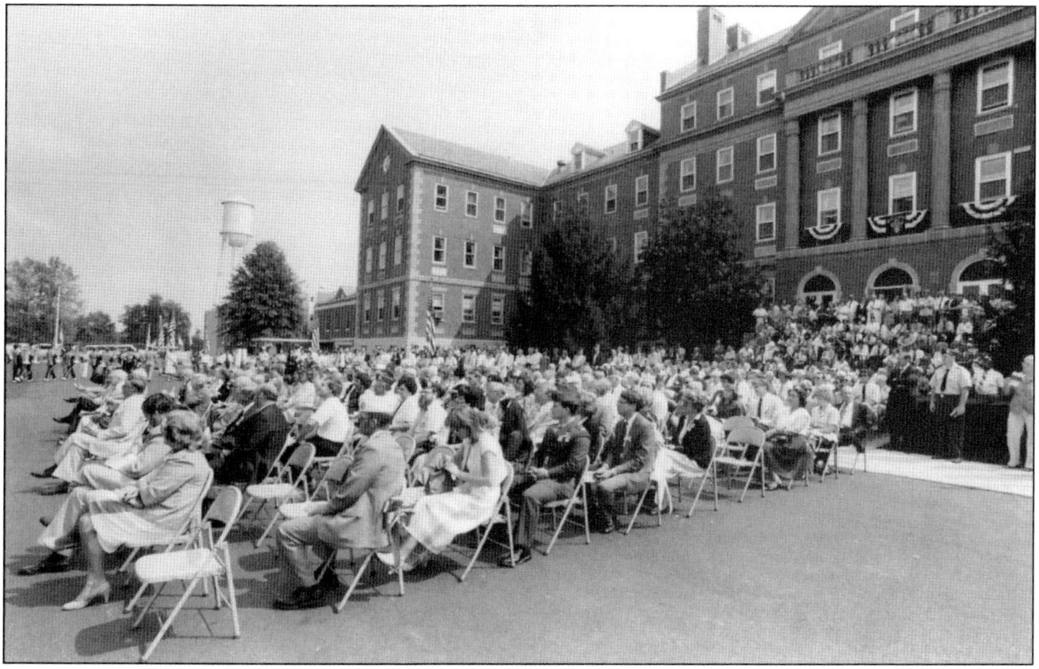

Over the years, the Huntington VA Regional Medical Center has grown dramatically in both size and the scope of its medical mission. Today, it is an integral part of Marshall University's School of Medicine. In this September 10, 1982, ceremony, two new buildings were dedicated at the center. An $11 million medical education building was completed and opened for use the year before, and a $9 million patient structure was opened that summer. (Courtesy of *H-D*.)

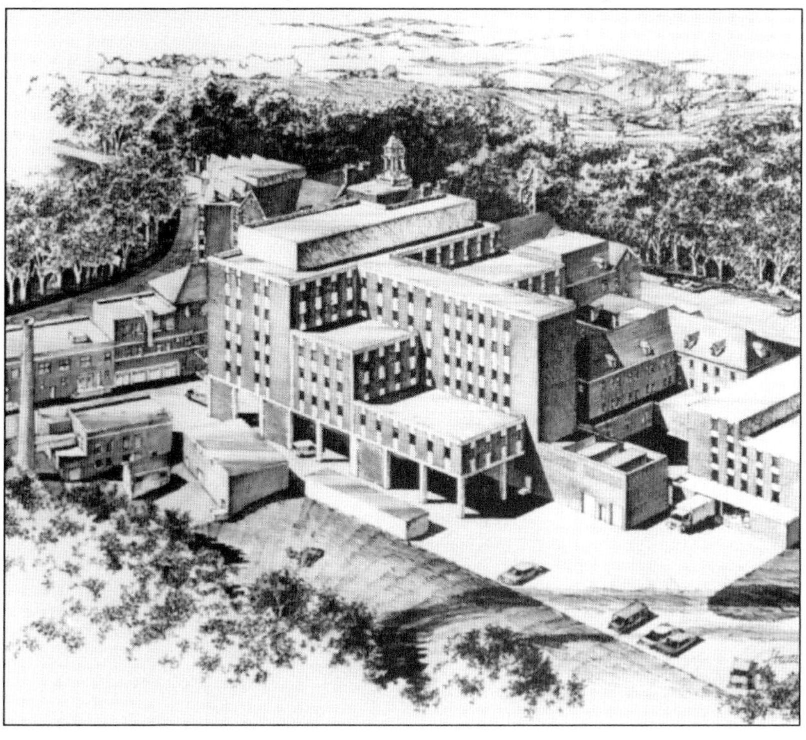

This artist's sketch dramatically shows how the Huntington VA Regional Medical Center has expanded over the years. The opening of the seven-story Robert C. Byrd Clinical Addition in 1993 almost doubled the center's size. (Courtesy of *H-D*.)

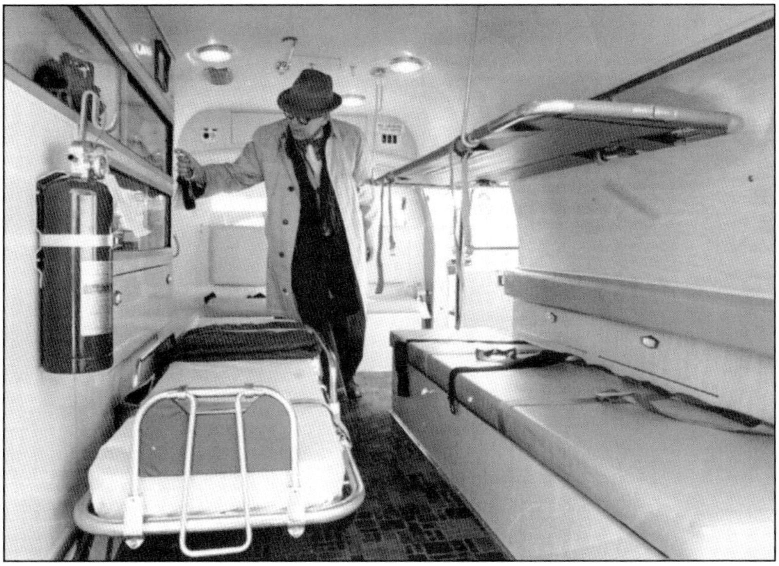

It is January 21, 1975, and Jack C. Capehart, president of the Wayne County Commission, is inspecting a new ambulance purchased for the Lavalette Fire Department. The county paid half the cost of acquiring the unit, and the state put up the other half. (Courtesy of *H-D*.)

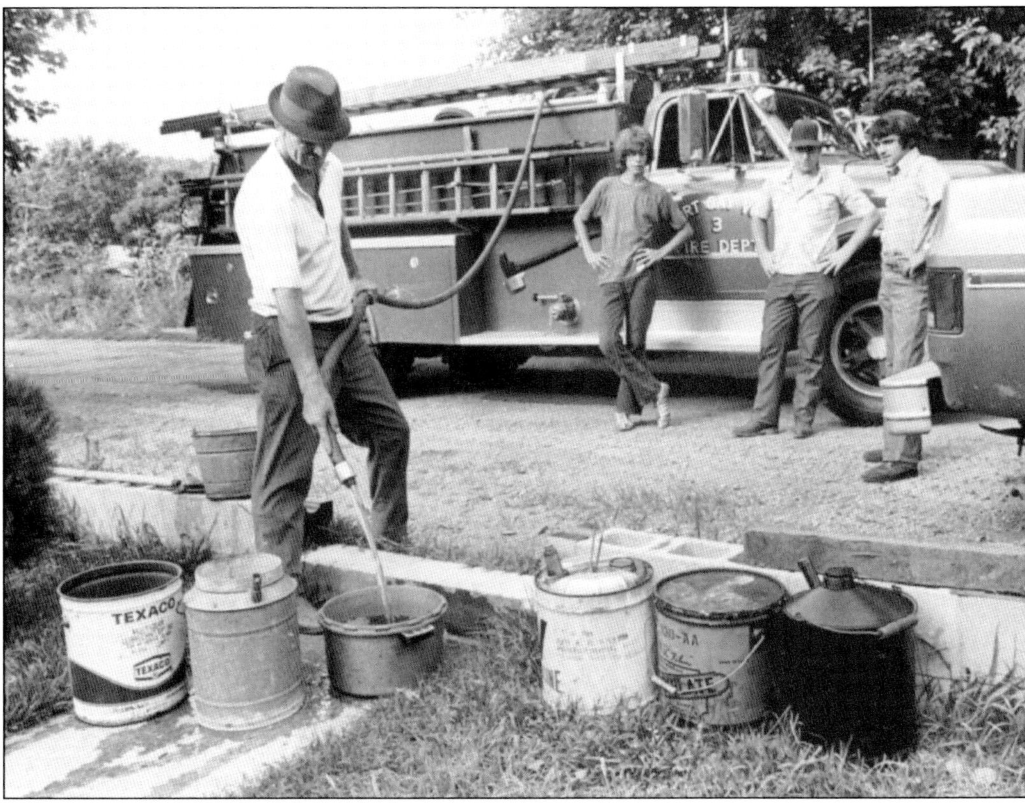

Firefighters do not spend all their time battling fires. They perform all manner of community services. In August 1975, a burned-out pump at the Fort Gay water plant left residents high and dry until the pump could be repaired. The Lavalette Volunteer Fire Department responded by sending two trucks to cruise the town, dispensing water to those with buckets, pots, and pans ready to fill. When the trucks ran dry, they crossed the Big Sandy River to Louisa, Kentucky, to refill their tanks. (Courtesy of *H-D*.)

Seven

School Days

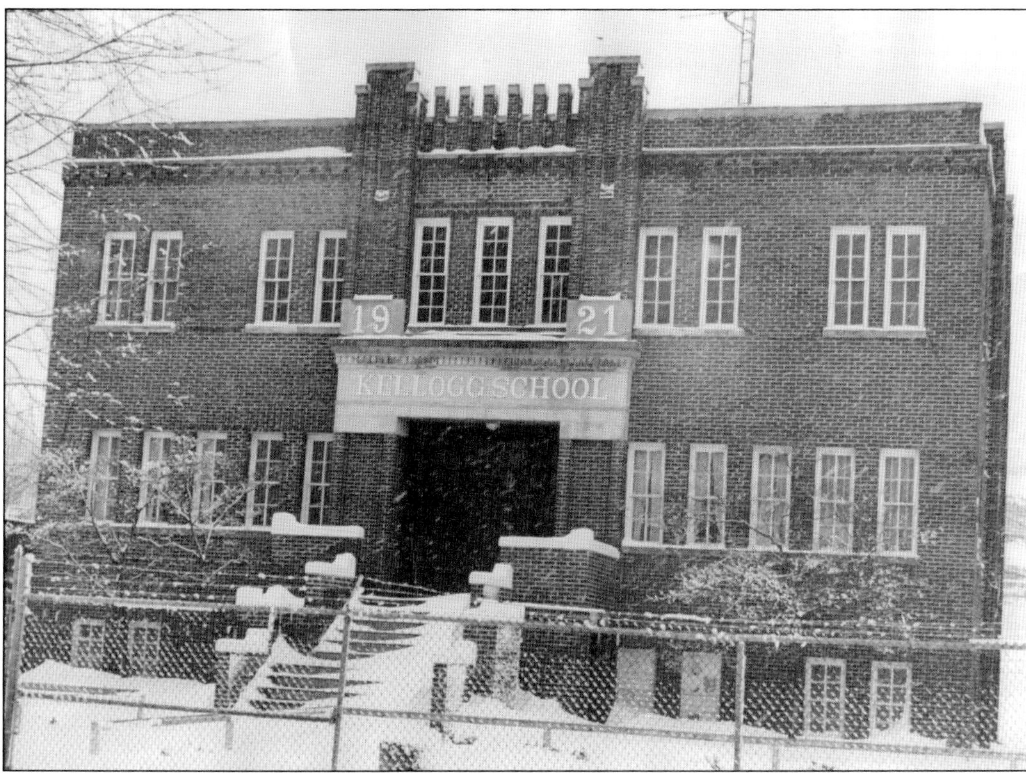

Wayne County still had many one-room schools in 1921, when the Ceredo Board of Education contracted with James A. Hughes to construct a new brick Westmoreland Public School Building. The contract may have said Westmoreland, but the name over the door when the building opened said Kellogg. The school, located on Piedmont Road, served the neighborhood until 1986, when it was demolished and replaced by a new building constructed nearby. (Courtesy of *H-D*.)

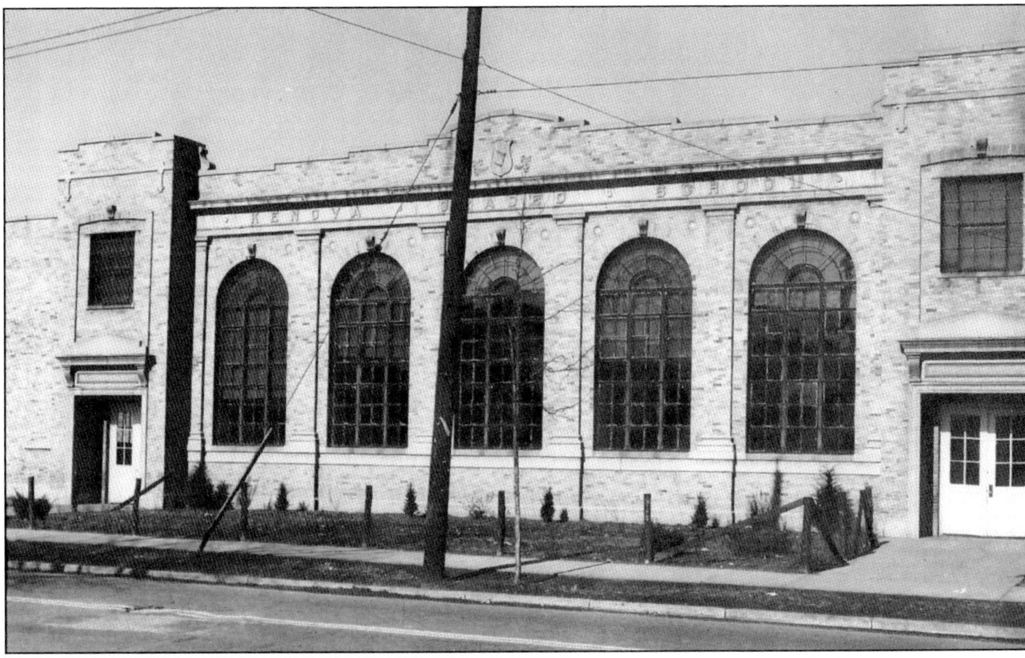

Originally built in 1939 and much added to over the years, Kenova Grade School was closed in 2011 when a large sinkhole developed on the school grounds. Students are slated to attend a new school to be built on the site of the demolished Ceredo-Kenova High School. Until the new school is ready, they are being taught in temporary trailers. (Courtesy of *H-D*.)

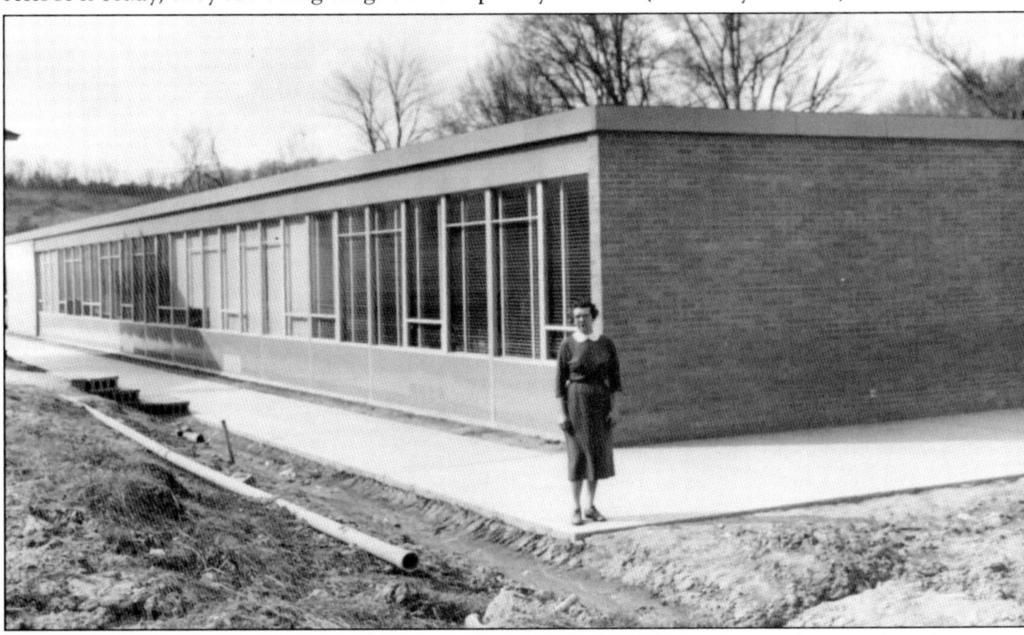

In a 1959 photograph, principal Caroline Cyrus is seen standing at a nearly completed six-room addition under construction at Buffalo Elementary School. Cyrus told the *Herald-Dispatch* she hoped another six-room addition could be built at the school but that would be dependent on voter approval of a levy that was coming up for a vote. The voters said yes, and the second addition was dedicated in 1961. (Courtesy of *H-D*.)

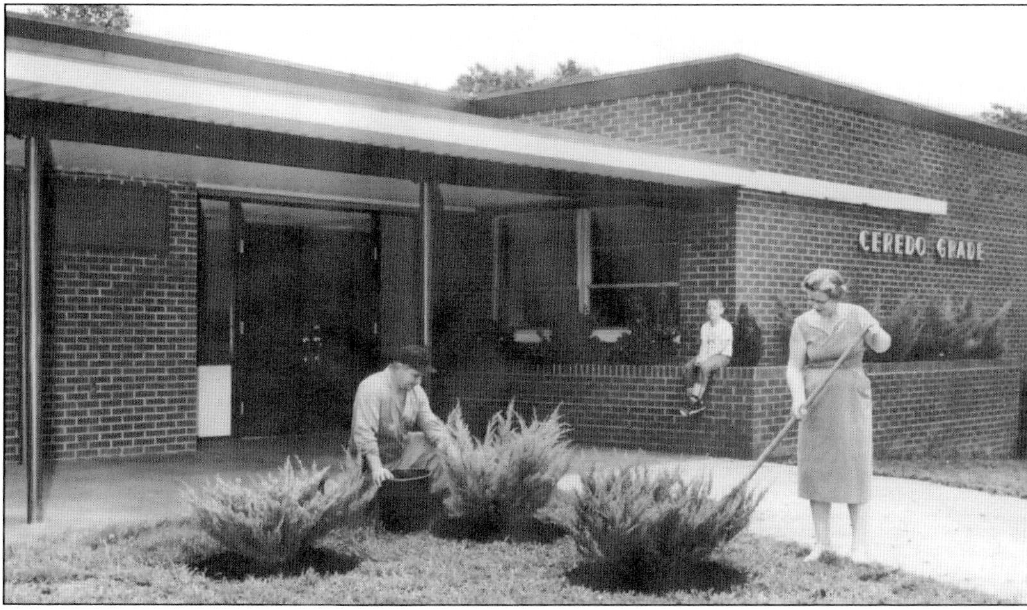

In 1957, a new Ceredo Grade School was constructed to replace the one destroyed in a spectacular fire the previous year. Here Bo Rowe and Mrs. Dale Massie are busy putting the finishing touches on a volunteer landscaping project at the new school. Massie's young son Bobby seems to be playing the role of sidewalk superintendent. (Courtesy of *H-D*.)

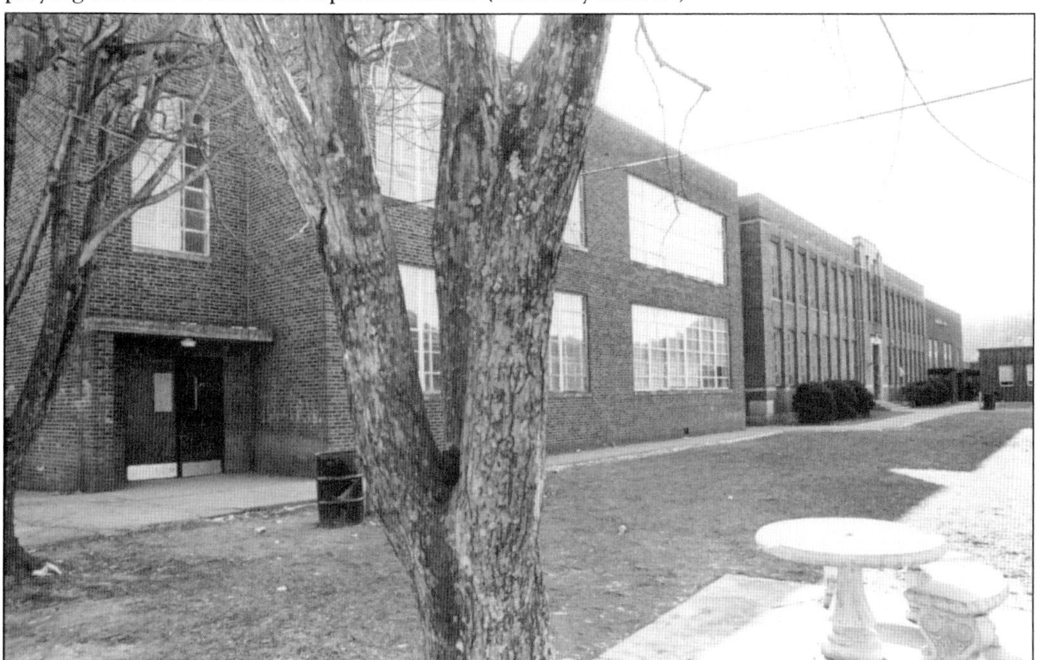

Constructed in 1927, with additions built over the years, Buffalo High School, pictured here in 1976, had about 500 students in the early 1990s. Vinson High School had about 400 and Ceredo-Kenova 340. The Wayne County Board of Education proposed to consolidate the three schools, and after considerable controversy, that is what was done. The three were joined to form Spring Valley High School. (Courtesy of *H-D*.)

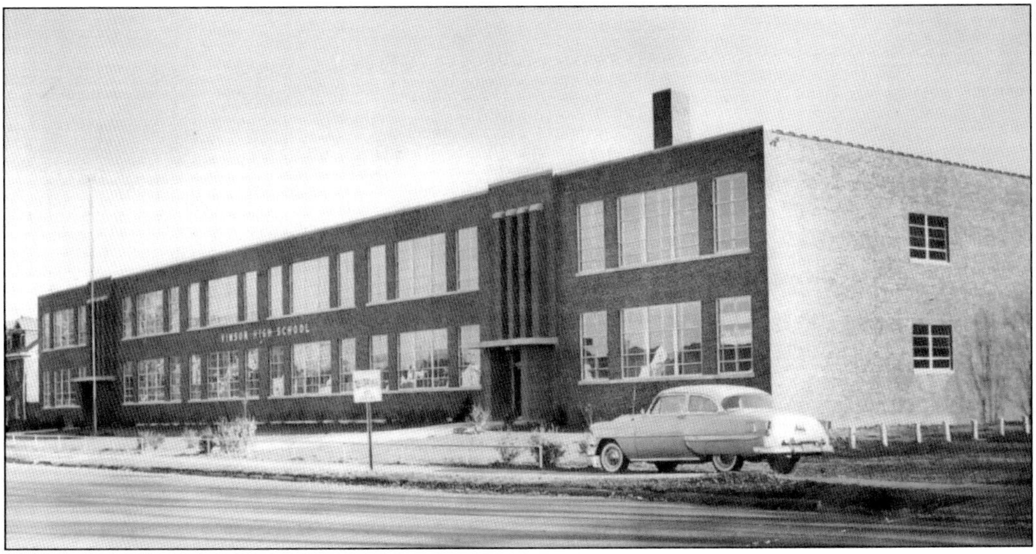

Prior to the adoption of the county unit system for West Virginia schools in 1933, Vinson School was nothing more than a junior high school, with older students moving on to Huntington High, Ceredo-Kenova High, or Buffalo High to take their final classes and graduate. But the growing Westmoreland population warranted a senior high school in the community. Thus, Vinson High was born, graduating its first class on May 1935. Its class of 1998 was its last. (Courtesy of *H-D*.)

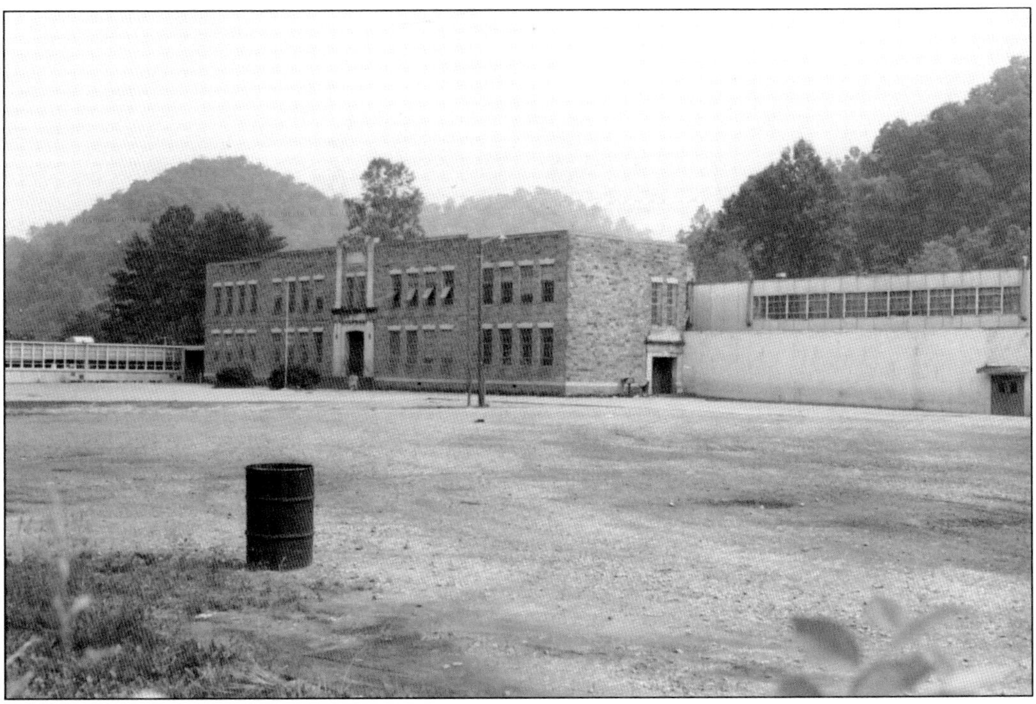

Dwindling enrollments also spelled consolidation for two other Wayne County high schools—Crum, shown here in 1973, and Fort Gay. Glenhayes was chosen as the site for the new school, and ground was broken in September 1986. Possible names considered for the new school included Adena High and Glenhayes High, but the name ultimately chosen was Tolsia. (Courtesy of *H-D*.)

Cousins Brian Stacy and Alvin Stacy peer out of a window at Crum High School on January 13, 1988, the last day of classes at the old school, built in 1938. Interviewed by a reporter for the *Herald-Dispatch*, most students indicated they were not sad to be leaving Crum behind and eager to see what was ahead for them at Tolsia High School, built at a cost of $3.6 million. Students at Fort Gay High, on their way to merge with their counterparts from Crum, also mostly welcomed the change, which would mean leaving behind their brownstone school building, constructed in 1931. (Courtesy of *H-D.*)

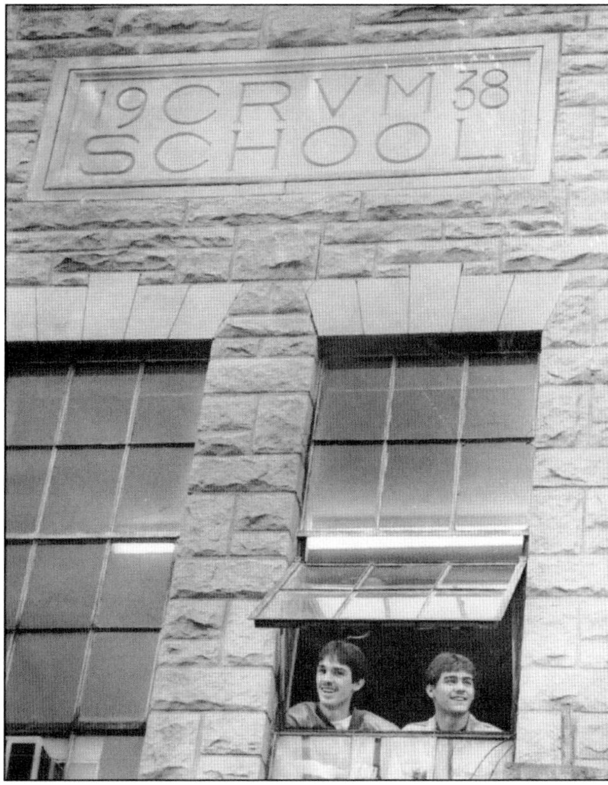

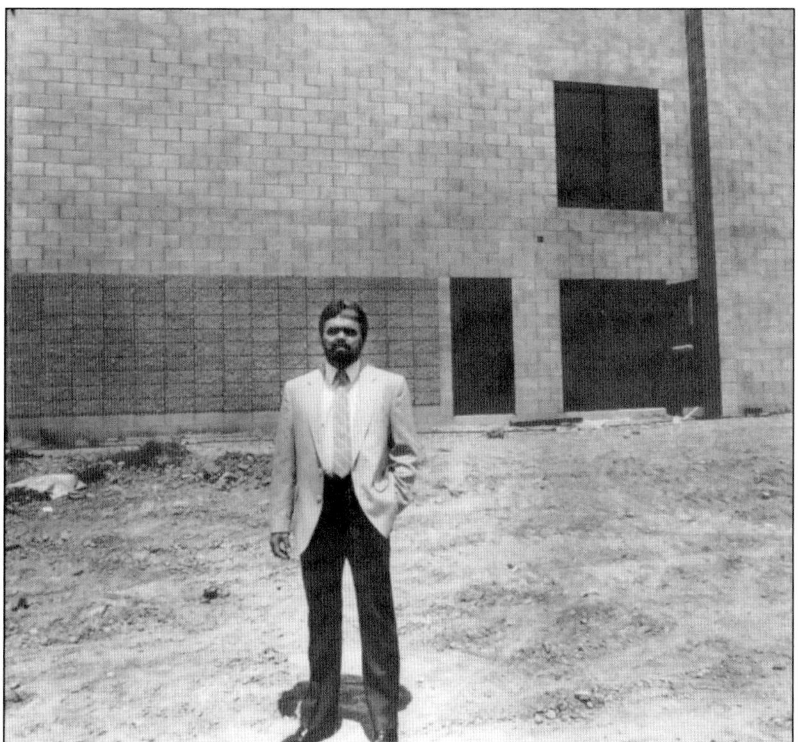

Principal Gary Adkins poses in August 1987 as the county's Tolsia High School nears completion. The school's unusual name is an acronym for the Tug, Ohio, Levisa, Sandy Improvement Association. The name was applied first to the highway that runs along the West Virginia side of the Big Sandy River and then to the new school. (Courtesy of *H-D.*)

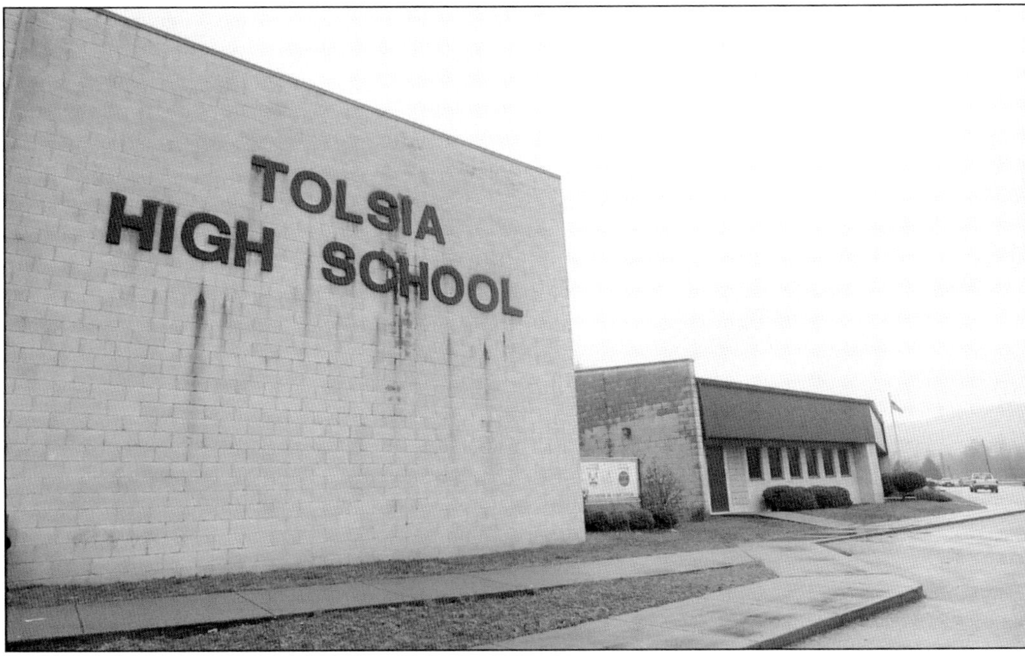

The new Tolsia High School opened on January 18, 1966, with only minor problems. The biggest problem he had those first few days, Principal Adkins said, "was when students got lost while trying to find a room." Later, he gave the school merger high marks, noting that it resulted in increased attendance, a decreased dropout rate, and higher test scores. (Courtesy of *H-D.*)

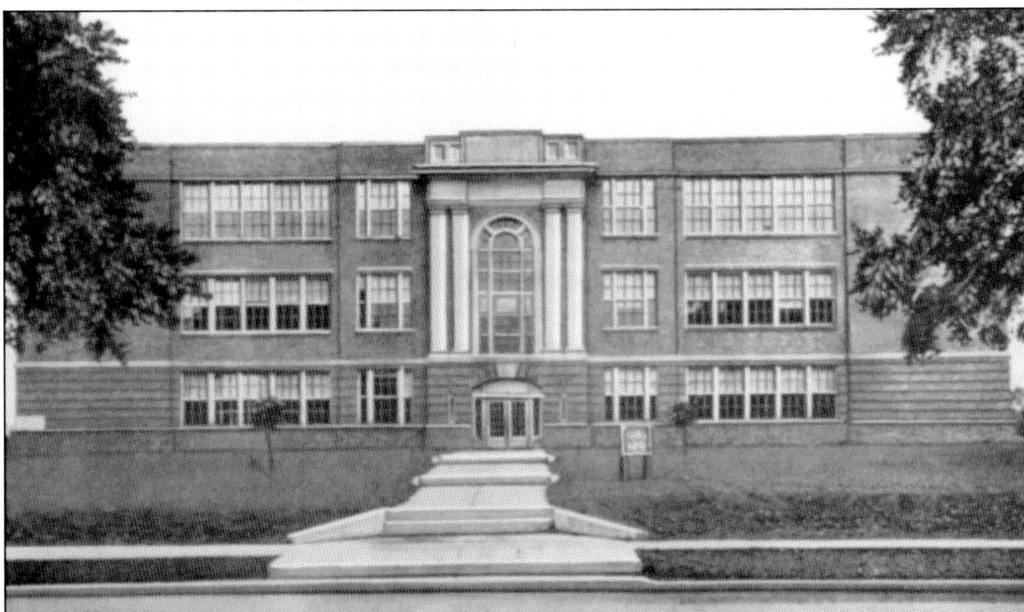
The cornerstone for Ceredo-Kenova High School was laid in 1921, and for decades the school was the cornerstone of the two communities, as young students followed their parents and grandparents through the school's doorway. Rooting for the school's sports teams was almost a religion for C-K fans. The marching band was a source of pride, and over the years, many band members have continued playing as members of the C-K Alumni Band. (Courtesy of *H-D.*)

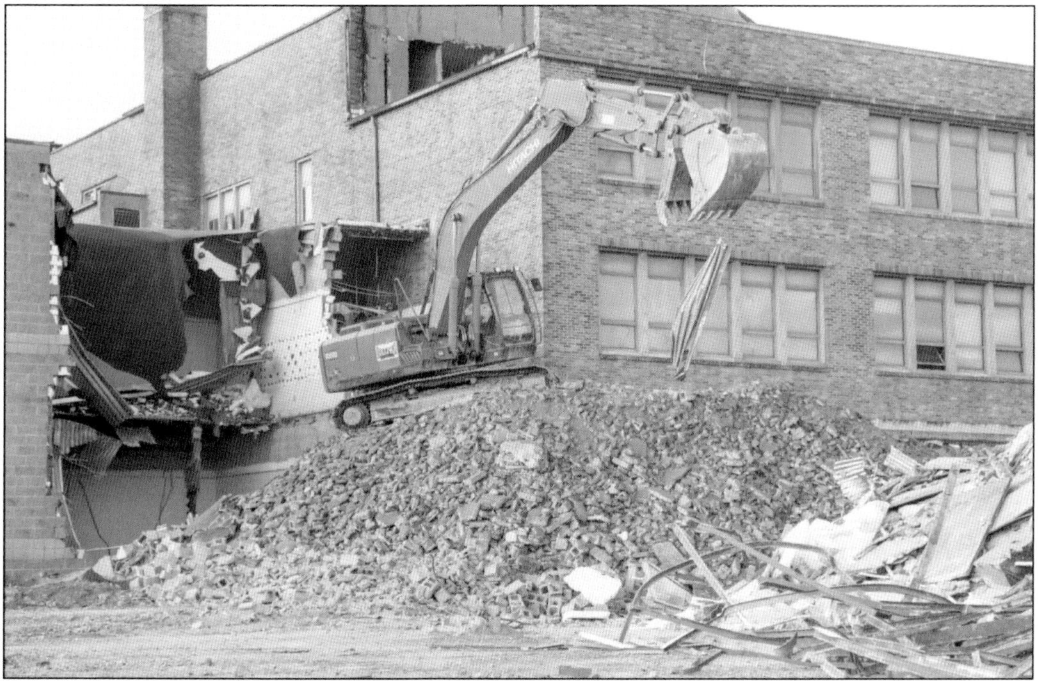

Ceredo-Kenova High is no more. It has been demolished to make way for a new C-K Elementary. But an important part of the school's storied past has been rescued from the wrecking crew. Thanks to a successful volunteer fundraising campaign, the school gym—the legendary Wonder Dome—has been rescued from the wreckers and will continue to provide colorful new chapters in the school's story. (Courtesy of *H-D*.)

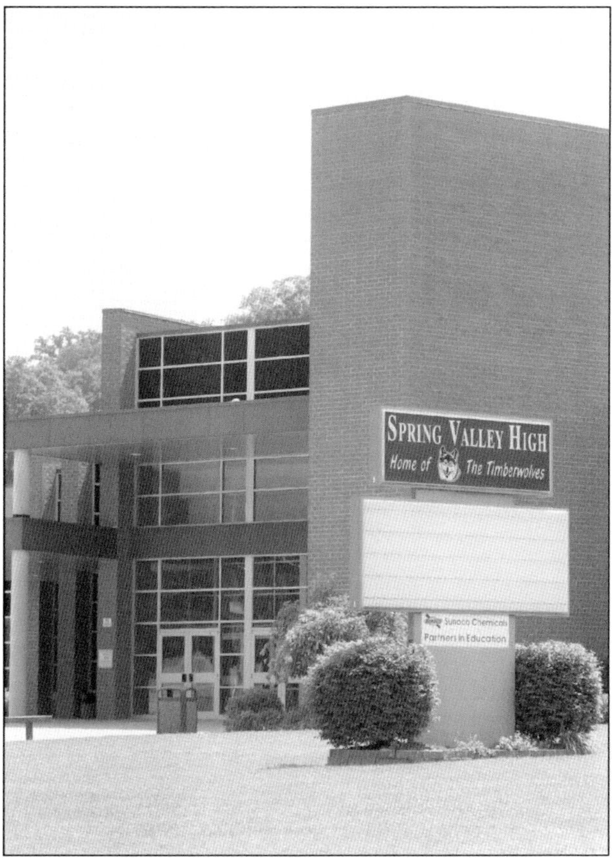

Spring Valley High School, located on Spring Valley Drive, is by far the largest of Wayne County's three high schools. It serves the northern part of the county, while Wayne High School serves the county's central section and Tolsia High School the county's southern section. The school bills itself as the "Home of the Timberwolves." (Courtesy of *H-D*.)

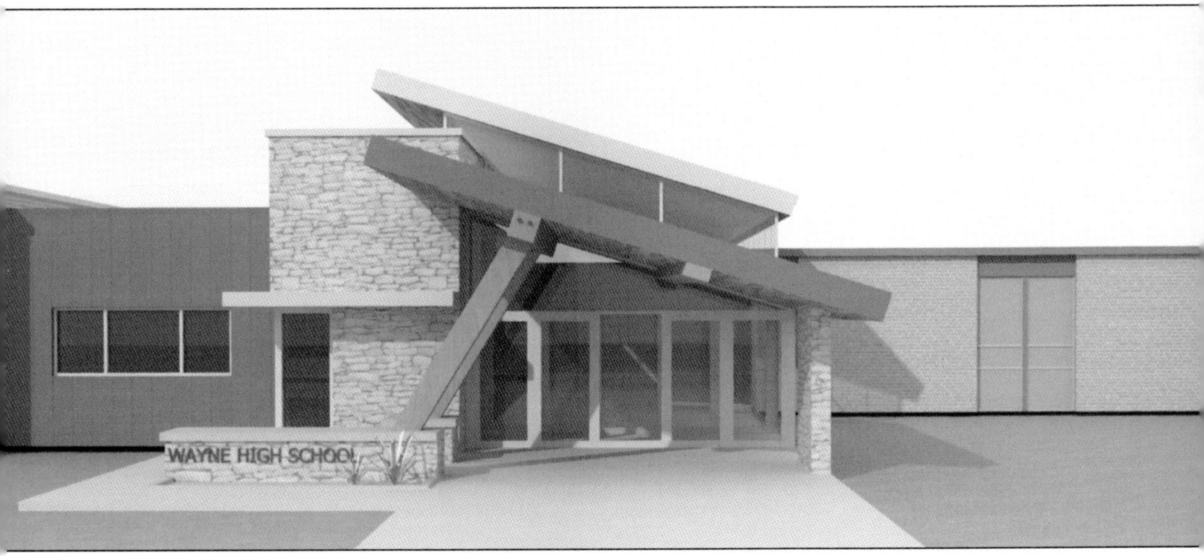

Wayne High School opened in 1921 in temporary quarters, moved into a new building in 1925, and awarded diplomas to 12 students in its first commencement. Over the years, the school saw the addition of more classrooms, a cafeteria, and a gym. In 1960, it moved to a new building, the one that currently houses the school on Craig Road. The school has a campus of 200-plus acres, with a nature trail, greenhouse, and outdoor recreation facilities. An extensive 2015 construction project at the school included this new entrance. (Courtesy of *H-D*.)

Eight

HOUSES OF PRAYER

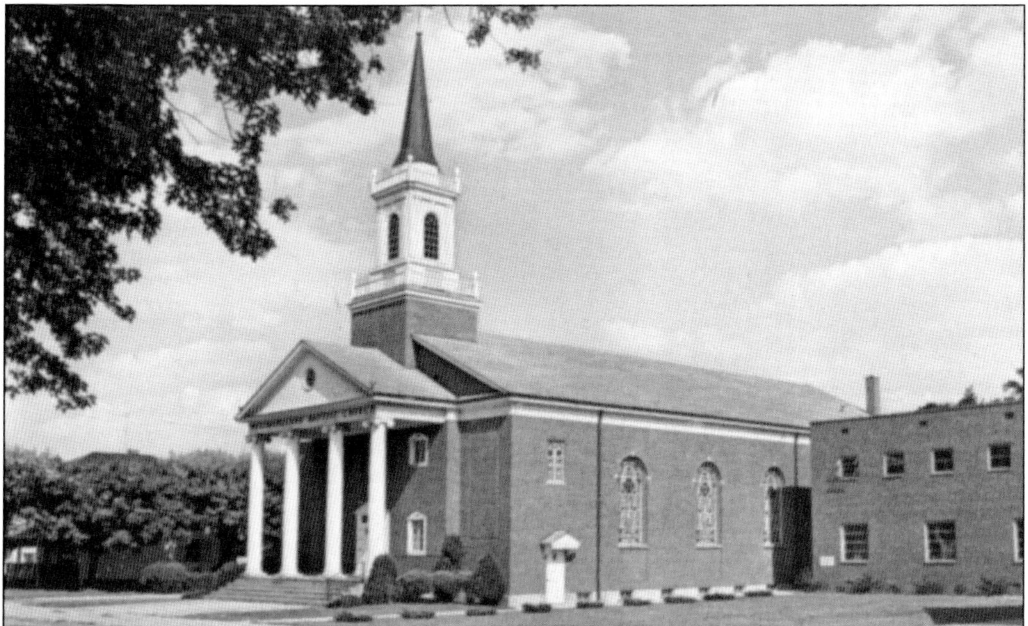

People in Wayne County take their religion seriously. By one unofficial count, Wayne County is home to more than three dozen churches, both large and small, including at least 15 Baptist churches. Westmoreland Baptist Church, located at 3401 Hughes Street, began as a mission of the Washington Avenue Baptist Church in 1915. In 1948, it became the first Southern Baptist church in West Virginia. The present sanctuary was built in 1955, refurbished in 1977, and again renovated in 2004. (Author's collection.)

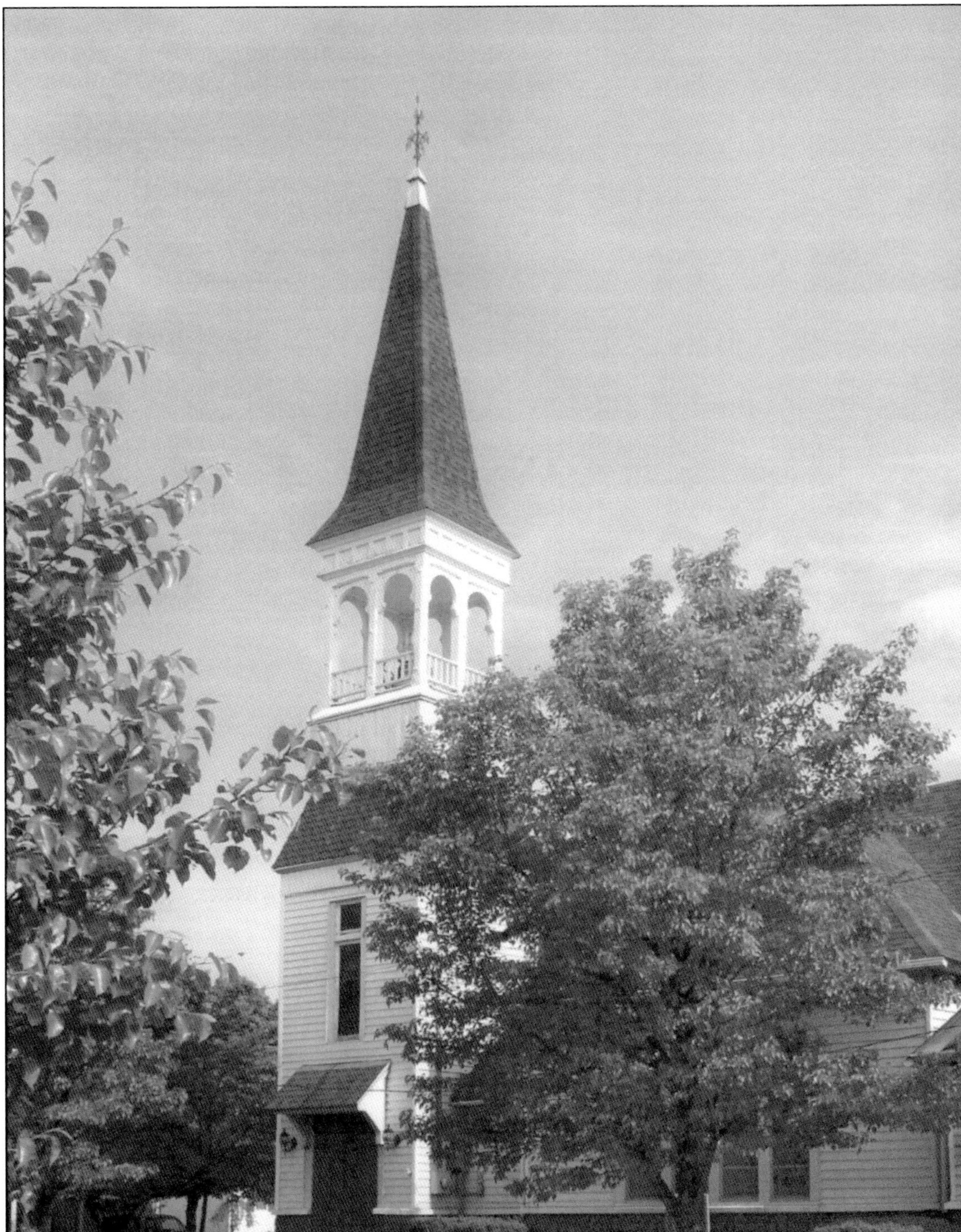

First Congregational Church, located at 600 C Street (US 60) in Ceredo, was built between 1885 and 1886. S. Floyd Hoard, the influential businessman who was president of the First National Bank of Ceredo, was a member of the congregation and is thought to have had a hand in the church's Craftsman design. In his *Buildings of West Virginia*, architectural historian S. Allen Chambers observes, "The presence of this relatively large Congregational church in a small West Virginia community reflects Ceredo's New England heritage." (Courtesy of *HQ*.)

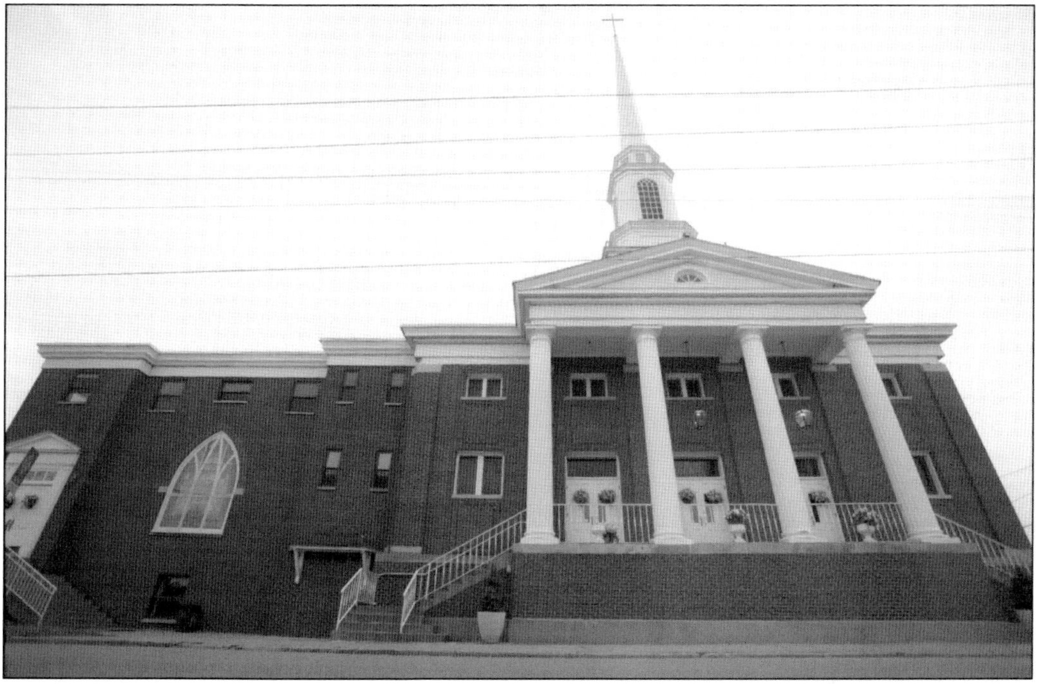

First Baptist Church of Kenova, 1120 Poplar Street, is one of Wayne County's largest churches. In 1957, it built a new education unit, designed to provide room for an additional 450 people in the church school, bringing its capacity to 1,000. A large education unit completed in 1952 had been expected to provide room for a decade or more of growth but by 1957 was already outgrown. (Courtesy of *H-D*.)

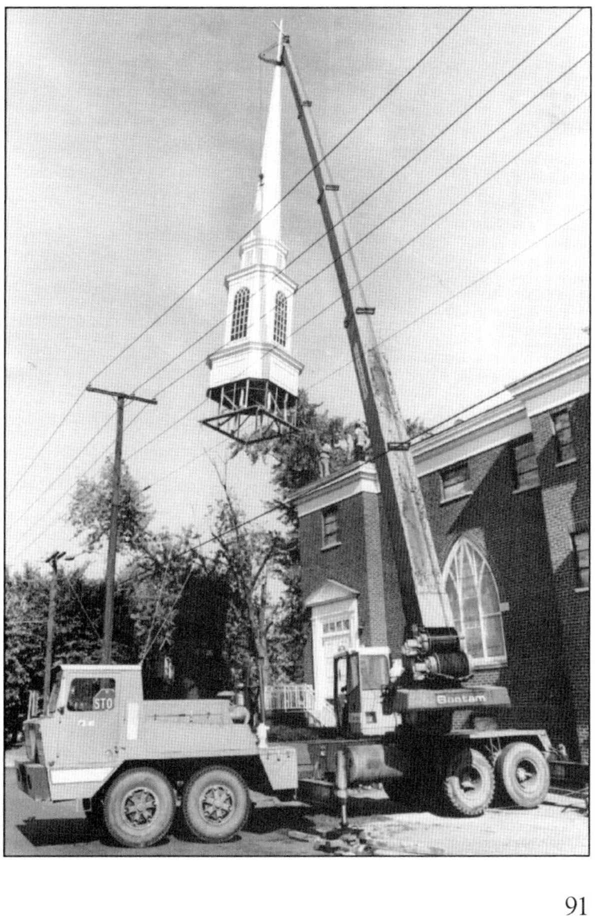

This is the church and this is the steeple—a new steeple. In March 1978, a thunderstorm with high winds blew down the old steeple at the First Baptist Church of Kenova. In October 1980, a new 80-foot steeple was purchased and installed at a cost of $46,000. "The steeple is a landmark in the community," associate pastor Dave Wilson told the *Herald-Dispatch*, "and the church felt that it should be restored. It is a symbol of our faith and commitment to God, and it shows the community that we are here." (Courtesy of *H-D*.)

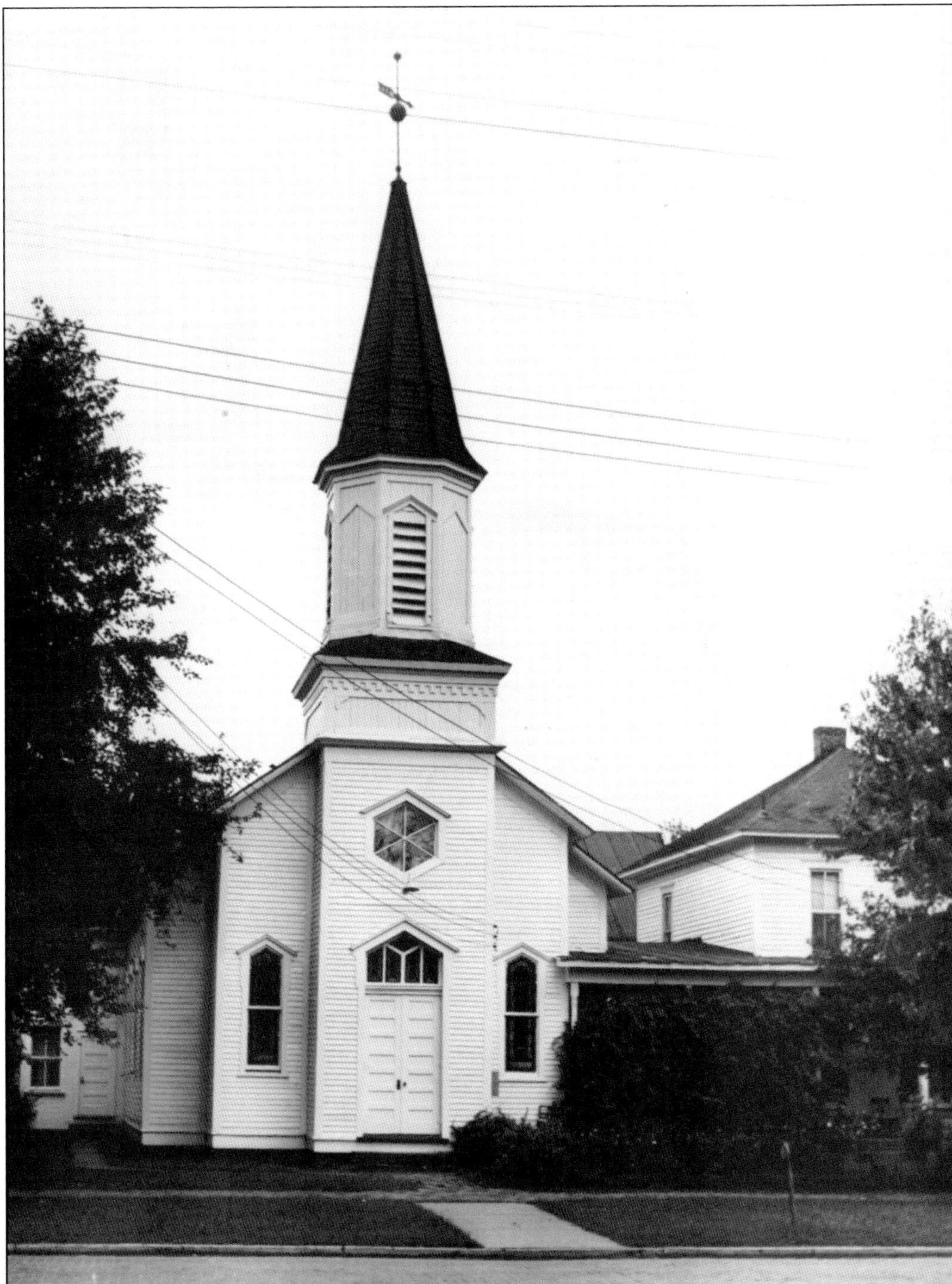

Ceredo United Methodist, 372 Main Street, celebrated its 125th anniversary in 2005. Here is what the church looked like in 1938—the year after the famed 1937 flood put three feet of water in the sanctuary. In a YouTube video, the Reverend Ron LeMaster, pastor at Ceredo UMC, describes it as "a little church with a big heart." The church, he says, has had its ups and downs over the years, "but we've always been a hospitable church." (Courtesy of *H-D*.)

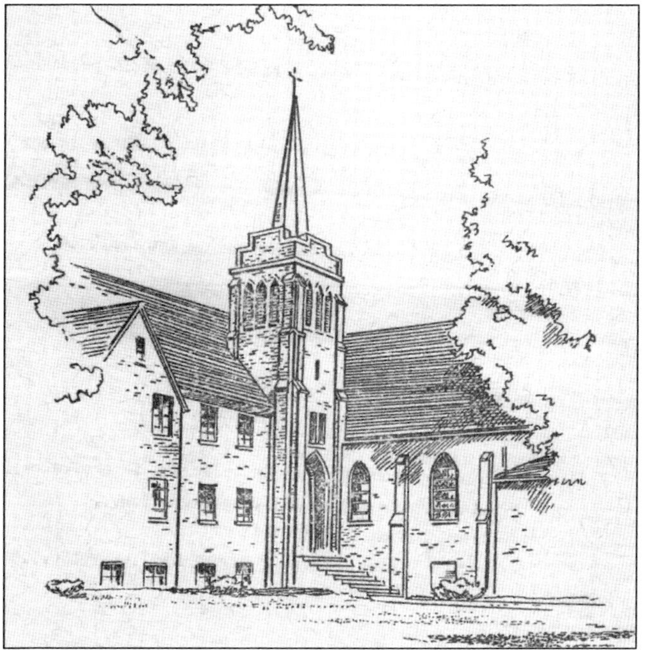

Westmoreland Methodist Church, located on Auburn Road at Kentucky Street, can trace its origin to a decision by a group of Westmoreland residents to organize a charitable organization they called the Helping Hand Society. In 1927, they decided to convert their society into a church and built a small frame structure to house it. Over the years, the congregation outgrew its original home and erected the current church in 1948. (Courtesy of Westmoreland Methodist Church.)

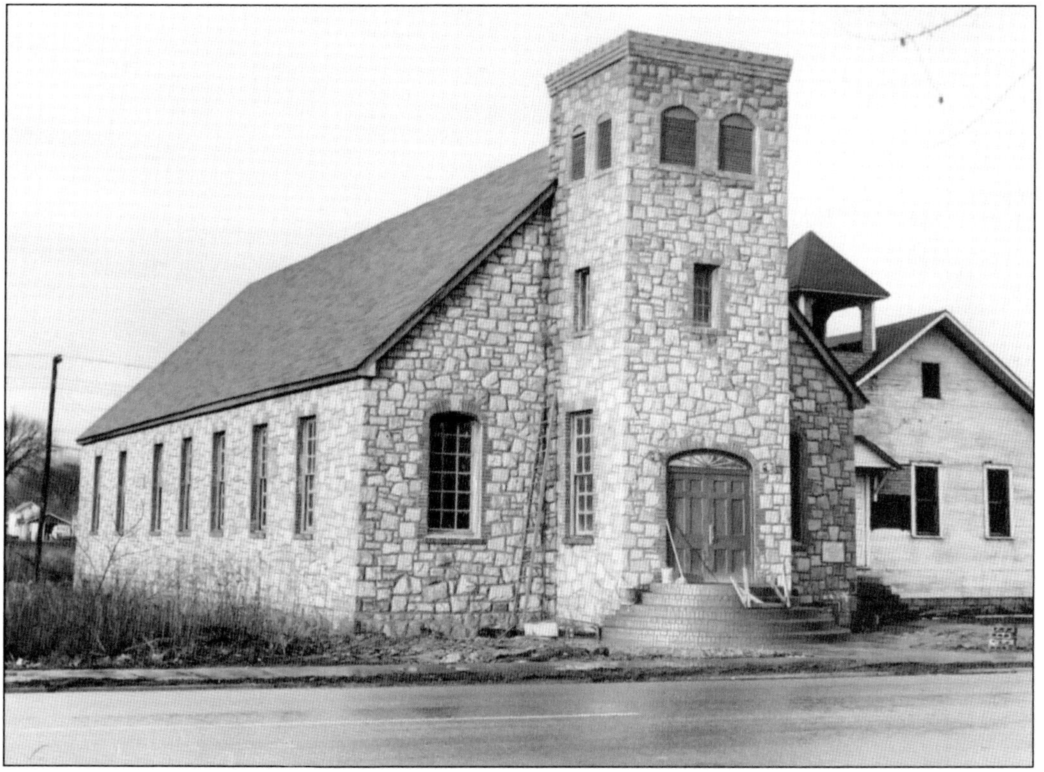

Kellogg Independent Holiness Church of God, 4430 Piedmont Road, was founded in 1921. This 1949 photograph shows the church's new stone sanctuary as it was nearing completion. Prior to the new church's construction, its members worshiped in the small frame building at the side of the new structure. (Courtesy of *H-D*.)

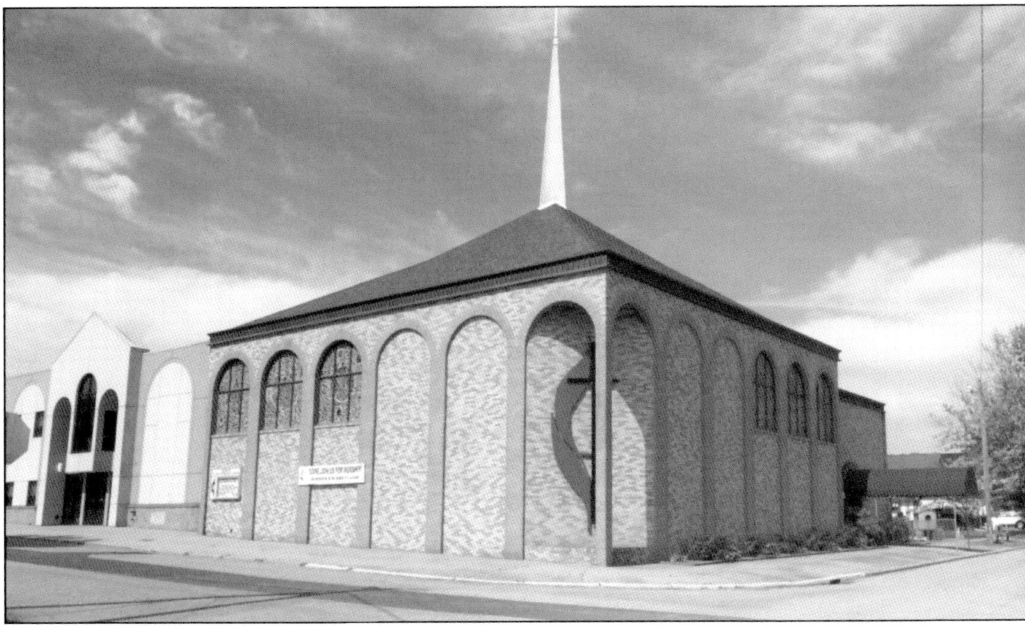

Kenova United Methodist Church was organized in 1894 and has steadily grown in the decades since. Its first building was on Sycamore Street. In 1911, the church moved to the 1500 block of Popular Street, where it was all but swept away by the 1913 flood. In 1924, a new church building was completed. In 2002, that building was razed to make way for a new structure with Sunday school rooms and a new church entrance. (Author's collection.)

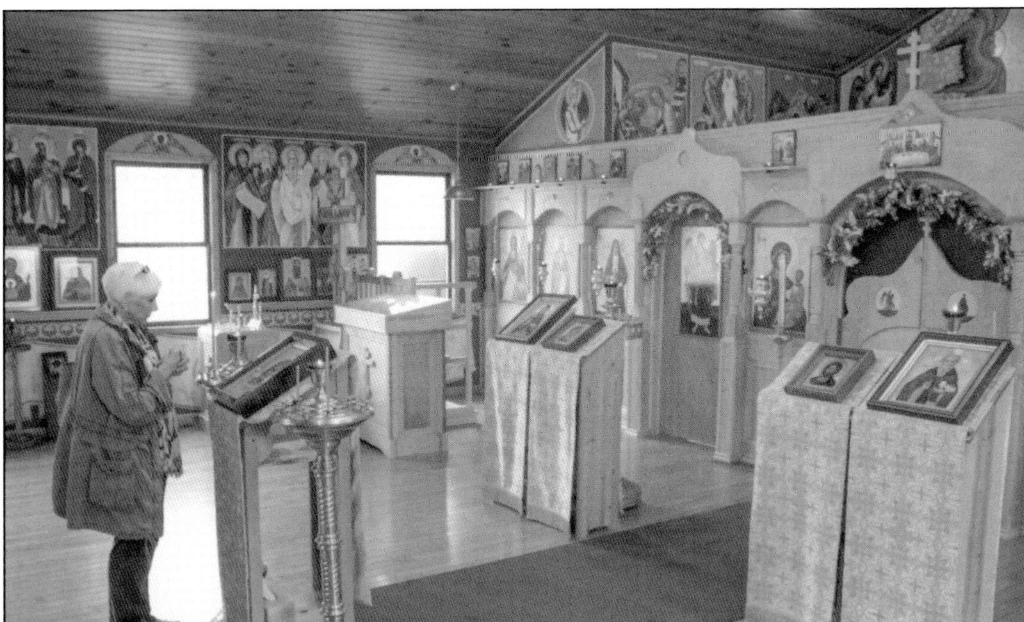

Christ the Savior Orthodox Christian Church is located on Route 152, about 15 minutes south of Huntington. A parish of the Eastern American Diocese of the Russian Orthodox Church, it was founded in 2002 in association with the Hermitage of the Holy Cross, a nearby monastic community of the Russian Orthodox Church. (Courtesy of *H-D*.)

Nine

Business and Industry

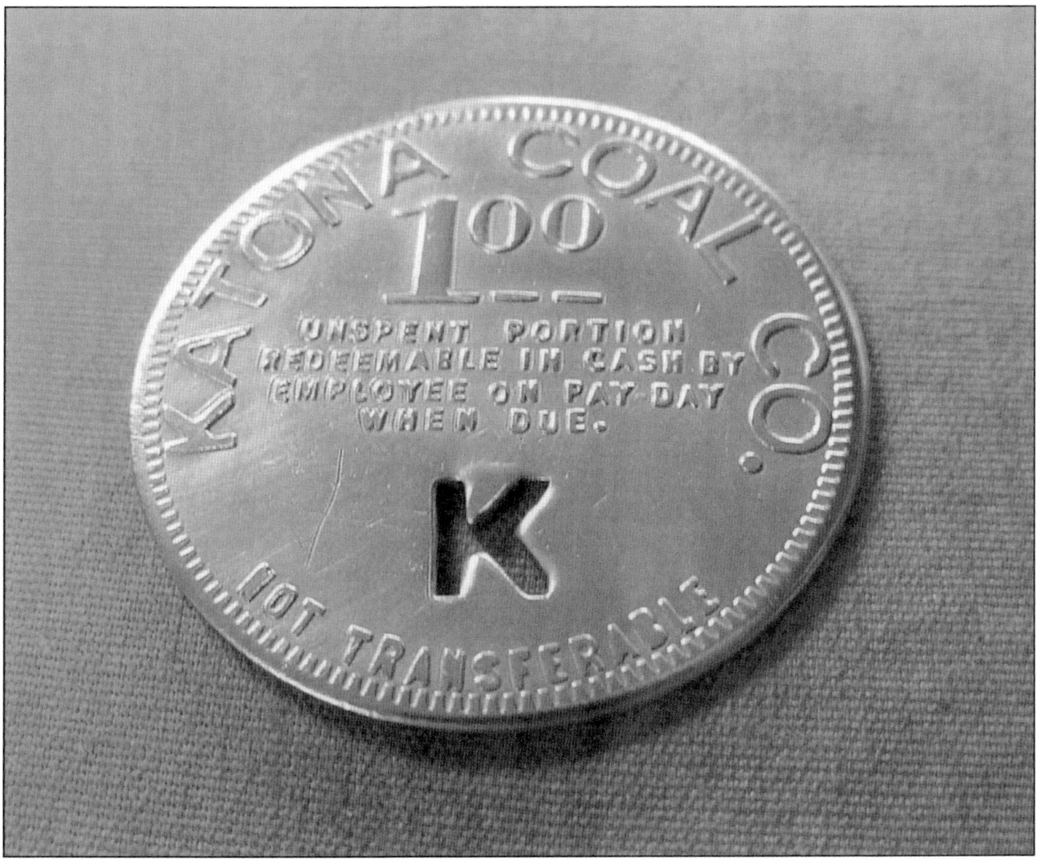

Although coal production in Wayne County never matched that of other coal-rich West Virginia counties, the county's mines provided a good living for generations of West Virginians. The Katona Coal Company was organized in 1920 by S.W. Perry, an Alabama native who came to Wayne County, obtained coal leases on 1,000 acres of land near East Lynn, and began operations. Like other coal companies, Katona Coal paid its miners with scrip, like the token shown here. The company closed in 1936, a casualty of the Great Depression. (Author's collection.)

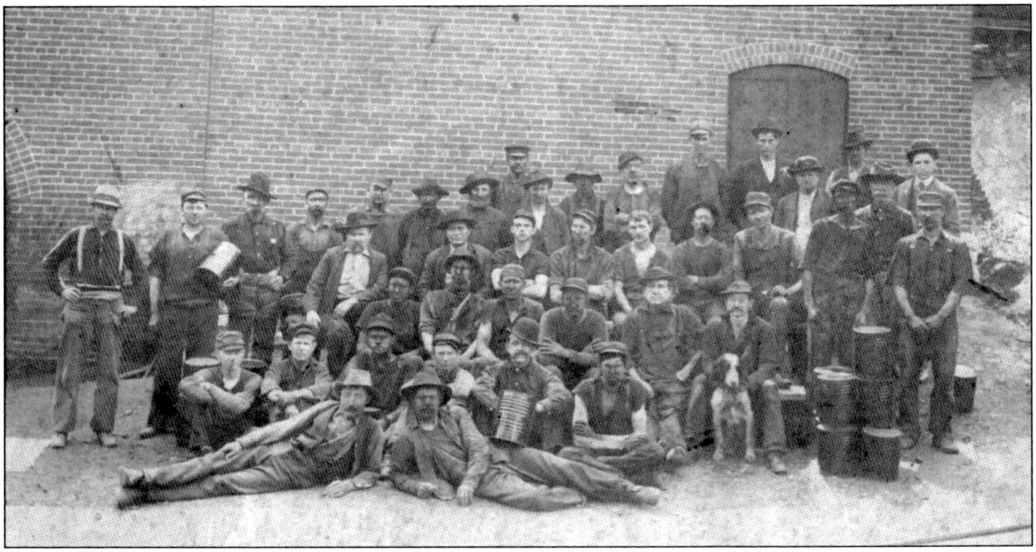

The Kellogg neighborhood in Westmoreland was named for B. Lafflin Kellogg, manager of the Phoenix Powder Company, which built a plant in the area where Camden Park now stands. On August 14, 1891, an estimated 100 kegs of powder exploded, destroying the building where they were stored and badly damaging the plant's other structures. Two men working in the building were never found. The plant was not rebuilt. (Author's collection.)

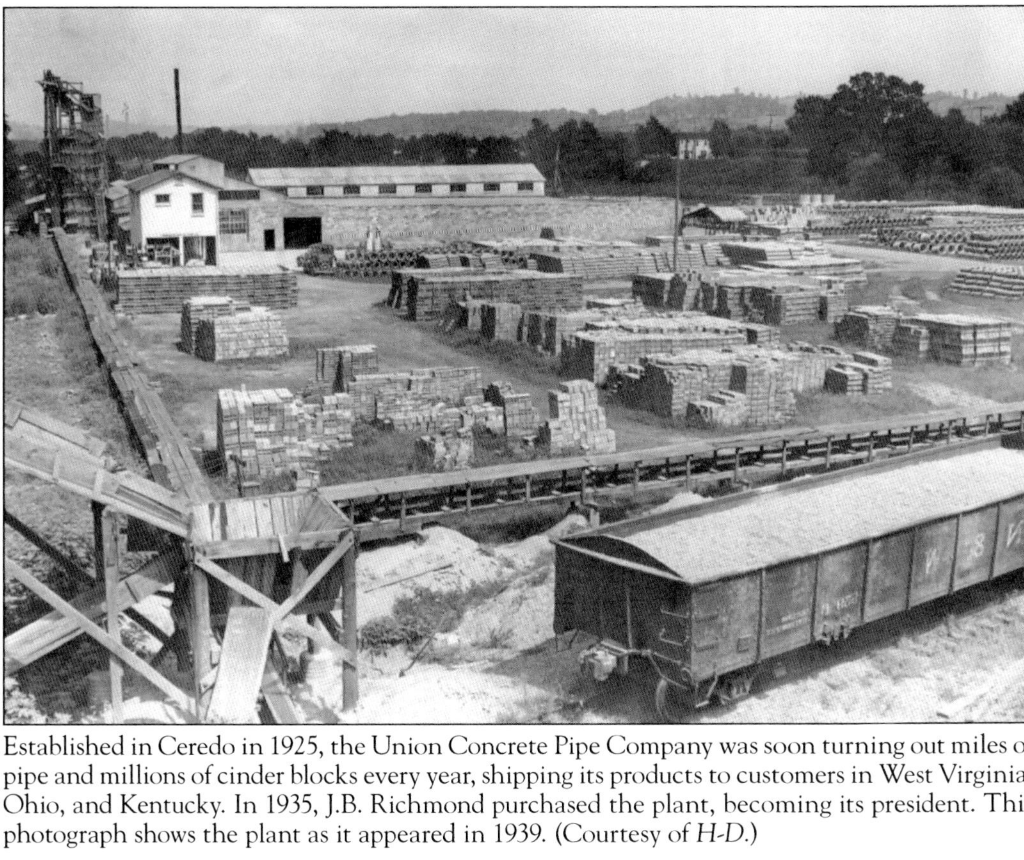

Established in Ceredo in 1925, the Union Concrete Pipe Company was soon turning out miles of pipe and millions of cinder blocks every year, shipping its products to customers in West Virginia, Ohio, and Kentucky. In 1935, J.B. Richmond purchased the plant, becoming its president. This photograph shows the plant as it appeared in 1939. (Courtesy of *H-D*.)

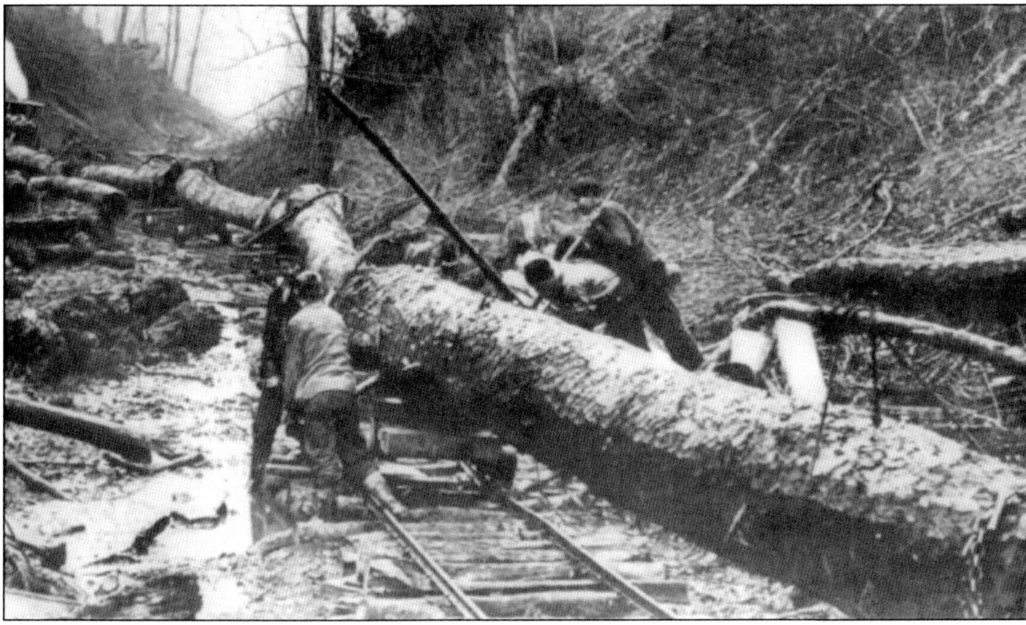

The timber industry has always stood tall in West Virginia. Logging operations such as this one on Jennies Creek in Wayne County date back to the state's earliest days. Only two states—Maine and New Hampshire—are more forested than West Virginia. In the early 1900s, clear-cutting nearly destroyed the state's woodland, but nature and better forest management have combined to bring the forests back. (Courtesy of MU.)

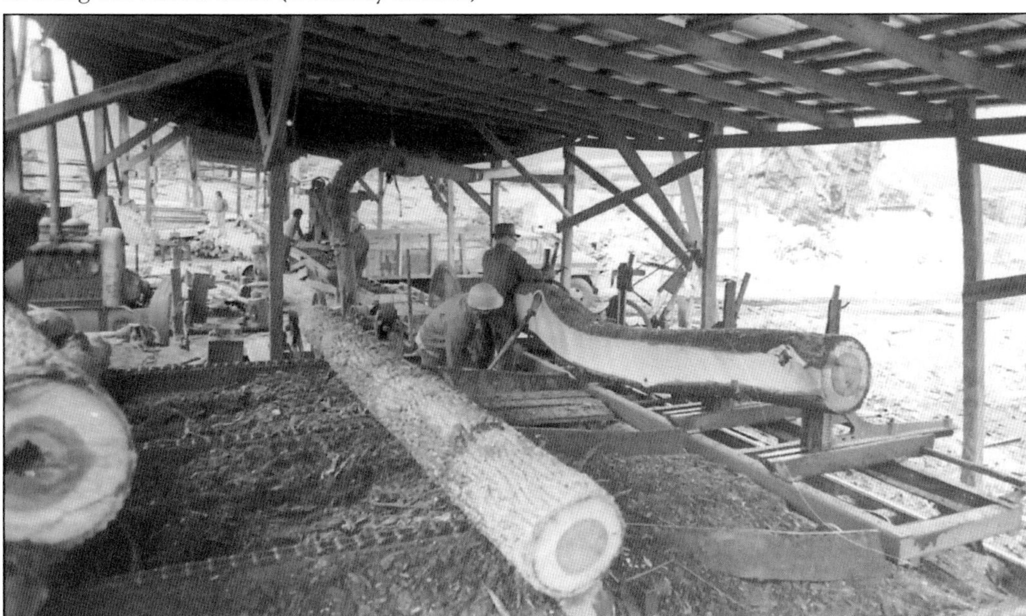

In 1909, West Virginia had more than 1,500 sawmills turning logs into lumber or other wood products. Today, the state has fewer than 200 sawmills. Nonetheless, they remain important to the economy in highly rural counties such as Wayne. Most of today's sawmills are small privately owned operations. This undated photograph features a sawmill at work on Craig Road in Wayne County. (Courtesy of *H-D*.)

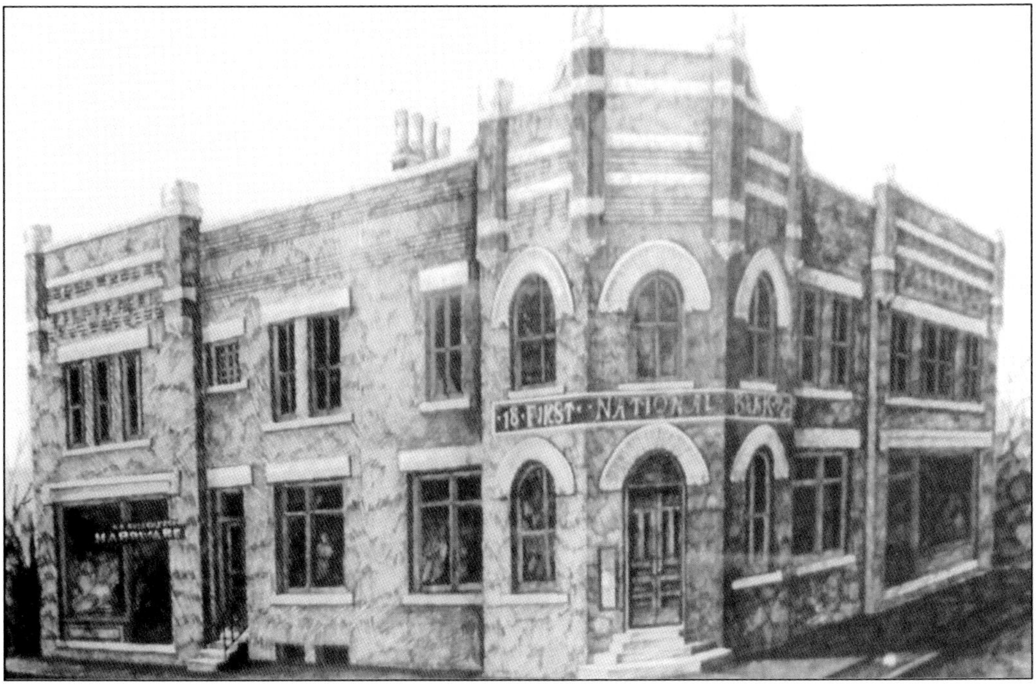

In the 1890s, Floyd Hoard designed and constructed a brick building on the southwest corner of Ceredo's Main Street and B Street for the new Ceredo Bank. His brother Pitt Hoard became the bank's president. Henry J. Stark joined the bank in 1918 and became its president when Pitt Hoard died in 1925. (Courtesy of *H-D*.)

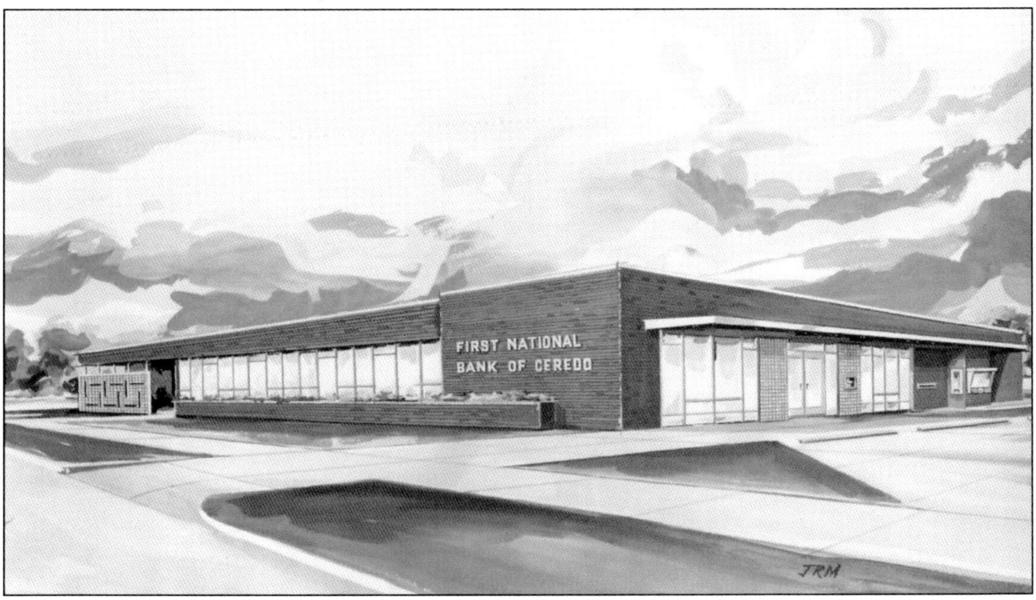

In 1959, the Ceredo Bank constructed this modern new building at First Street and US 60. A far cry from the bank's original 1890s home, the new bank included a customer's lounge, a combination conference and recreation room, soft music piped through the building, electronic banking and filing equipment, and a closed-circuit television system linking the tellers' area with the bookkeeping and accounting departments. (Courtesy of *H-D*.)

When Henry Stark stepped down as Ceredo Bank president in 1962, he was succeeded by his son Pitt H. Stark. Pitt Stark was active in business and civic affairs. An Eagle Scout as a boy, he served on the board of the Tri-State Scout Council. He also served on the board of Logan Hardware and was chairman for the Cabell-Wayne United Way campaign. (Courtesy of *H-D*.)

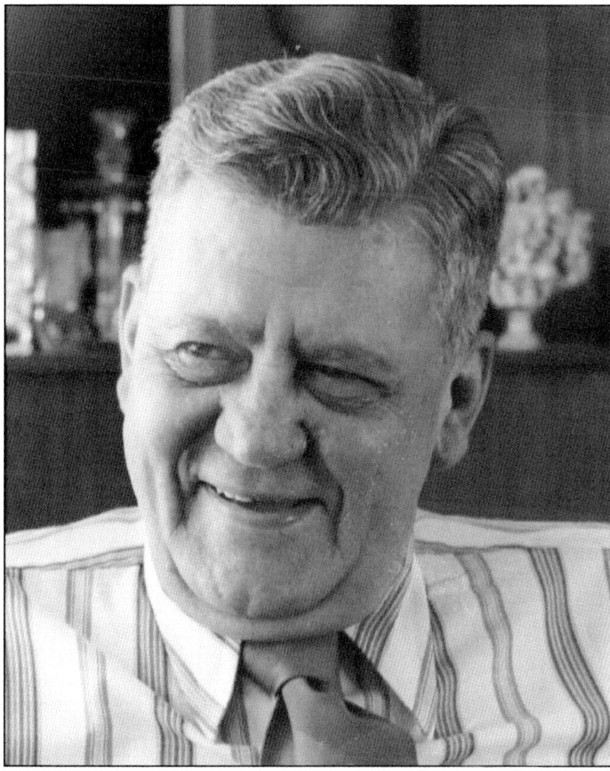

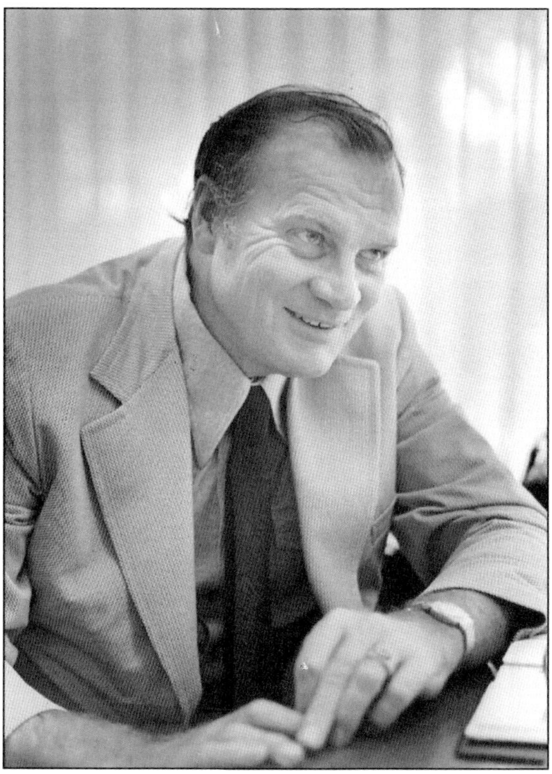

On Pitt Stark's retirement in 1980, his brother Floyd Stark became president of Ceredo Bank. Like this brother, he was a concerned and highly involved member of the community He was the founder of the Ceredo Beautification Committee, the first president of the C-K Little League, and a volunteer coach for the C-K Junior High basketball team. (Courtesy of *H-D*.)

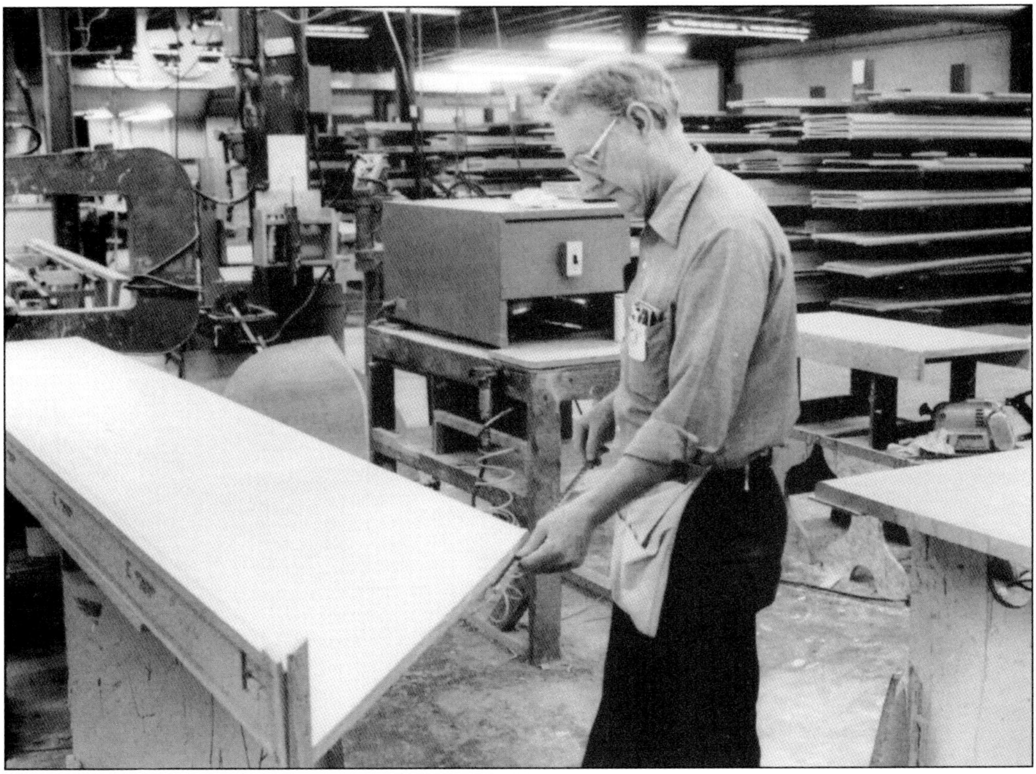

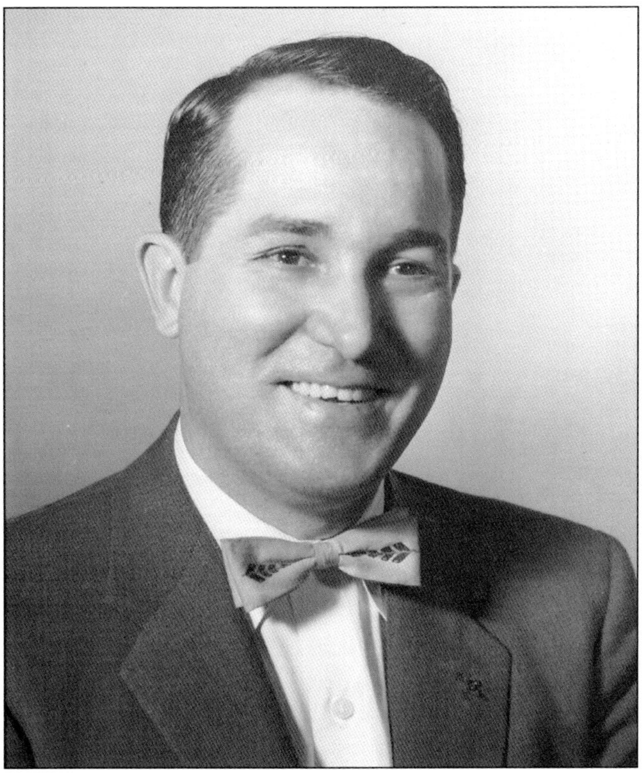

Chandler's Plywood Products is one of Wayne County's oldest businesses. Known for its kitchen designs, it also serves a wide range of commercial customers, crafting everything from hotel front desks to bank teller counters. This 1988 photograph features chief shop foreman Max Walters at work in the company's Waverly Road shop. (Courtesy of *H-D*.)

In the 1930s, Denvil Chandler spent his nights and weekends making wooden novelties in a back-porch workshop. In 1943, he took a big gamble when he quit his day job and formed the company that became Chandler's Plywood Products. Over the years, he was joined by brothers Paul, John, Edgel, and Leroy. (Courtesy of *H-D*.)

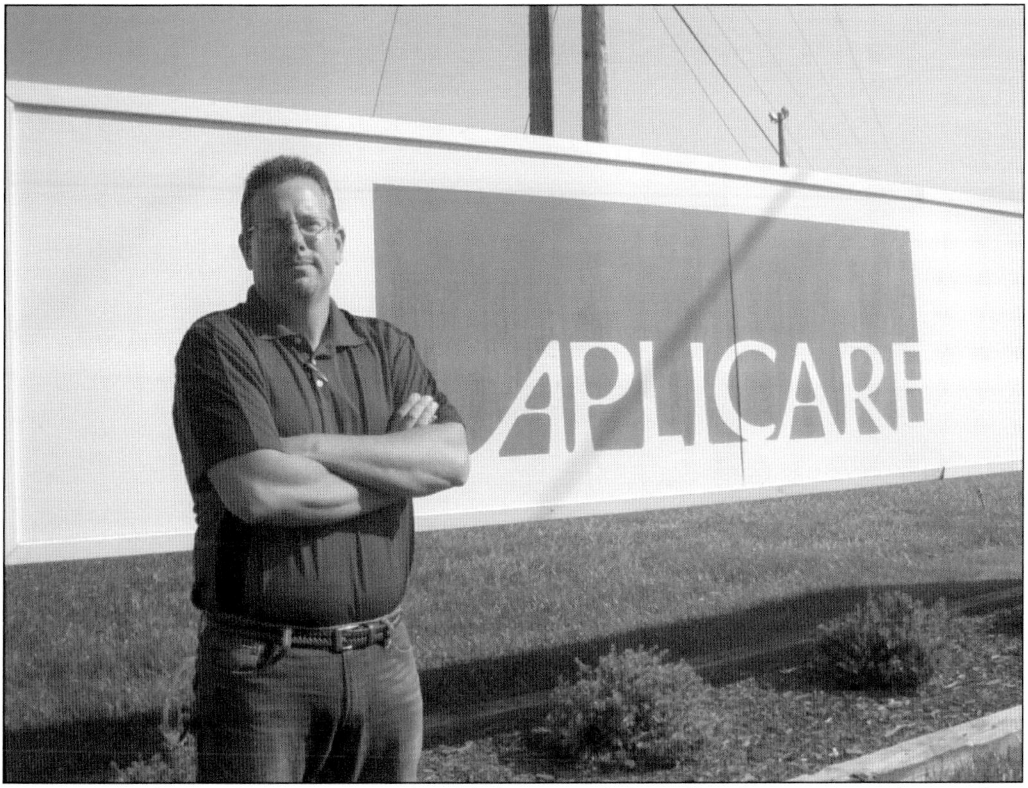

Anyone who has undergone surgery has likely noticed the yellow hue on their skin at their incision. That would be povidone iodine, a product manufactured and bottled in Wayne County and then shipped for use around the world. Aplicare, located in Prichard, also makes and sells other hospital products. After its recent acquisition of the plant, the Clorox Company invested $300,000 in capital improvements, prompting plant manager Paul Carico, pictured here, to predict a bright future for it. (Courtesy of *H-D*.)

In 2014, Italian automobile parts maker Alevard Sogefi announced it would spend $20 million to upgrade its Prichard plant, which manufactures parts for Ford, General Motors, Toyota, Subaru, and other automakers. "Business is good," Troy Thomas, the plant's general manager, said in an April 2015 interview. "The plant is operating 24 hours a day, seven days a week." (Courtesy of *H-D*.)

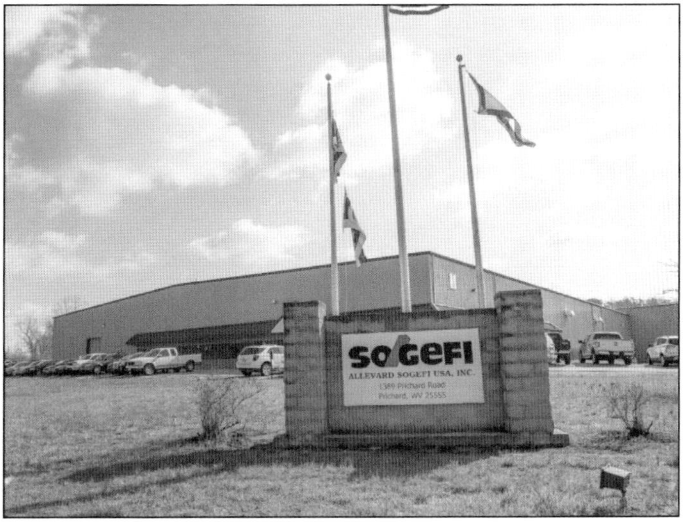

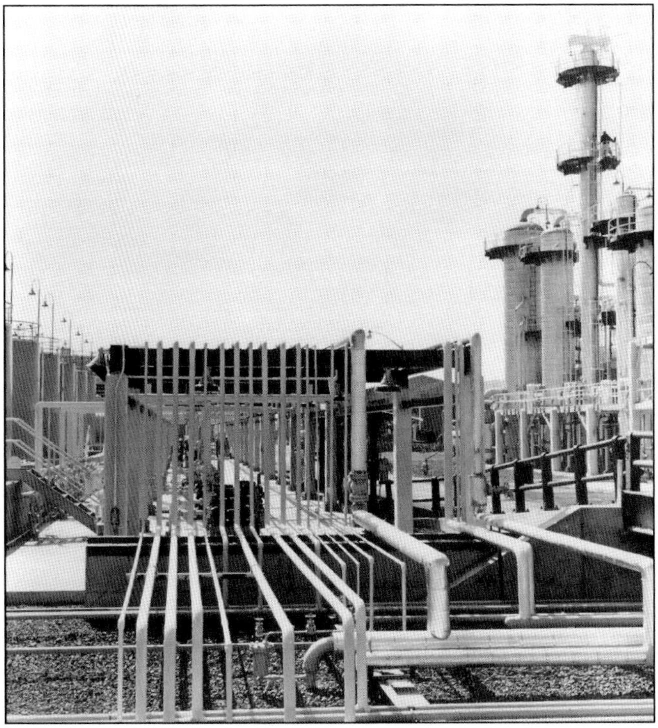

In October 1961, officials of Montecatini of Italy and Novamont, its US subsidiary, gathered with local leaders at Neal on the Big Sandy River in Wayne County to dedicate the company's first American plant. The plastics plant, the first of its kind, was designed to use feedstock low-cost propylene gas produced as a by-product at the Ashland Oil (now Marathon) refinery located across the river in Kentucky. (Courtesy of *H-D*.)

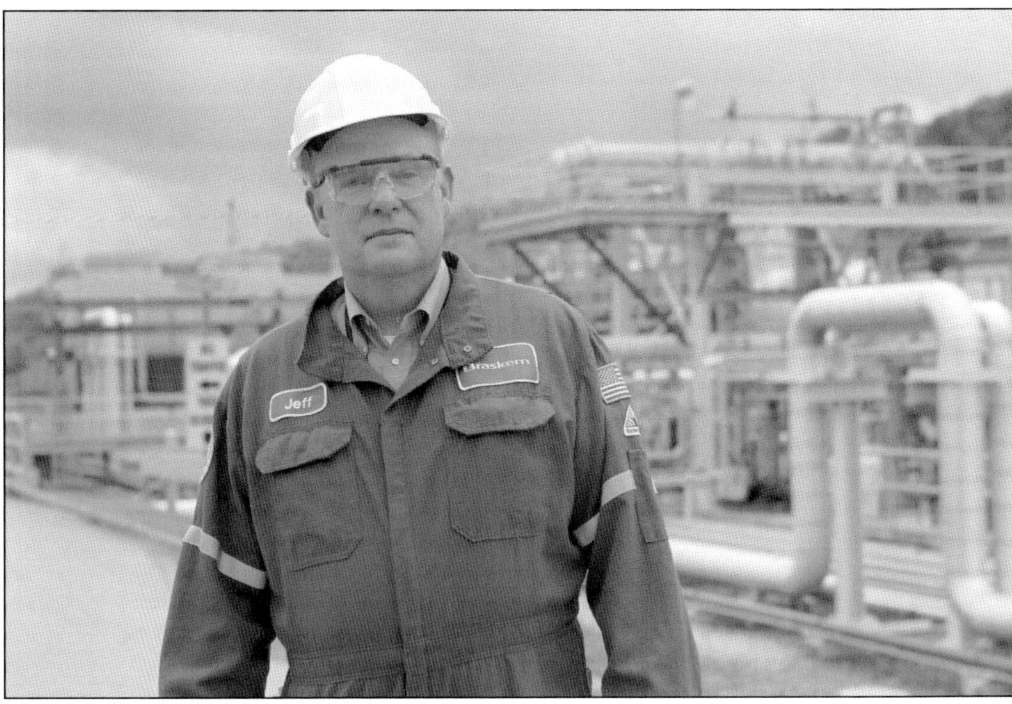

After the Novamont polypropylene plant opened at Neal in 1961, it went through a series of ownership changes. Today, it is owned and operated by Braskem America, the Philadelphia-based arm of a Brazilian company. Under the leadership of manager Jeff Blatt, pictured here, the 100-acre plant produces 500 million pounds of polypropylene each year. (Courtesy of *H-D*.)

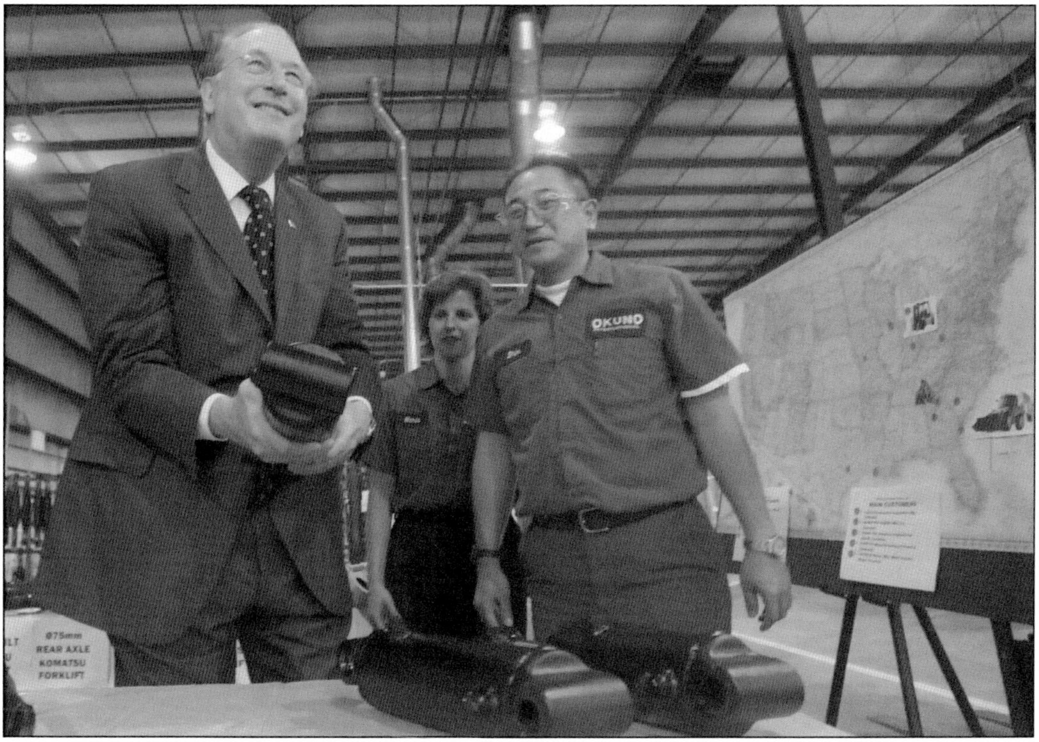

US senator Jay Rockefeller looks over finished products with Shin Okuno and Maria O'Reilly at the Okuno International facility in Prichard. The hydraulic cylinder–manufacturing company moved to Wayne County in the A. Michael Perry Industrial Park in 2000. (Courtesy of *H-D*.)

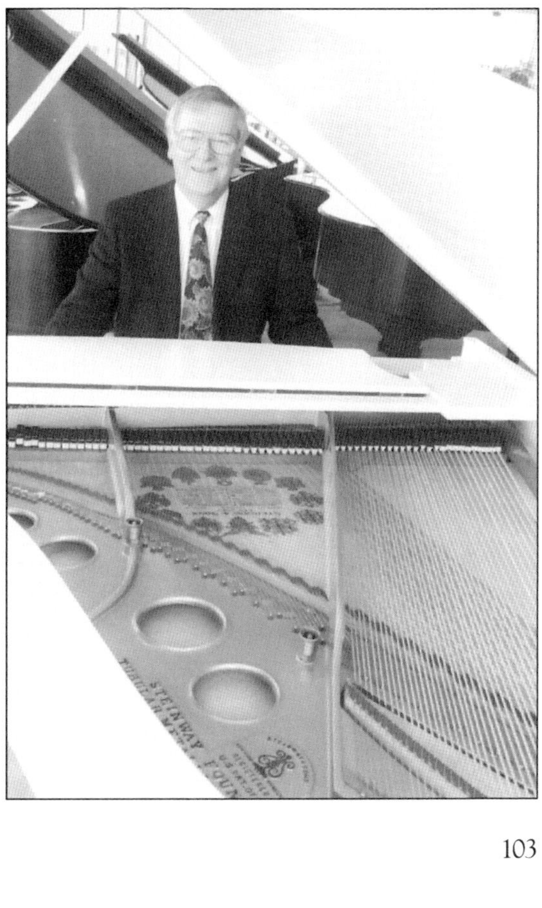

After 55 years of selling pianos, Dan Ferguson retired and closed his Ceredo music store in 2013. Interviewed by the *Herald-Dispatch* as he worked at closing his store, Ferguson said his ultimate desire was always to own his own store, and he never really thought about doing anything else. (Courtesy of *H-D*.)

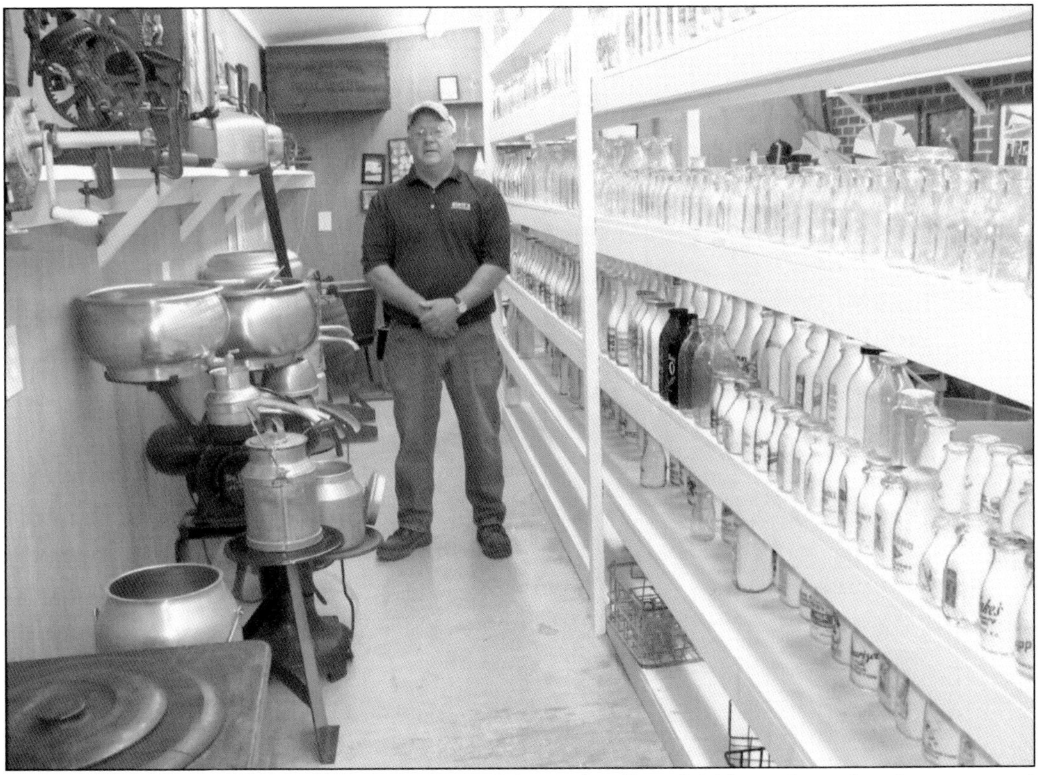

For more than 40 years, the Blatt Dairy Farm delivered milk to 3,000 residential and commercial customers in Wayne and Cabell Counties. Like most all family dairies, Blatt Dairy is long gone. Later, Mike Blatt operated Blatt's Greenhouse in Lavalette. But along the way, he never lost his fascination with the humble milk bottle and is shown here displaying part of his collection, which numbers more than 800 bottles. There is a story behind each glass vessel, he says. (Courtesy of *H-D*.)

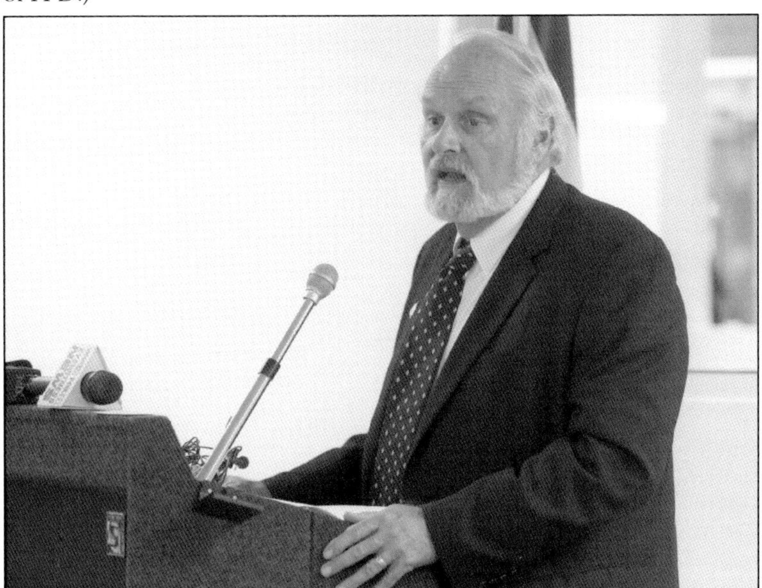

Don Perdue of Kenova is a retired pharmacist and a longtime member of the West Virginia House of Delegates. Today, however, he is wearing an additional hat. He is the executive director of the Wayne County Economic Development Authority, which is working to build business and industry in the county. (Courtesy of *H-D*.)

Ten

FAMILIAR FACES

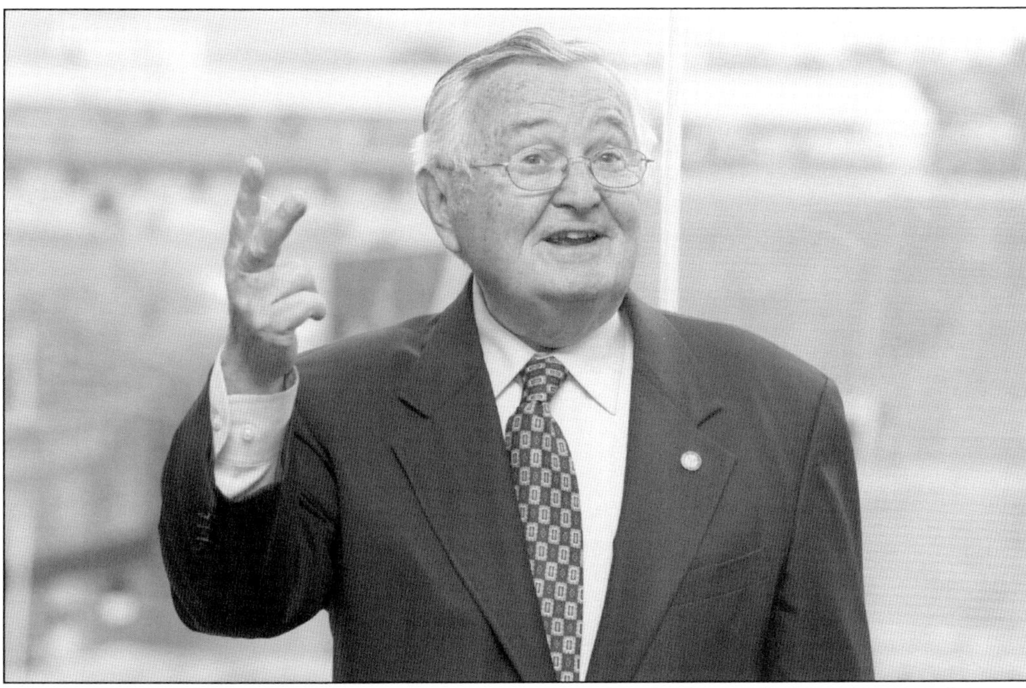

A. Michael Perry, who died on February 25, 2015, was a key leader in the West Virginia business community throughout his long career. As chairman and CEO, he helped guide Key Centurion Bancshares, the state's first billion-dollar banking organization, through its growth to become Banc One (now a unit of J.P. Morgan Chase). Active in a long list of organizations, he served as chairman of both the West Virginia Bankers Association and the West Virginia Chamber of Commerce. On weekends, he happily shed his suit and tie, donned work clothes, and prowled antique stores and estate sales, looking for vintage items to add to his growing collection. (Courtesy of *H-D*.)

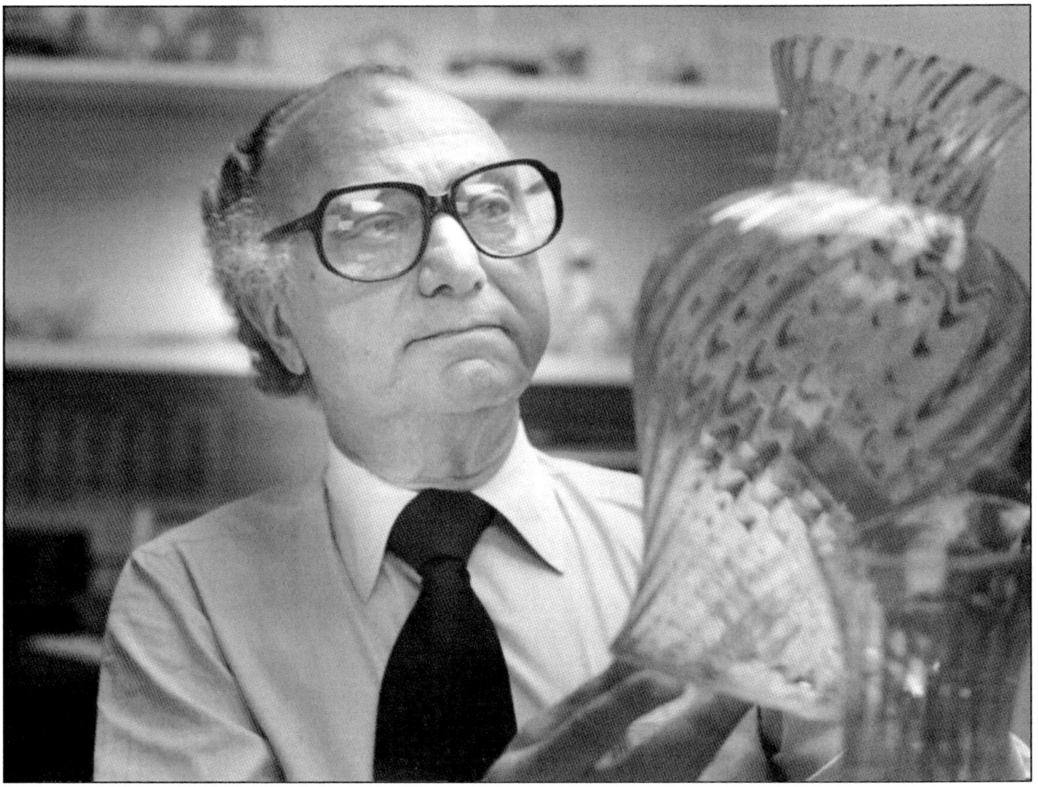

In his own words, Alfred Knobler had "$5,000 and a lot of chutzpah" when he came to Wayne County in 1949 and started Pilgrim Glass in Ceredo. Over the years, the company gained a well-deserved reputation for quality tableware and art glass. In 2001, Pilgrim went the same sad route as most of West Virginian's glassmakers when Knobler reluctantly closed its doors. He was 93 when he died in 2007. (Courtesy of *H-D*.)

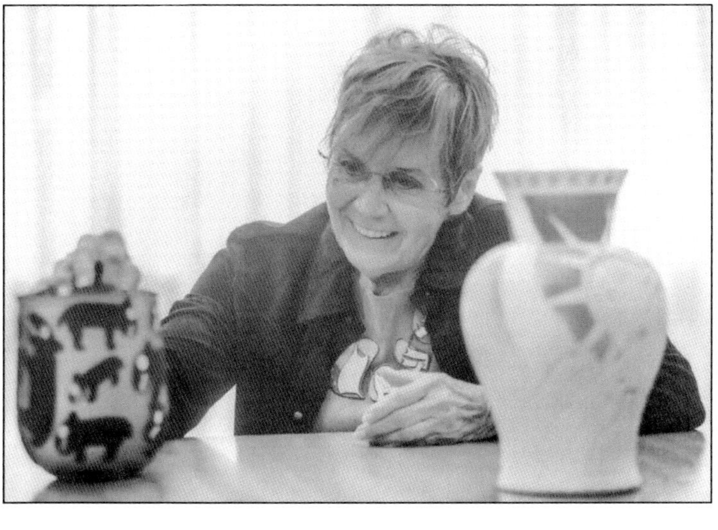

Artist Kelsey Murphy specializes in glass cameo carving, an exacting art that demands both skill in design and great dexterity in execution. For a number of years, she worked closely with entrepreneur Alfred Knobler and Pilgrim Glass. Since Pilgrim closed, she and fellow artist Robert Bornkamp have worked on their own, producing glass designs that collectors treasure. (Courtesy of *H-D*.)

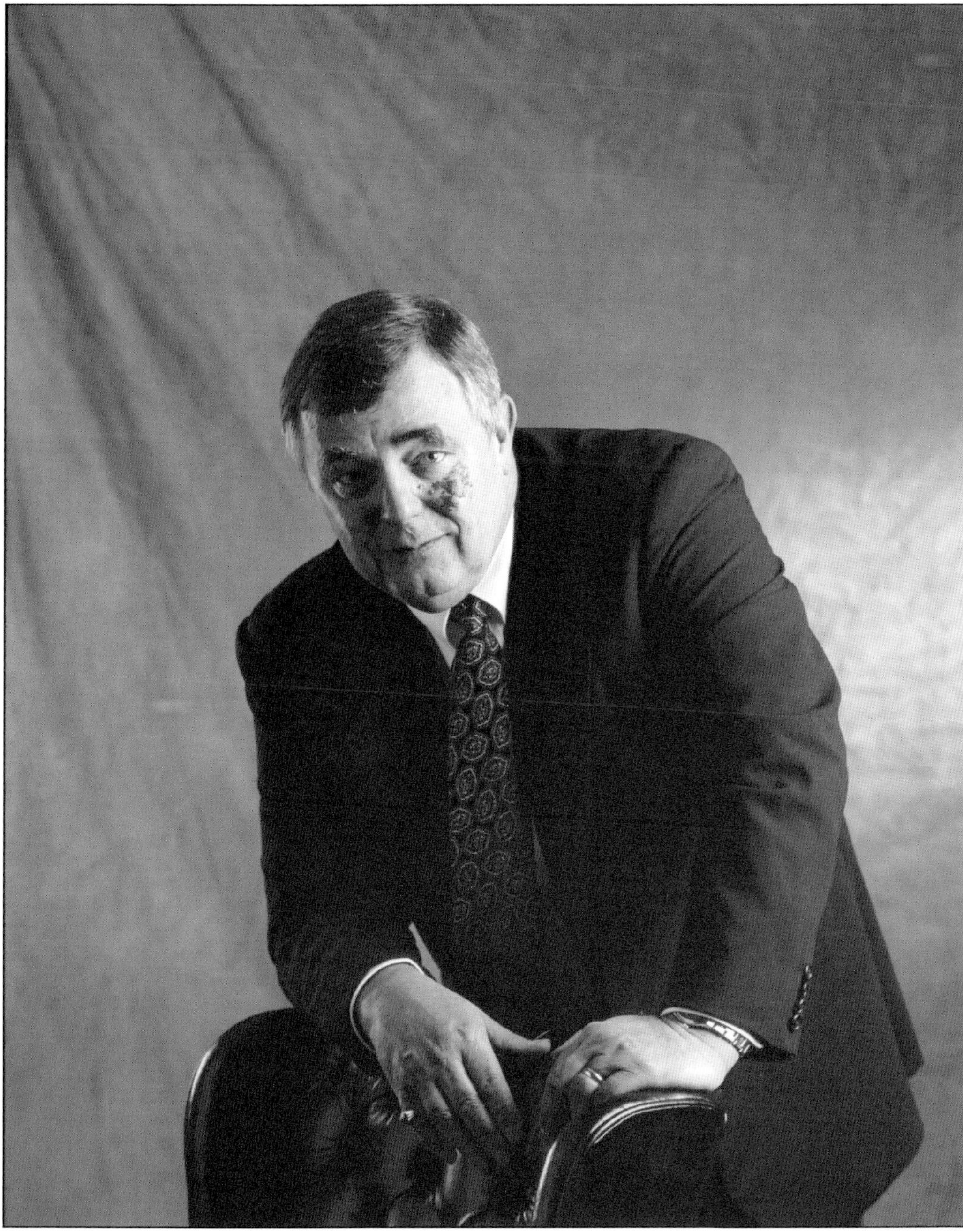

Marshall Reynolds grew up just a stone's throw from Wayne County's Camden Park, where he worked as a teenager. When the First Huntington National Bank denied a young West Huntington businessman a modest $2,500 loan for his business, he stormed out of the bank, vowing "I'll own this damn bank one day." Reynolds made good on that pledge 15 years later. Reynolds is one of West Virginia's best-known and most successful entrepreneurs. Starting with Chapman Printing, where he once worked as a delivery boy, he has assembled a network of printing properties, banks, manufacturing companies, real estate holdings, a hotel (downtown Huntington's Pullman Plaza), and other ventures. (Courtesy of *HQ*.)

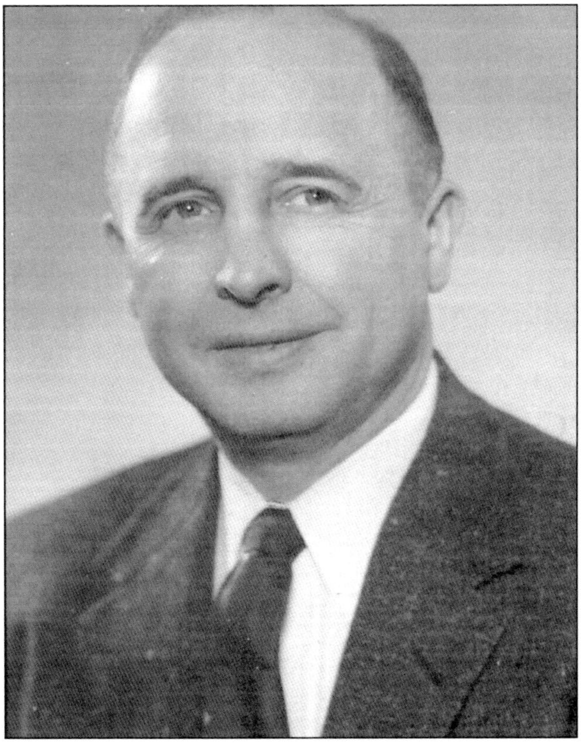

Charles H. "Jackie" McKown (1907–1997) captained the Marshall College basketball team in 1928 and was president of his senior class. An educator, he was a teacher, coach, and principal at Wayne County High School. And in a distinguished legislative career, he represented Wayne County in the West Virginia Senate for 30 years. (Courtesy of *H-D*.)

US Marine Corps colonel Justice M. Chambers (1908–1982) of Westmoreland was awarded the Medal of Honor for the valor he displayed in the battle for Iwo Jima in 1945. After the war, he served as staff advisor to the US Senate Armed Services Committee. The US 60 bridge connecting Cabell and Wayne Counties was named for him in 2004. The span stands not far from his boyhood home. (Courtesy of *H-D*.)

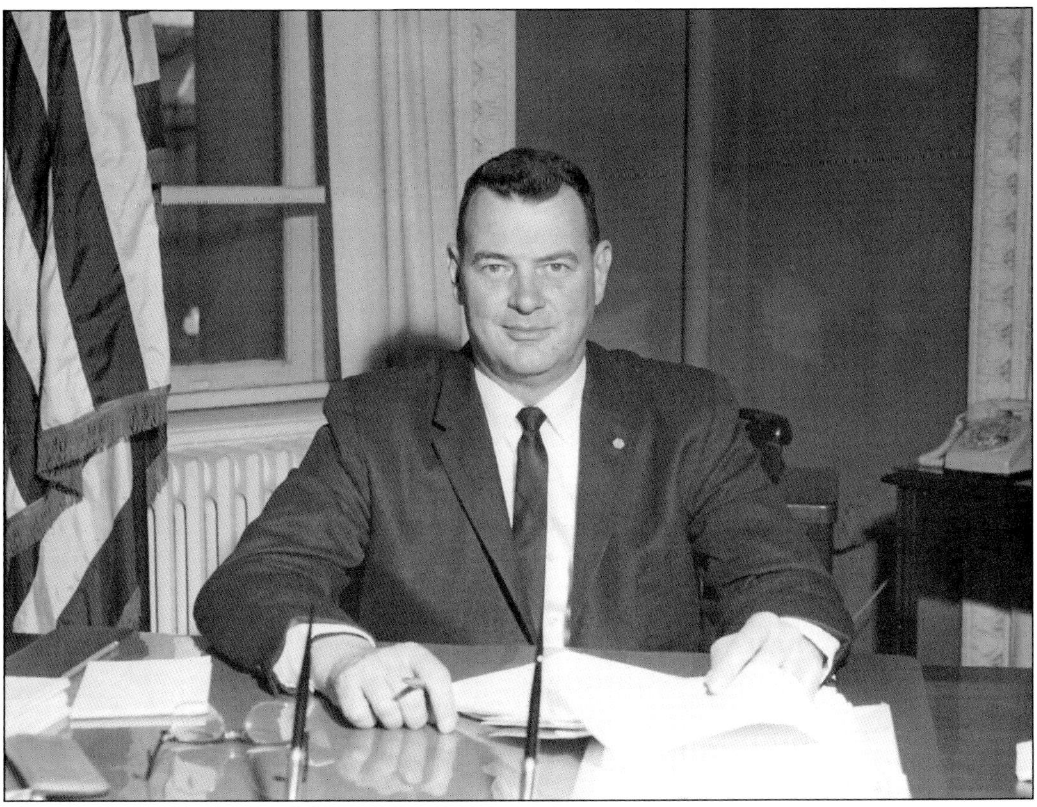

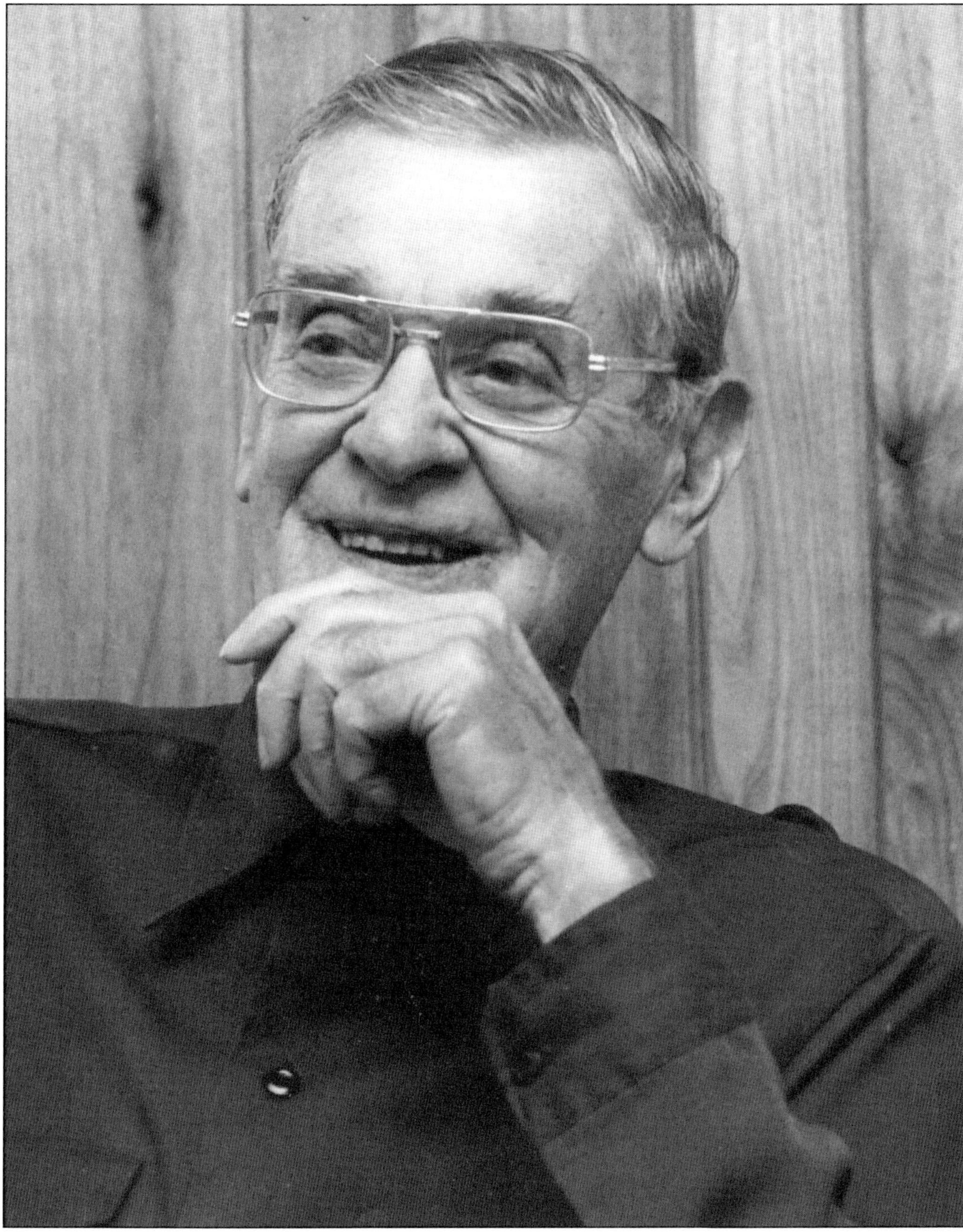

Wayne County political patriarch Milton J. Ferguson, who died in 1995 at age 92, was a skilled lawyer, powerful politician, knowledgeable historian, and, as his family and friends would gladly attest, a heckuva storyteller. Earning his law degree at West Virginia University in 1929, he served briefly in the legislature and began his career as a trial lawyer. After an unsuccessful bid for governor in 1956, he was appointed US attorney for the Southern District of West Virginia. At various times in his long career, he served as state tax commissioner, mayor of Wayne, and Wayne County prosecuting attorney. He served for 32 years on the Tri-State Airport Authority, which named its Milton J. Ferguson Field in his honor. (Courtesy of *H-D*.)

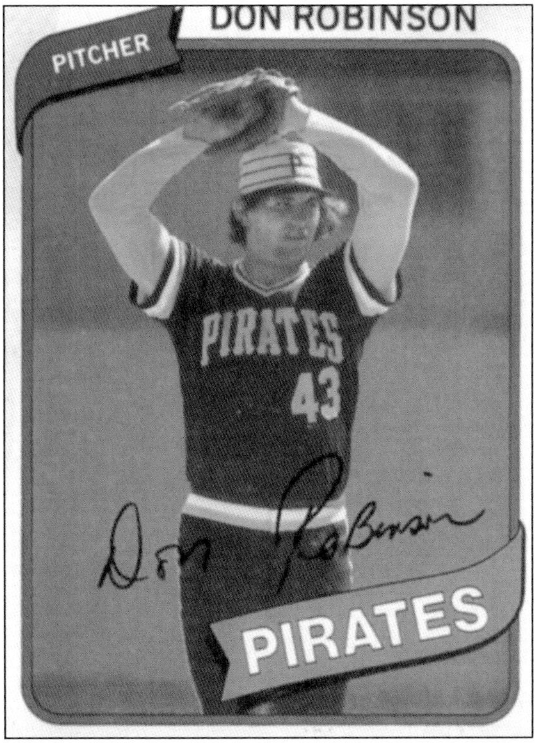

Don Robinson of Kenova, known as "Donnie," wore four different uniforms—the Pittsburgh Pirates, San Francisco Giants, California Angels, and Philadelphia Phillies—during his 14-year career in Major League Baseball. Regarded as one of the best-hitting pitchers of his day, he won three Silver Slugger Awards in 1982, 1989, and 1990. He is shown here on a bubblegum card from early in his career. (Author's collection.)

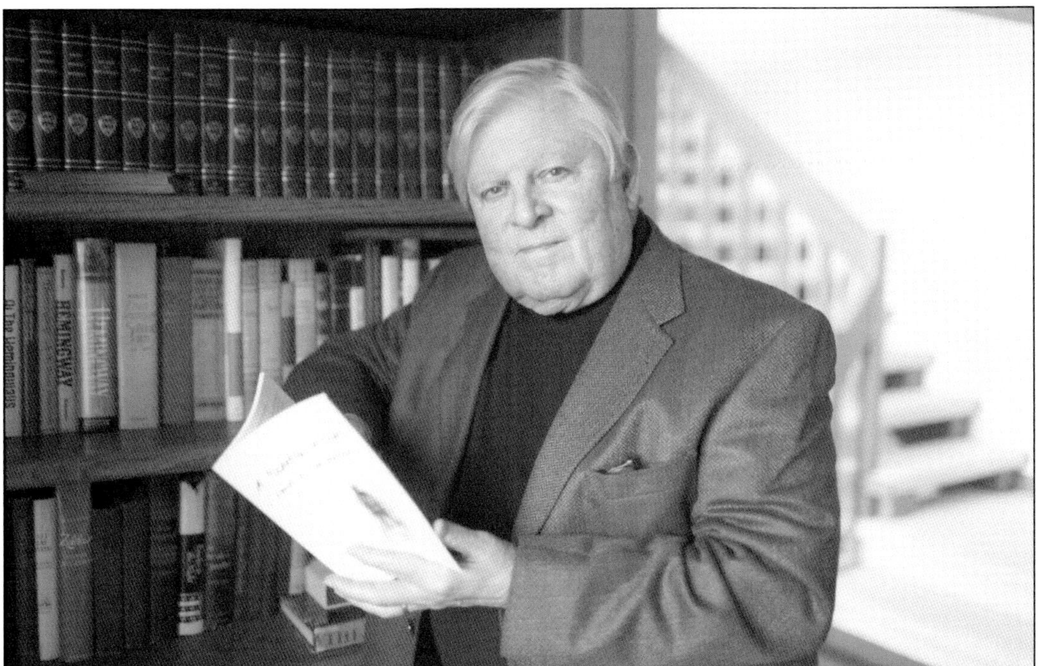

Vinson High School graduate Don Hatfield rose from part-time sports reporter to become executive editor, president, and publisher of the *Herald-Dispatch*. He followed that by becoming vice president of Gannett West in Arizona. When he retired after 47 years of newspapering, he and his wife, Sandy, moved from Tucson back to Huntington. (Courtesy of *H-D*.)

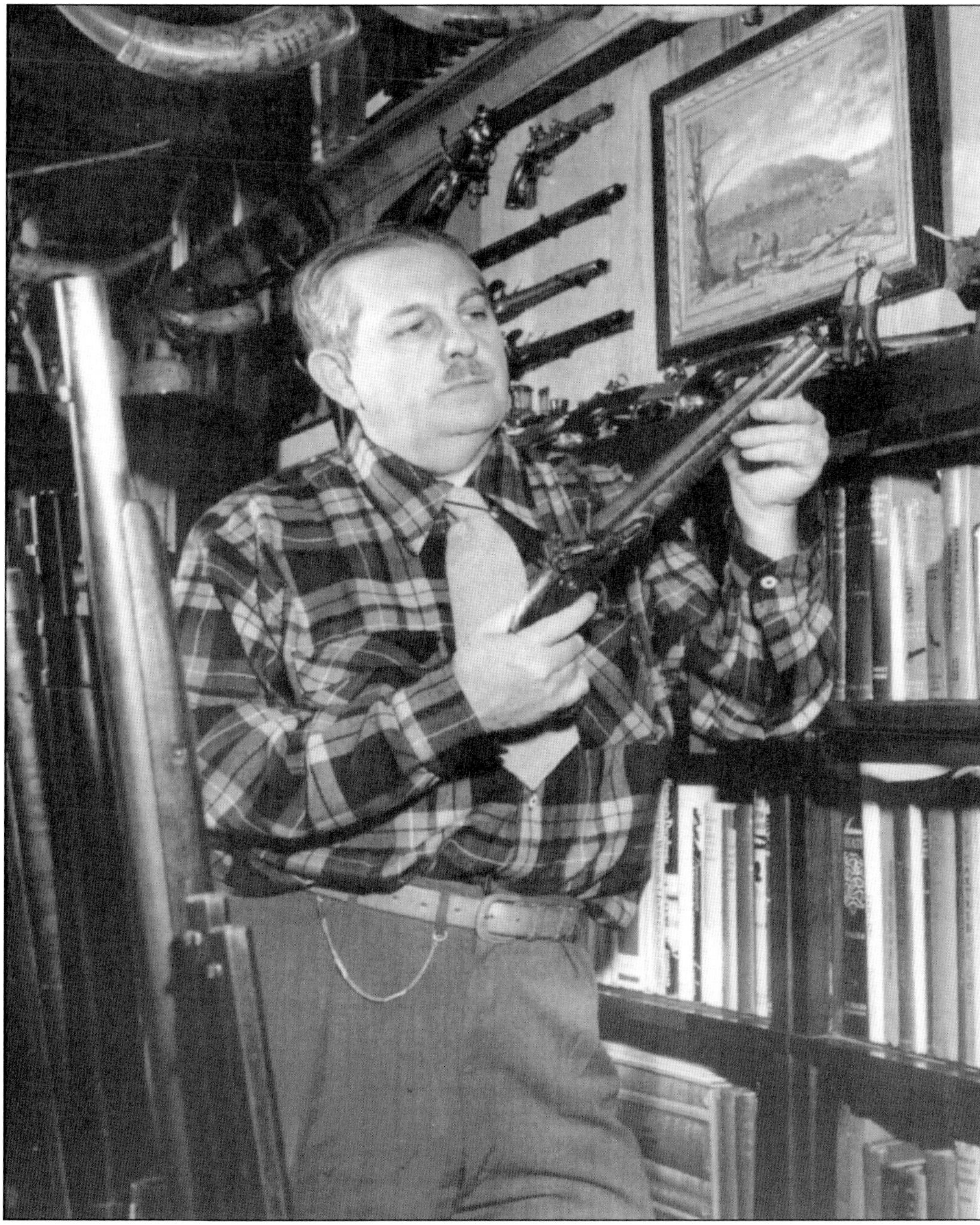

Herman P. Dean (1897–1978) packed several lifetimes of experiences into his busy eight decades. A businessman, he owned Huntington's former Standard Printing & Publishing Co. A newspaperman, he published the weekly *Wayne County News*. A church and civic leader, he taught Sunday School at Huntington's Central Christian Church for 30 years and aided a long list of charitable endeavors. A world traveler, he visited not just familiar tourist spots but such remote regions as the Canadian Yukon, where he even lived with the Eskimos for two years. He loved hunting, fishing, and collecting antique guns. He spent a lifetime amassing his collection of firearms and then presented it to the Huntington Museum of Art for future generations to admire and enjoy. (Courtesy of the Huntington Museum of Art.)

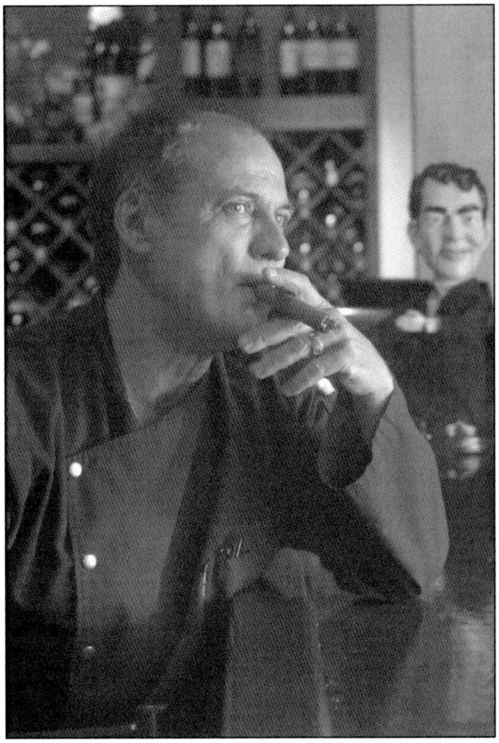

Early on, it appeared that Clarksburg, West Virginia, native Rocco Muriale's career might be in music. He majored in music at Fairmont State University and was picked to play in the US Army Field Band. But he turned down the chance to play in the military band in favor of working with his parents and uncle who had opened a Clarksburg restaurant, and that experience planted the seed of a dream for him. (Courtesy of *HQ*.)

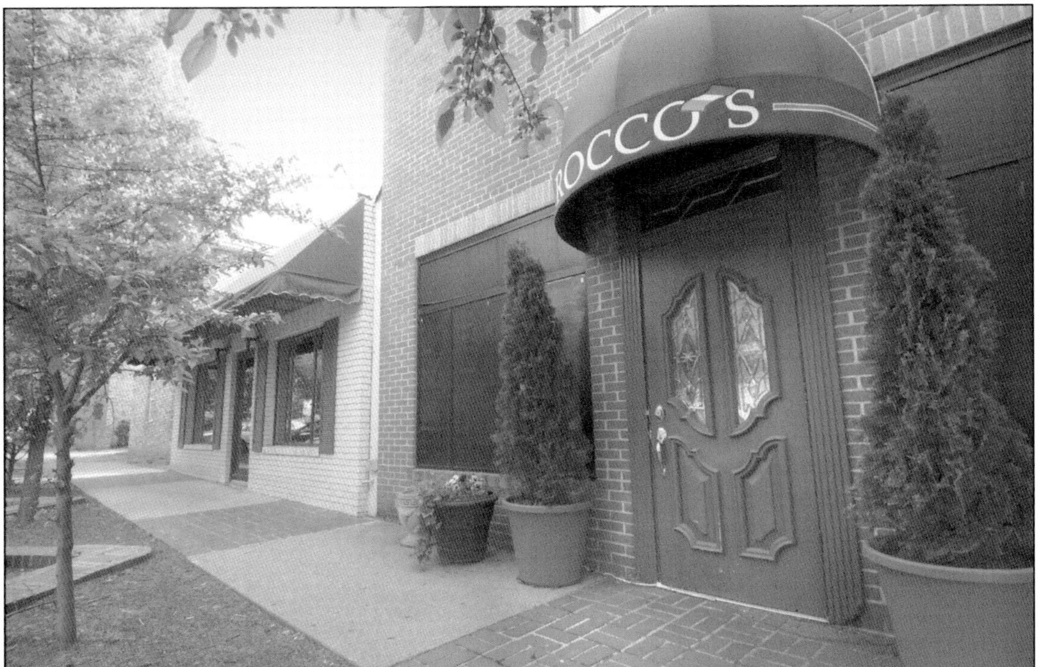

In 1977, Muriale opened Rocco's, a small Italian restaurant, on Main Street in Ceredo. Over the years, Rocco's has grown significantly, both in size and reputation. Today, it is one of the region's most popular restaurants. In 2005, Muriale began selling a selection of Italian specialty food items in the region's supermarkets. (Courtesy of *HQ*.)

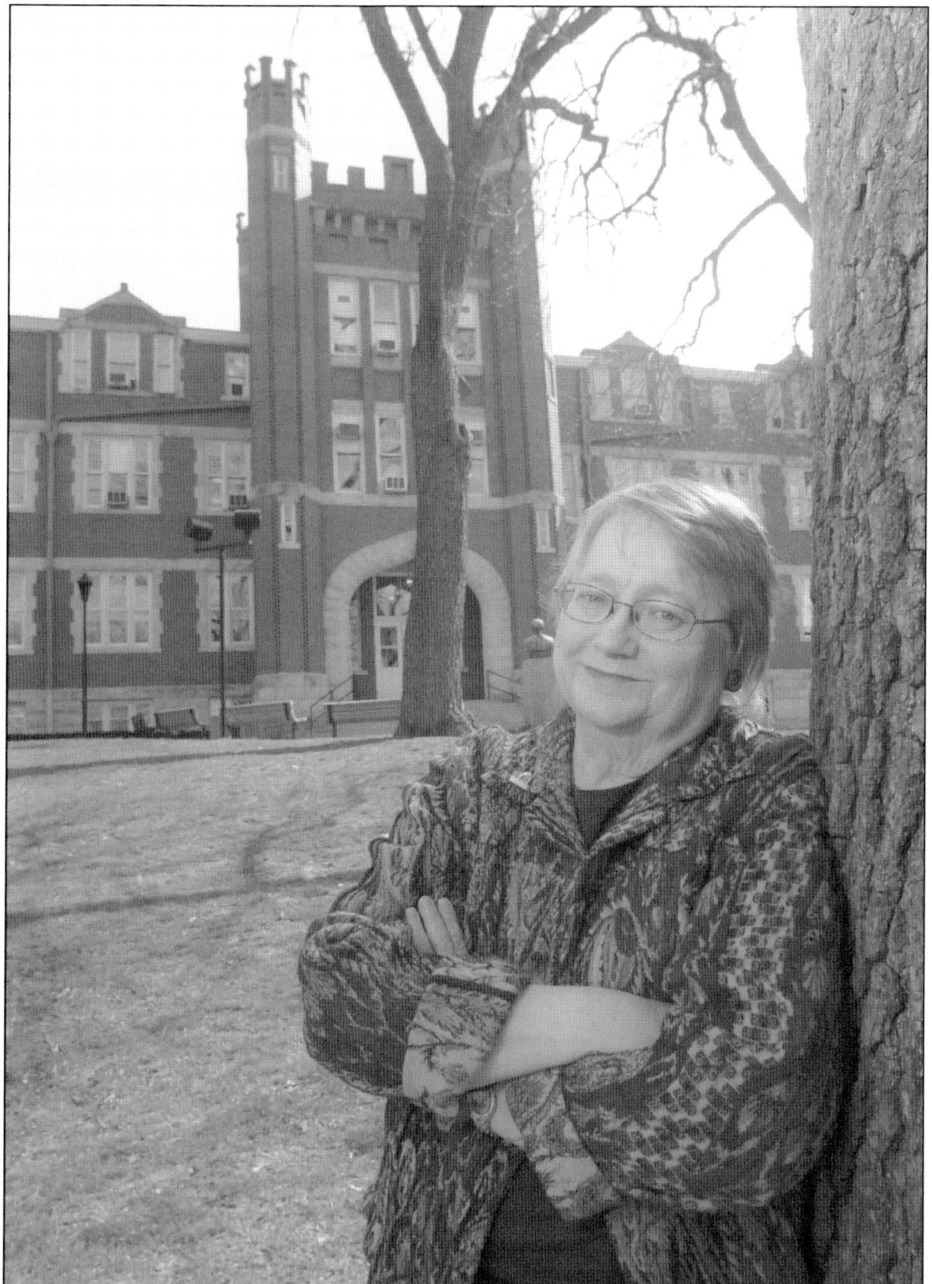

A native of Kenova, Dr. Sarah Denman retired in 2008 after 39 years in education, including 33 at Marshall University. She had been with the university since 1975, when she was hired as part of the team that helped establish the former Marshall Community and Technical College. She steadily rose in the university's ranks, retiring as provost and senior vice president for academic affairs. She earned her bachelor's degree at Marshall and then taught at Ceredo-Kenova High School while completing her master's. She received her doctorate in higher education administration from West Virginia University in 1986. On her retirement, she noted she had served with nine presidents during her years at Marshall. (Courtesy of *H-D*.)

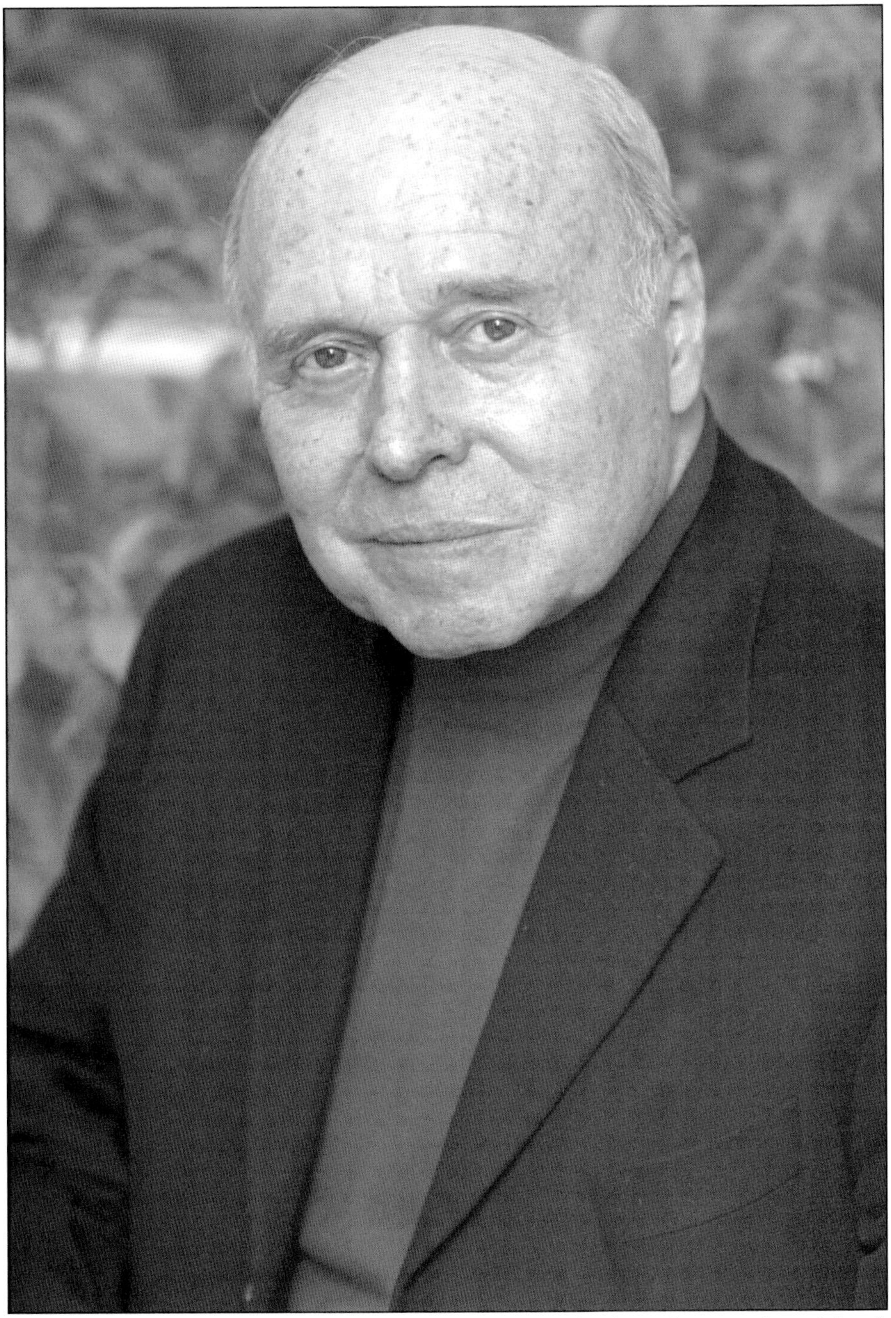

A Wayne County native, Dr. Charles McKown played a pivotal role in the growth and development of the Joan C. Edwards School of Medicine at Marshall University, stepping down in 2011 after 22 years as the school's dean. McKown earned his bachelor's degree at West Virginia University and his medical degree at the Medical College of Virginia. He joined the Marshall medical faculty in 1975, following an already impressive career at the McGuire VA Hospital in Richmond, Virginia; Walter Reed Army Medical Center in Washington; and the National Institutes of Health in Bethesda, Maryland. Some think he may have gotten the bug for public service from his father, the late Charles H. "Jackie" McKown. (Courtesy of *H-D*.)

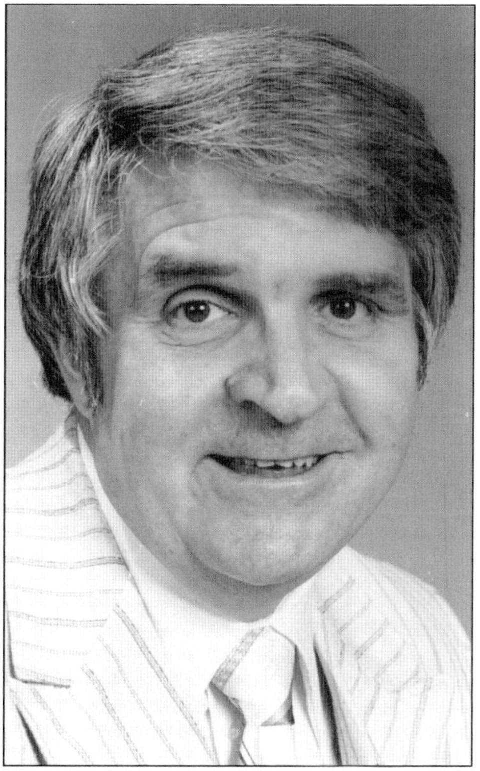

In his half-century of reporting for Huntington's newspapers—first for the *Advertiser* and later for the *Herald-Dispatch*—Jack Hardin (1926–2011) of Ceredo wrote thousands of news stories, but he excelled with stories from the police beat. Knowing every local police officer and firefighter by their first name gave him unprecedented access to news happenings—and his readers were the beneficiaries. (Courtesy of *H-D*.)

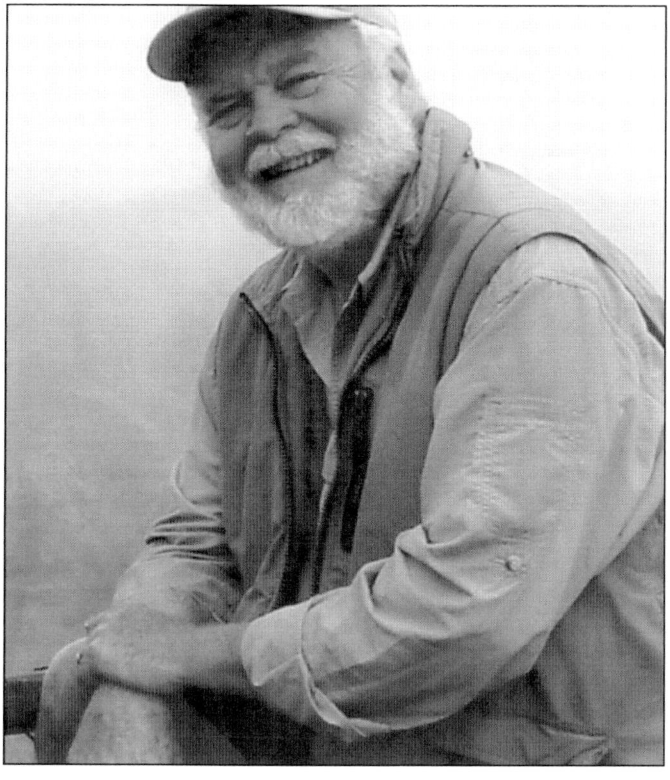

Lee Maynard's first novel, *Crum*, was a fictionalized account of his boyhood in the tiny Wayne County community of that name. The book had so many four-letter words that Tamarack, the state's official arts and crafts marketplace, refused to stock it. Two sequels proved equally outrageous, leaving some readers shaking their heads but delighting his many fans. And that, Maynard insists, is fine by him. (Courtesy of Lee Maynard.)

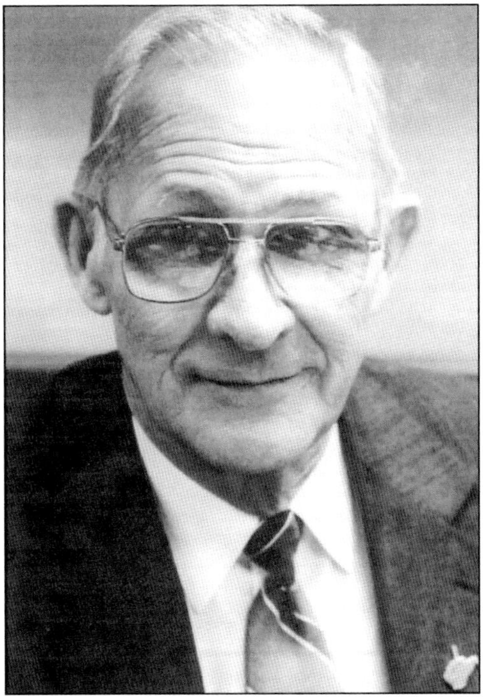

Pearl E. Booth, who died in 2014 at age 84, was a familiar face in Wayne County politics for decades. He served 30 years as a county commissioner, completed one term as assessor, and was a longtime member of the Tri-State Airport Authority. Booth, who retired from the insurance industry, was eulogized by Rep. Nick Rahall for his efforts at bringing economic development to the county. (Courtesy of *H-D*.)

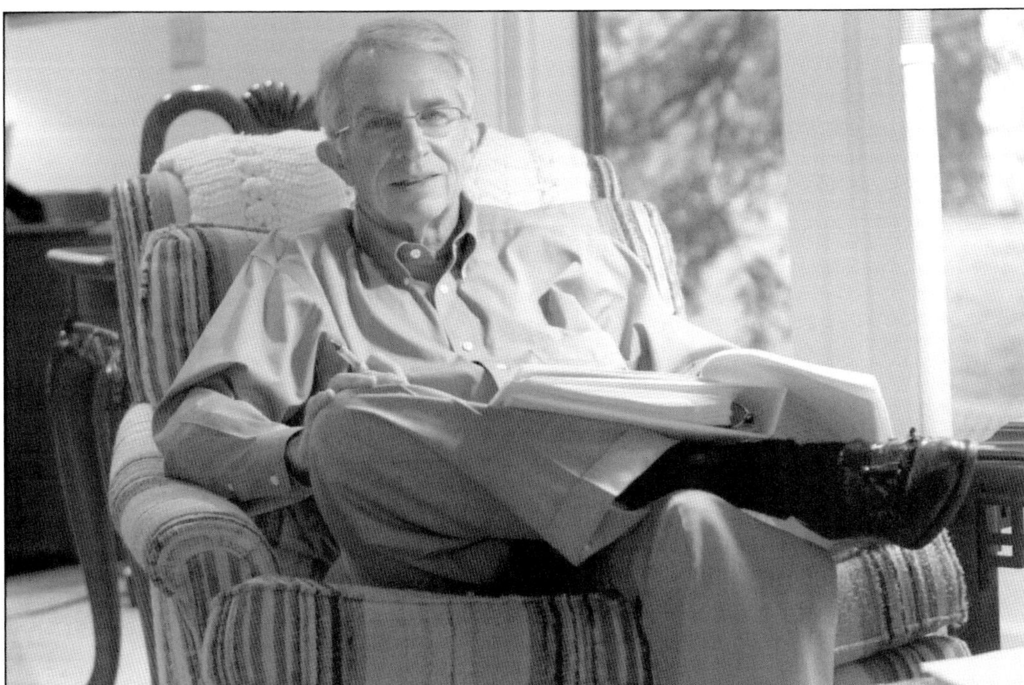

Born in Huntington, Menis Ketchum was raised in Wayne County and educated in Wayne County schools before attending Ohio University in Athens, Ohio. He earned his law degree at West Virginia University in 1967, then returned to Huntington where he practiced law with his father, Chad Ketchum. He was elected to a 12-year term on the West Virginia Supreme Court of Appeals in 2008. (Courtesy of *H-D*.)

Madison Monroe "Buzz" Nutter (1931– 2998) played high school football at Vinson High School and college ball at Virginia Tech, where he became the school's first player drafted into the NFL. A center, he was drafted by the Washington Redskins, then played for the Baltimore Colts and later for the Pittsburgh Steelers. (Author's collection.)

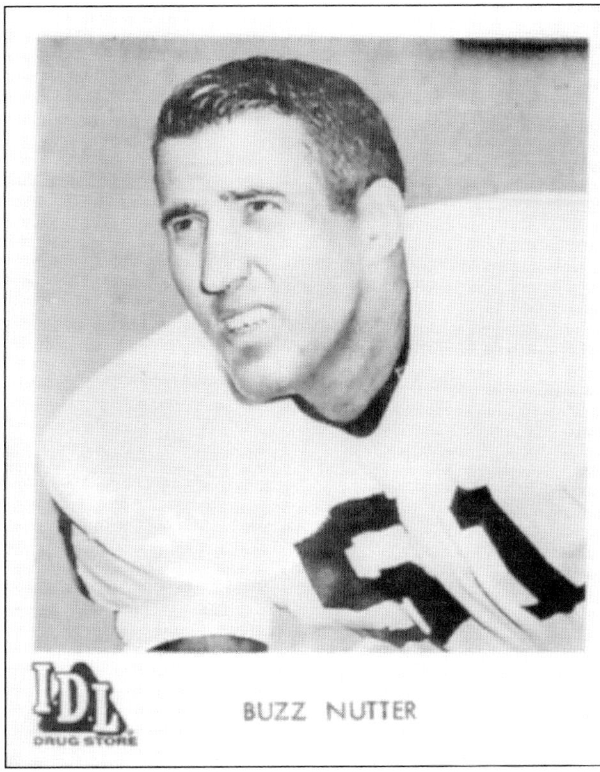

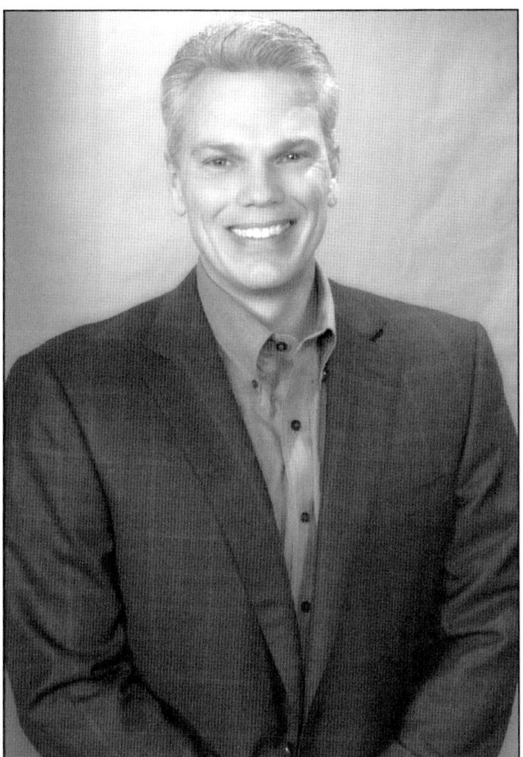

Rescued from the wreckers who demolished the former Ceredo-Kenova High School, the school's former gymnasium will continue in use as the C-K Alumni Gym thanks to a community fundraising campaign. The campaign got a big boost from Brad Smith, a C-K grad and president and CEO of Intuit Inc. Smith contributed $100,000 to the campaign. (Courtesy of *H-D*.)

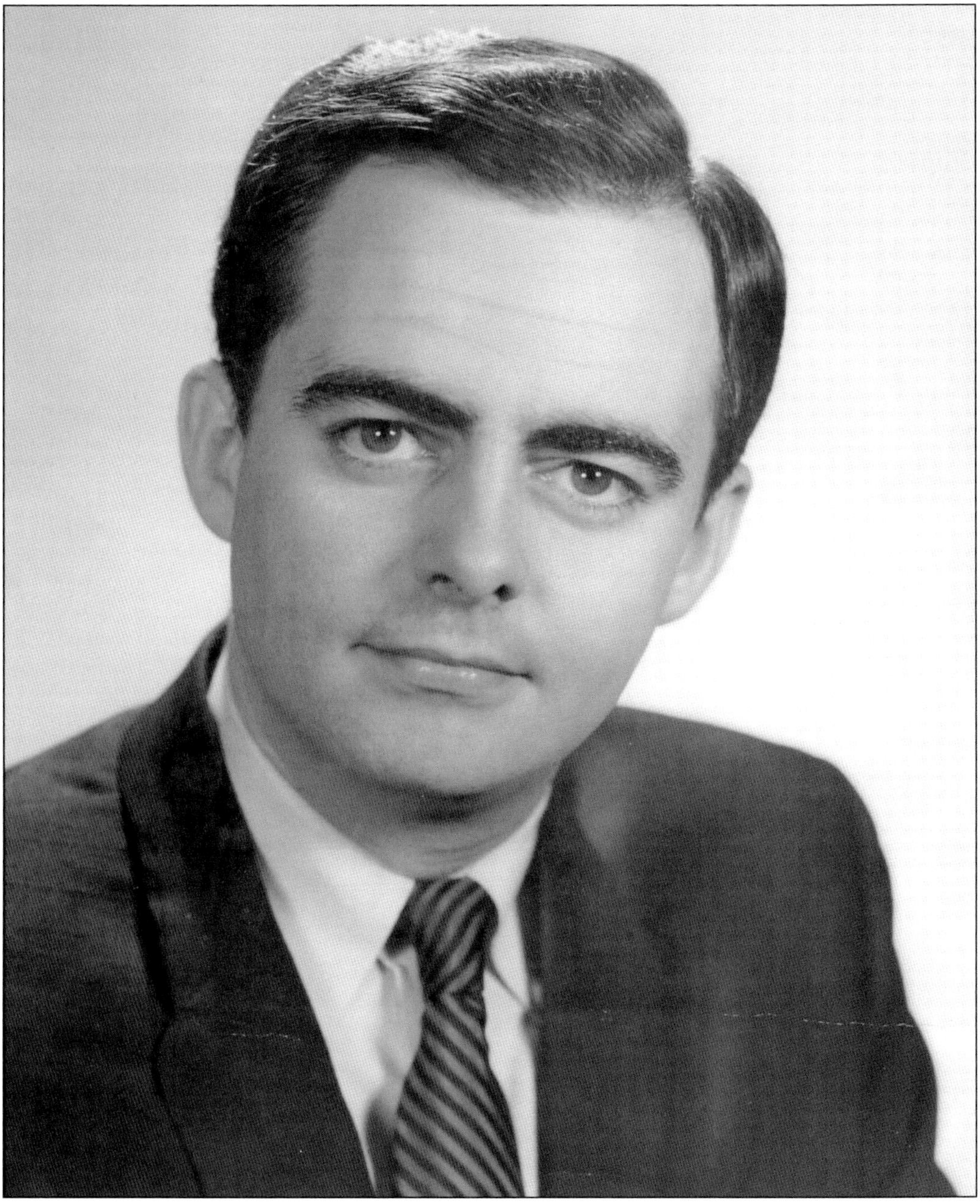

In 1979, Bill Stewart, a Vinson High School graduate and former television newsman in Huntington, was covering the Nicaraguan revolution for ABC News when he was summarily murdered by Nicaraguan National Guard forces. The footage of Stewart's killing was smuggled out of the country by his crew and sent to New York, where all three major American networks ran it on their evening news broadcasts and repeatedly rebroadcast the clip in the following days. Millions of viewers in the United States and worldwide reacted with shock and outrage toward the regime of Nicaraguan strongman Anastasio Somoza Debayle. Pres. Jimmy Carter labeled the murder "an act of barbarism that all civilized people condemn." The Somoza regime was overthrown less than a month after Stewart's murder. (Courtesy of *H-D*.)

Walter F. "Lefty" Rollins (1922–1992), a graduate of Ceredo-Kenova High School, attended West Virginia University and graduated from the Cincinnati College of Mortuary Science. He was co-owner of the Rollins Funeral Home in Kenova but best known for his service in the West Virginia Legislature—18 years in the House of Delegates (where he became majority leader) and four years in the state senate. (Courtesy of *H-D*.)

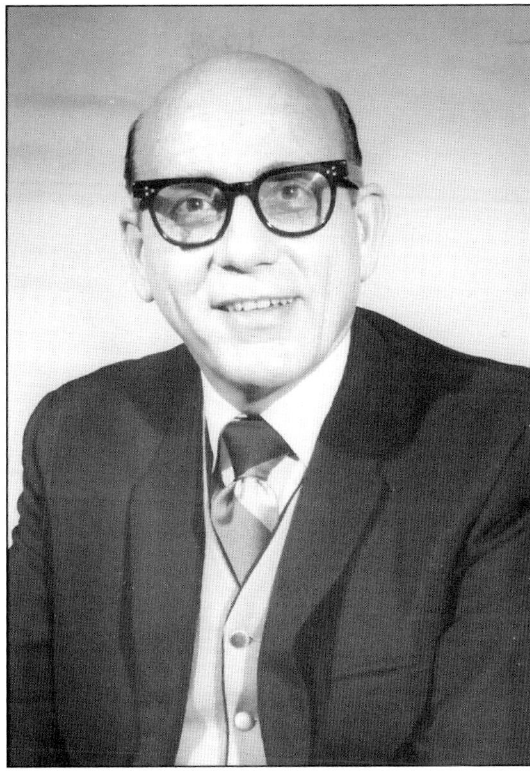

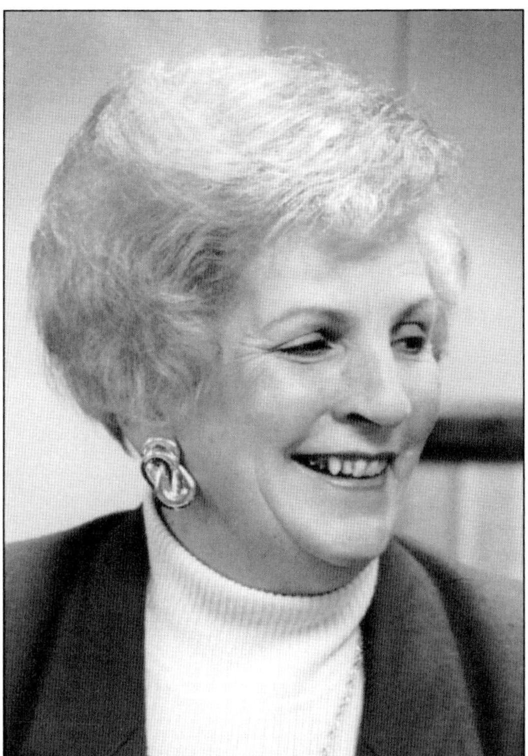

Her responsibilities at the family-owned Rollins Funeral Home kept Lucy Rollins (1928–2009) more than busy, but she nevertheless always had time for a worthy community project. She was the founding mother of the C-K Football Mothers Club, chartered the C-K Health Services Scholarship Committee, and cofounded the Kenova Volunteer Fire Department Advisory Board. She was inducted into the Kenova Hall of Fame in 2001. (Courtesy of *H-D*.)

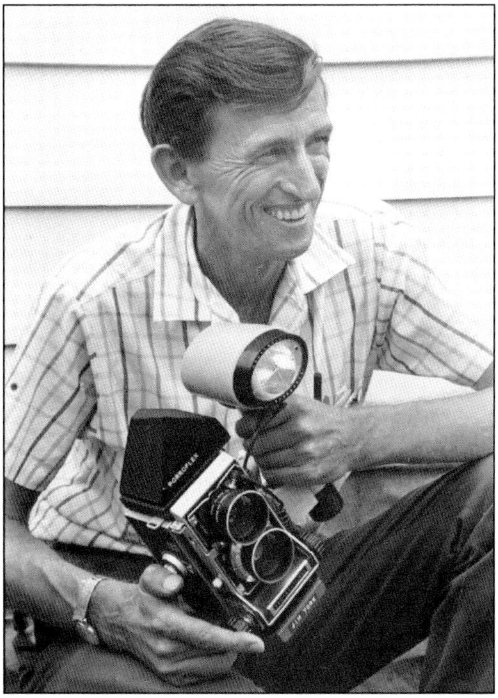

It seems fitting that Jim York's photograph be included in this book, as he snapped many of the images. York worked as a freelance photograph for the *Herald-Dispatch* and the *Wayne County News* after a heart problem forced him to retire from his job at Allied Chemical Corp. He was serving on Kenova City Council when he suffered a fatal heart attack in 1989. (Courtesy of *H-D*.)

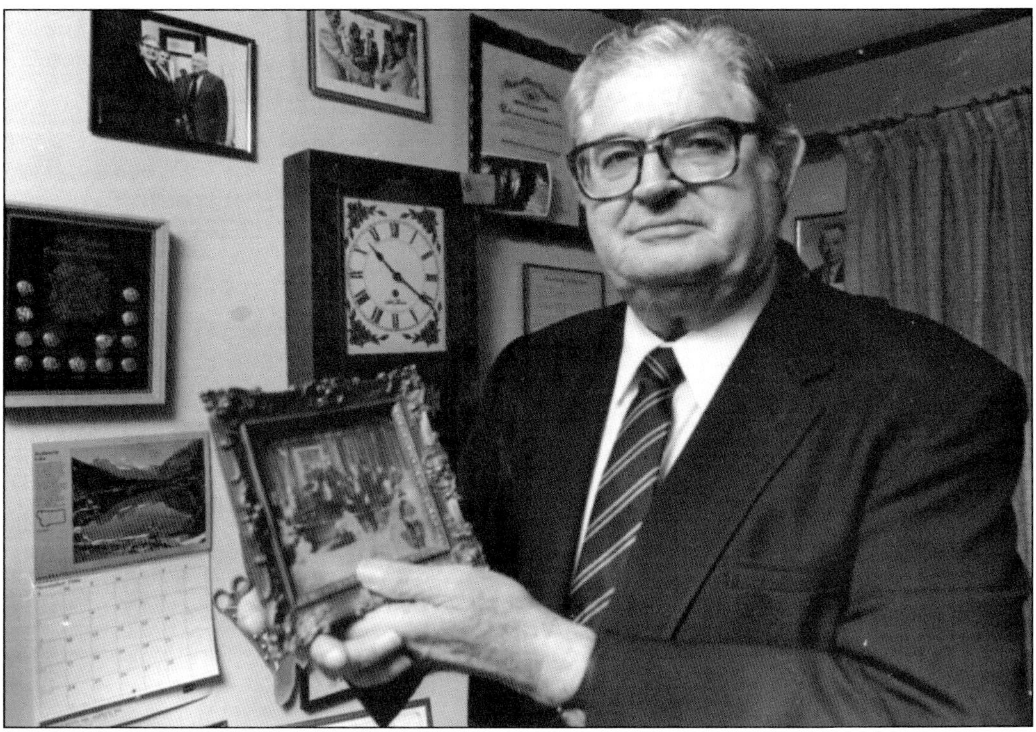

Lucian Fry, who ran the Wayne County Democratic Party for more than three decades, died in 1990. He was 83 years old. He started his political career in 1939, when he was elected sheriff of McDowell County. After serving in World War II, he returned to Wayne County, where he served four terms in the House of Delegates, from 1978 to 1986. (Courtesy of *H-D*.)

Known throughout Wayne and Mingo Counties as the "Judge," Charles W. Ferguson (1892–1976) served on the Circuit Court bench for 38 years before his retirement in 1966. Reared on a farm near Elmwod, two miles south of Wayne, he was a World War I veteran. Prior to his election as judge, he served 12 years as Wayne County prosecuting attorney in Wayne County. (Courtesy of *H-D.*)

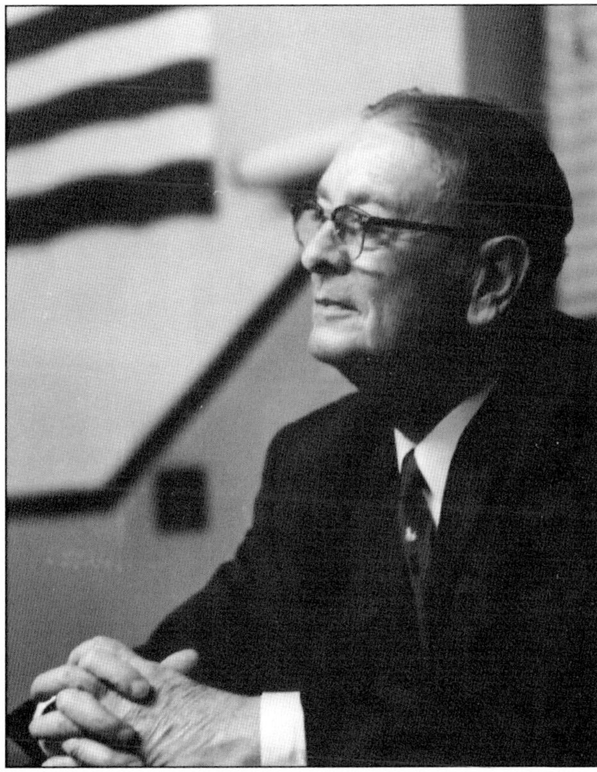

The curtain came down on a judicial era in 1984, when circuit judge C.W. Ferguson III announced he would not seek another term. The younger Ferguson succeeded his father when the elder Ferguson retired as judge in 1966. The two men had served a combined 56 years, meaning few in Wayne County could remember a time when there was not a C.W. Ferguson on the bench. (Courtesy of *H-D.*)

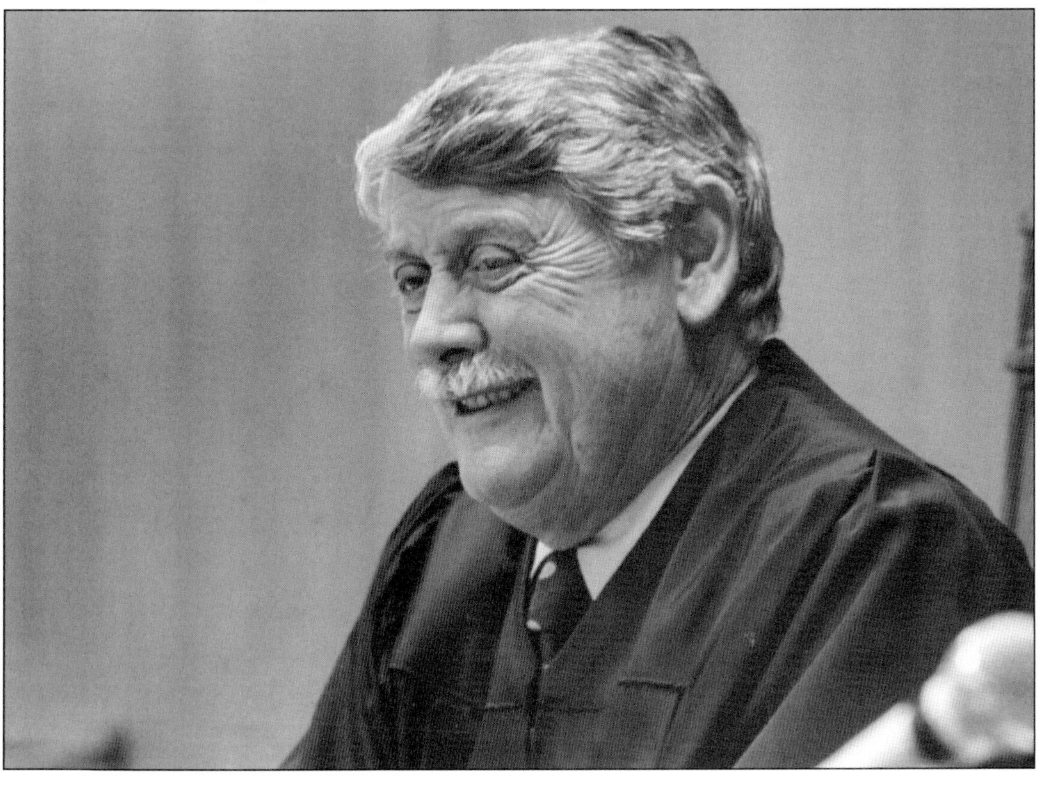

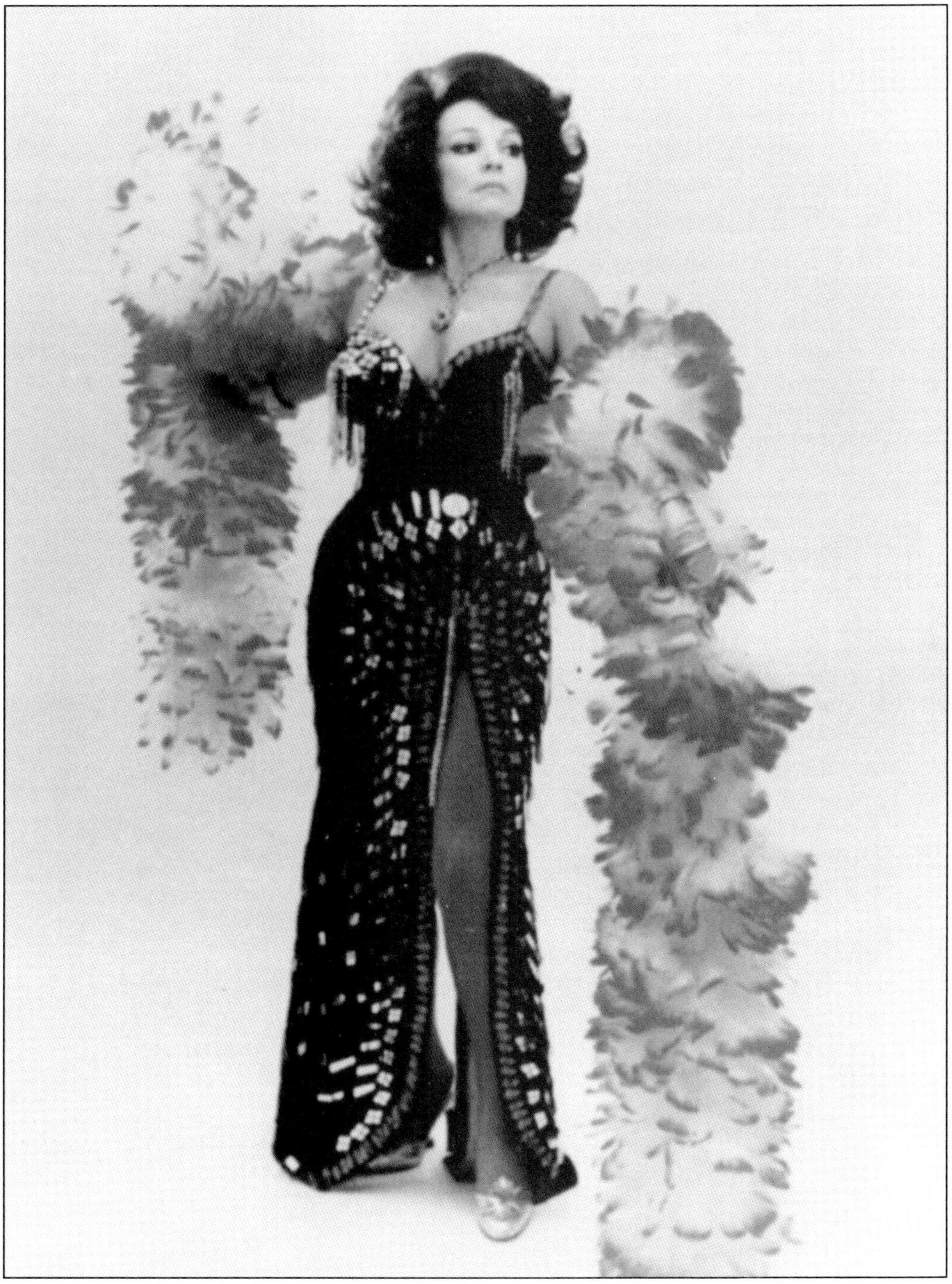

Blaze Starr was born as Fanny Belle Fleming in 1932 on a farm near Wilsondale in Wayne County. She left home at 14, worked at a Logan drive-in, then caught a bus for Washington. When a date took her to a burlesque club in Baltimore, Maryland, she told the owner she could do a better job than any of his dancers. The next night she showed up to prove it. Impressed, owner Sol Goodman became her manager and rechristened her "Blaze Starr." Soon she was the star attraction at Goodman's club. In 1959, while performing in New Orleans, she met Louisiana governor Earl Long. They began an affair that horrified Long's friends and delighted his foes. When Long died of a heart attack, Starr returned to burlesque, bought Goodman's club, and became a Baltimore legend. (Courtesy of the West Virginia Humanities Council.)

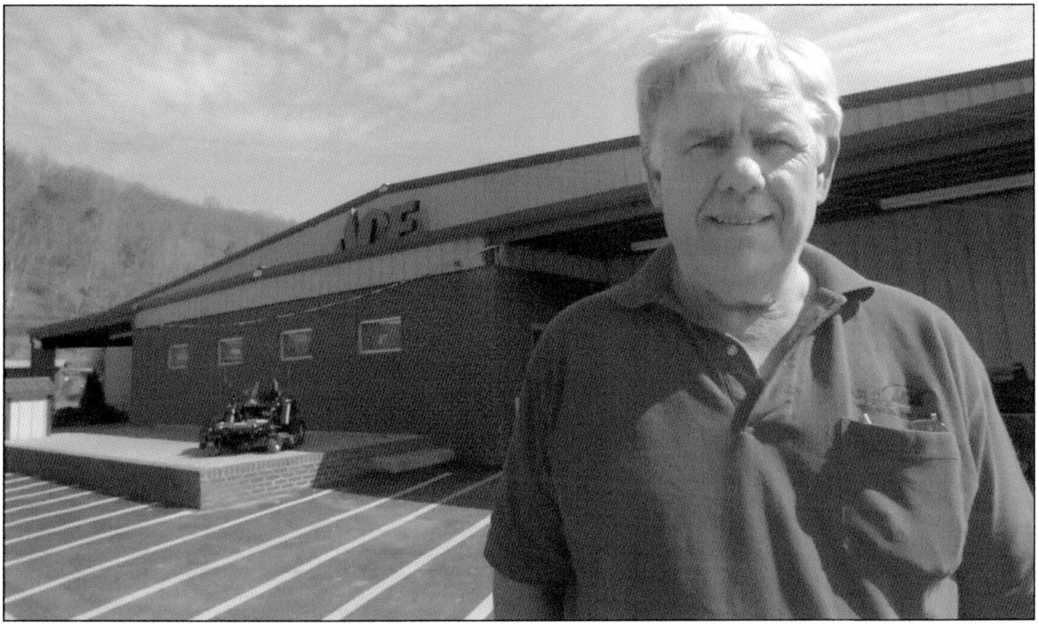

Owner Kenny Queen recalls that when he first opened his small hardware store in Lavalette in the early 1970s, he served maybe 10 or 12 customers a day. By the time the store observed its 10th anniversary, that figure had grown to 300 customers each day. Today, Kenny Queen Ace Hardware is a three-store chain. In 2012, Queen bought and renamed Kenova Box, a century-old business. And he has also opened a location in Wayne. (Courtesy of *H-D*.)

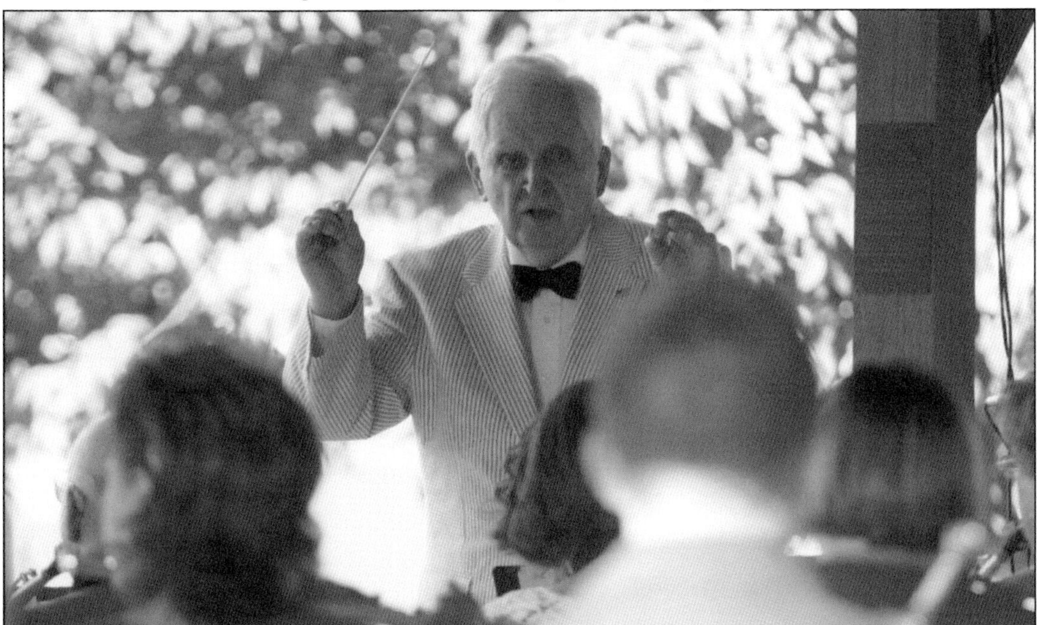

Charles Oshel, former director of the Ceredo-Kenova High School band, today wields his baton to lead the C-K High School Alumni Band, a dedicated group of musicians who keep the music playing and the memories of the old school alive. Founded in 1990, the band gives more than 20 concerts a year. (Courtesy of *H-D*.)

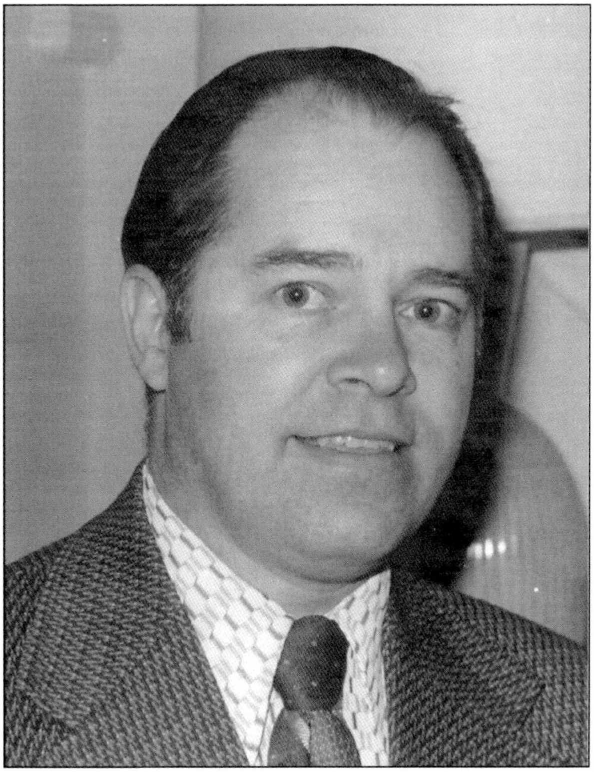

Dr. Joseph Billups, a Kenova dentist for 40 years, was dedicated to his patients and community. A member of the C-K Alumni Band, he was a past president of the Ceredo-Kenova Chamber of Commerce and on the board of directors for the C-K Credit Association and the Kenova Police Civil Service Commission. A US Army veteran, he was a member of American Legion Post 93. Dr. Billups was 83 when he died in 2013. (Courtesy of *H-D*.)

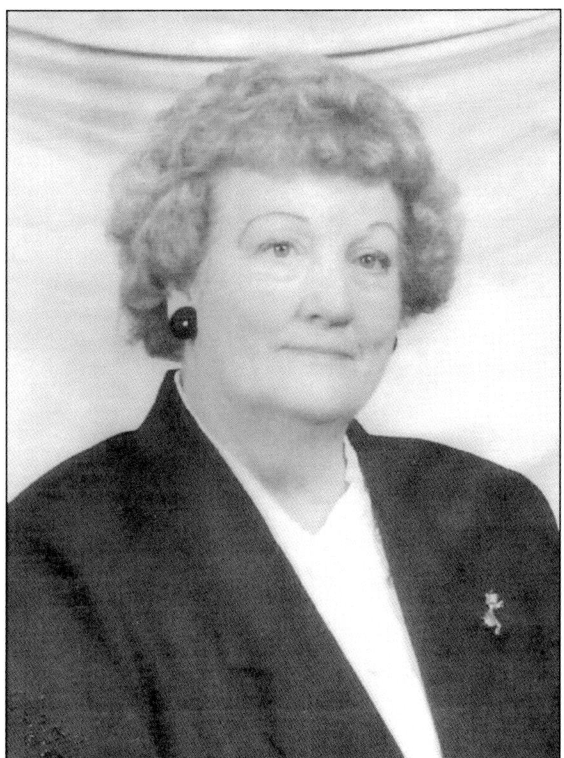

Betty Spry, a longtime Wayne County educator, died in 2014 at age 81. She was a teacher at Kenova Grade School, an assistant principal at Buffalo Elementary, and principal at Farmdale Grade School. She served on the Kenova City Council from 1999 to 2003 and again from 2011 until her death. (Courtesy of *H-D*.)

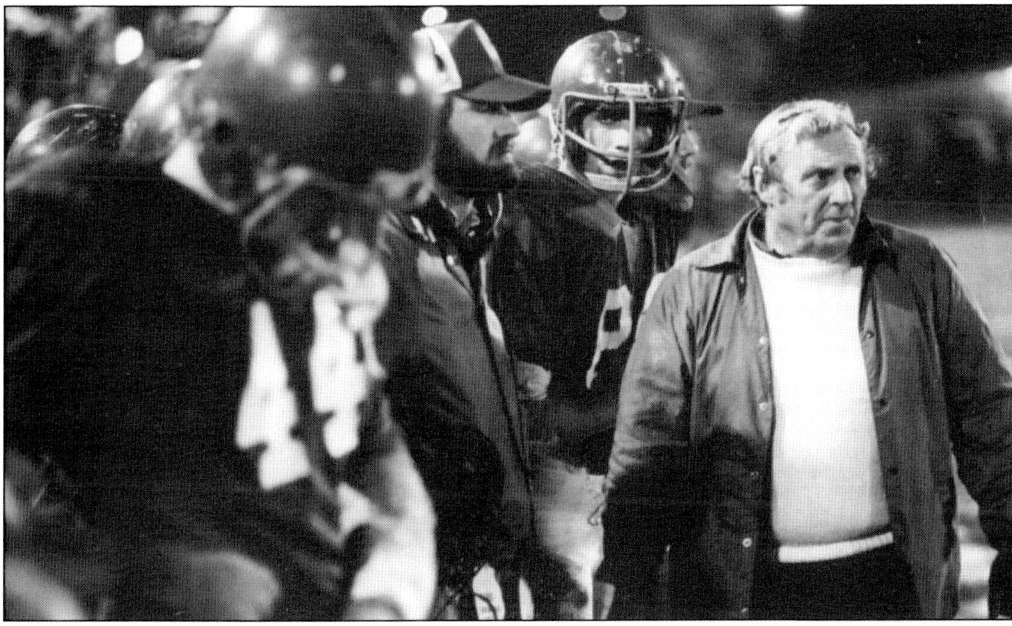

When Ceredo-Kenova High School merged with Buffalo and Vinson High Schools in 1998 to form Spring Valley High, it wrote an end to the rich history of each school. At C-K High School, it brought down the curtain on a storied football program. Carl Ward, shown here on the sidelines during a 1980 game, coached the C-K Wonders to 10 state titles between 1963 and 1983. (Courtesy of *H-D.*)

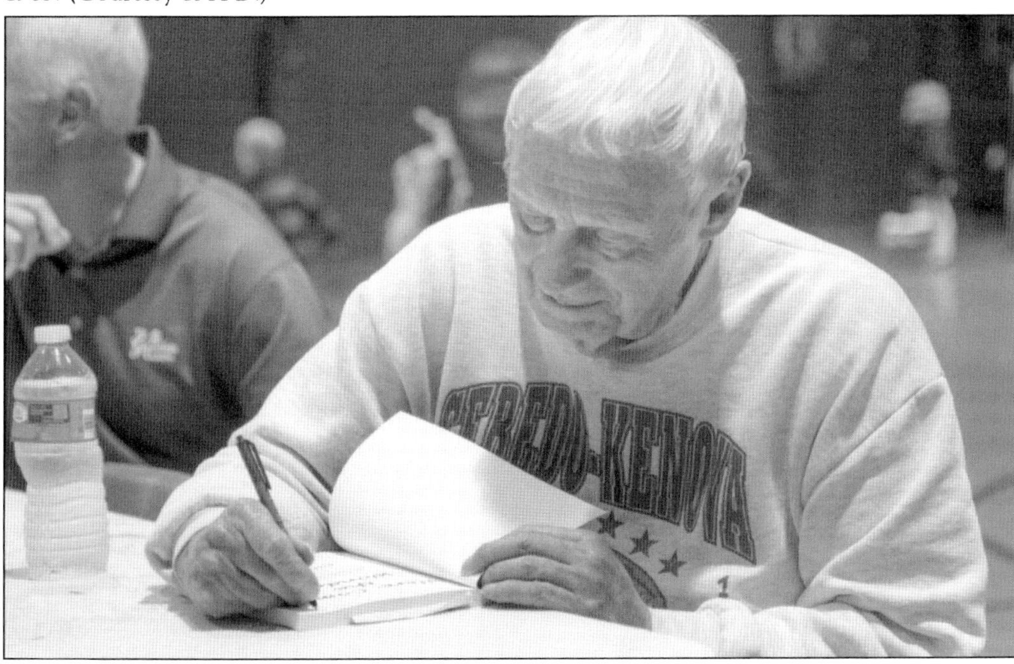

On October 20, 2014, former Ceredo-Kenova High School head coach Carl Ward signs a copy of *Here Come the Wonders*, a book by Rick Chaffin that details the history of C-K football. Proceeds from the book will be used to help restore the gym, the only part of the old school preserved after the rest was demolished. (Courtesy of *H-D.*)

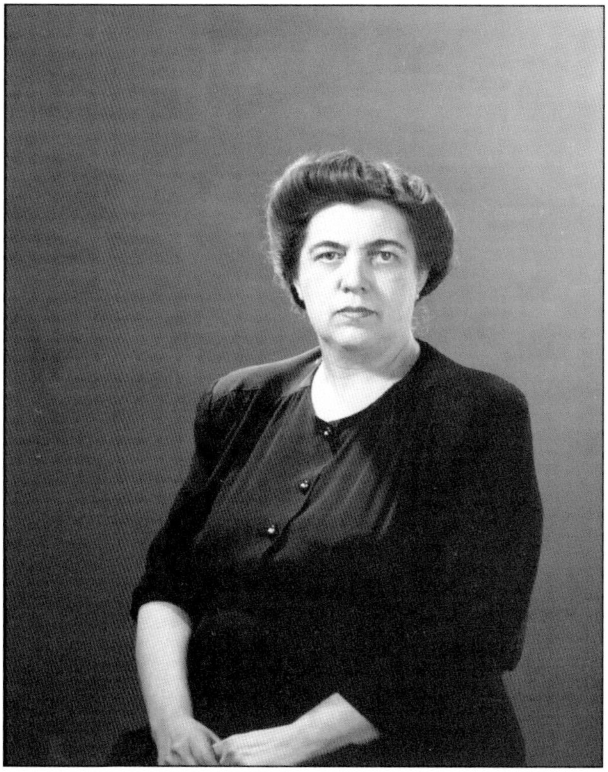

Doris C. Miller (1903–1993) was a teacher, newspaper writer, church secretary, and poet. Born at Shoals in Wayne County, she was proud of her Wayne County roots. At age 18, she began teaching at a rural school in Wayne County. She later wrote for the Huntington newspapers and was secretary at Central Christian Church. Her column Poetry Today was a Sunday feature in the papers for more than 15 years. (Courtesy of *H-D*.)

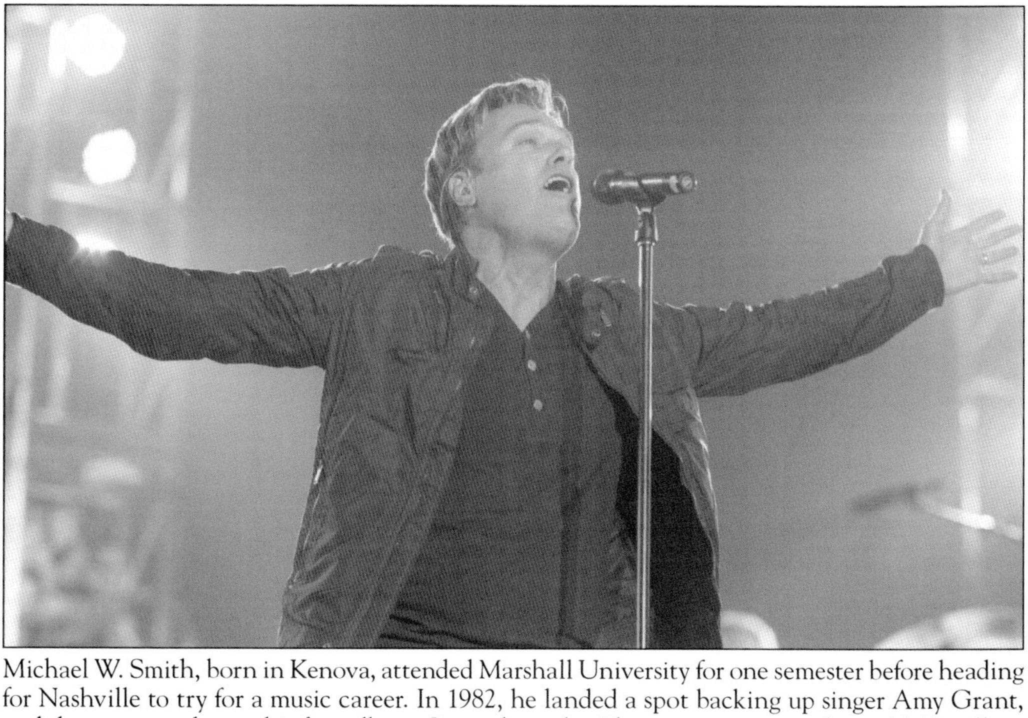

Michael W. Smith, born in Kenova, attended Marshall University for one semester before heading for Nashville to try for a music career. In 1982, he landed a spot backing up singer Amy Grant, and the next year he cut his first album. Since then, the Christian music icon has sold 15 million albums, scored 28 No. 1 hits, written 10 books, and won a flock of awards. (Courtesy of *H-D*.)

James P. Hammer of Kenova organized the J.P. Hammer Lumber Company in 1938 and built it into one of the largest and most successful lumber operations in the region. Born near Dingess in Mingo County, he was a past president of the Appalachian Hardwood Manufacturers Association, the National Hardwood Lumber Association, and the West Virginia Chamber of Commerce. He died in 1995 at age 90. (Courtesy of *H-D*.)

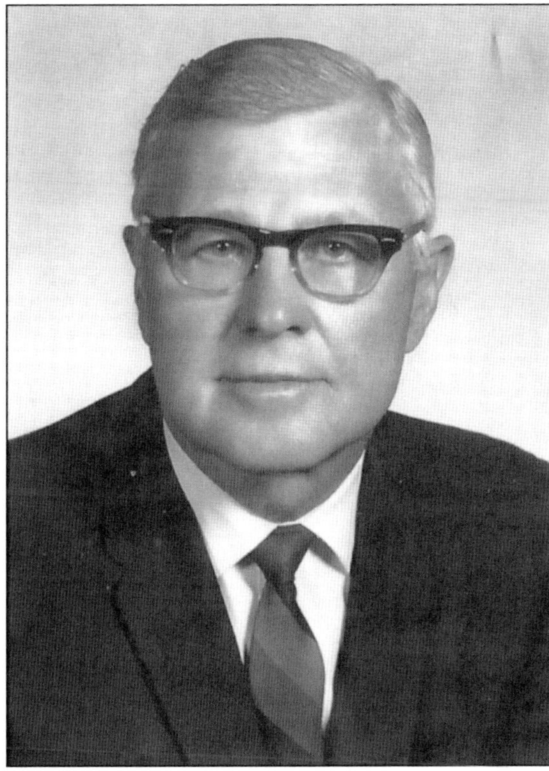

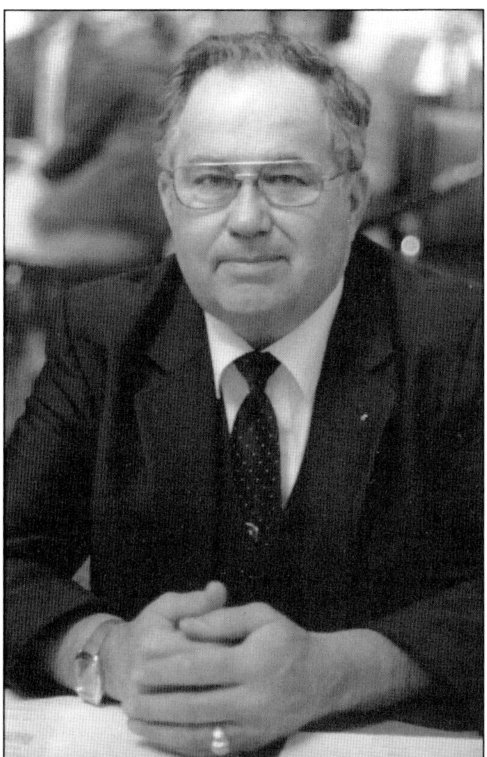

Mack Jarrell, DPM, graduated from Ceredo-Kenova High School and served in the US Navy in World War II and the Korean Conflict. While practicing as a podiatrist, he also taught school at South Point (Ohio) High School. As a young man, he served on Ceredo City Council and nearly 30 years later was elected to represent Wayne County in the West Virginia Senate. He died in 2014 at age 78. (Courtesy of *H-D*.)